The Associational State

POLITICS AND CULTURE IN MODERN AMERICA

Series Editors
Margot Canaday, Glenda Gilmore,
Michael Kazin, Stephen Pitti, Thomas J. Sugrue

Volumes in the series narrate and analyze political and social
change in the broadest dimensions from 1865 to the present,
including ideas about the ways people have sought and wielded
power in the public sphere and the language and institutions of
politics at all levels—local, national, and transnational. The series
is motivated by a desire to reverse the fragmentation of modern
U.S. history and to encourage synthetic perspectives on social
movements and the state, on gender, race, and labor, and on
intellectual history and popular culture.

The
ASSOCIATIONAL STATE

American Governance
in the Twentieth Century

Brian Balogh

PENN

UNIVERSITY OF PENNSYLVANIA PRESS

PHILADELPHIA

Published by
University of Pennsylvania Press
Philadelphia, Pennsylvania 19104-4112
www.upenn.edu/pennpress

Printed in the United States of America on acid-free paper
1 3 5 7 9 10 8 6 4 2

A Cataloging-in-Publication record is available
from the Library of Congress
ISBN 978-0-8122-4721-3

Contents

Introduction

Toward an Associational Synthesis

Americans are frustrated with government. Partisan gridlock has driven public opinion of Congress to historic lows. Budget deficits loom and the wealth gap expands. The price of homeland security requires citizens to share their homes, or at least their cell phones, with Big Brother. And a host of foreign economic competitors threaten to eclipse the American Century. Even those idealistic souls inclined to give Washington the benefit of the doubt wondered during the Obama administration if their faith had been misplaced after enduring the botched rollout of the Affordable Care Act (ACA)—the most important government domestic-policy initiative since the Great Society.

Historiography does not rank high on the list of causal factors fueling this frustration. Indeed, Google's top listings for "historiography" link to Princeton, not *Politico*, CUNY rather than CNN. Yet aligning the fundamental framework that informs the interpretation of political events in the mass media with a perspective forged by cutting-edge scholarship might begin to redefine the kinds of questions that citizens ask, influencing both expectations and demands.

There was a time when scholarship *did* align with the network news and the *New York Times*. For the middle third of the twentieth century a powerful perspective on the historical evolution of politics in the United States engaged leading scholars in New Haven *and* the journalists writing for the *New York Times*, academics in Cambridge *and* anchormen at CBS. It was called the "Progressive synthesis," and it was forged by pioneers like Charles Beard and popularized by professors like Arthur Schlesinger Jr. at Harvard, John Morton Blum at Yale, and William Chafe at Duke. The Progressive synthesis featured the march of powerful liberal presidents who represented the people against self-interested groups that hid behind conservative ideology to maintain the status quo or roll back any hint of reform. Many political historians have moved on from the Progressive synthesis, but some opinion makers in the United States (most importantly, elected officials) have not. They continue to demarcate political time and the polity's future through the ideological clash of liberalism and conservatism. They measure progress toward either ideal through the discourse of big or limited government, individual initiative or collective will. The failure to infuse the nation's narrative with post-Progressive scholarly interpretations contributes to some of the frustration with politics today because the analytical lens through which politics is understood does not fit the underlying structural challenges that face the nation. Nor does the old Progressive synthesis capitalize on the hybrid solutions that Americans have crafted to satisfy their insatiable demands for collective action while assuaging their enduring fears of big government.

The battle over the ACA epitomizes this dilemma. Pundits raged over the government's power grab (Fox News) or the failure to procure a unitary payer system (MSNBC). Yet the ACA illustrated America's historical commitment to combining federal financing with voluntary and private-sector mechanisms to deliver health care. Lost in the liberal versus conservative framework was the history of conservative business interests acknowledging that the private sector could not profitably finance care for America's elderly, for instance, and the history of liberal administrations turning to the voluntary and the market sectors to administer the resulting Medicare program. Such public/private partnerships have been the norm for much of American history, and a long line of historians has documented this genealogy. Yet the manner in which these associations were forged and the ways that they evolved have not been expressed in the popular lexicon. Oblivious to this history, elected officials do battle with straw men rather than focusing on the hard work of ensuring the proper balance between government oversight of institutions on the one hand, and autonomy for the intermediaries that citizens historically have preferred over the state, on the other hand—from private physicians to Blue Cross and Blue Shield, to for-profit insurance companies and hospitals. Nor have citizens fully appreciated who wins and who loses as long as the nation's political history is framed along ideological rather than more materially based perspectives—from class and occupation to demographics and region to technological disruption.[1]

I hope that the essays in this book will provide a historical interpretation that speaks to opinion makers as the Progressive synthesis once did, a perspective that explains political phenomena that shape citizens' lives today.

Scholars have dismantled virtually every component of the Progressive synthesis, but they have failed to do the one thing that might displace that easy story as the nation's guide to its own history. They have failed to aggregate our case studies and theoretical insights into a perspective that is designed to travel from the ivory tower to Main Street. We must strive to align the exciting interpretations of political history that have displaced Beard and Schlesinger with the mass media's headlines that remain frozen in time and that explain less and less each decade.

Alignment does not mean capitulation. By the turn of the twenty-first century, as liberalism explained less and less, some scholars turned to what looked like a new framing device, conservatism, in order to treat much of the political action that had been neglected, from tax revolts to the rediscovery of religious motivation in politics. At a time of increasing partisan rancor and the proliferation of media outlets arrayed along ideological lines, historicizing the ideological debate and linking it to critical elections comported with headlines and tweets. But did focusing on conservatism instead of liberalism constitute a new approach to understanding our history?

As a framework for capturing the sweep of twentieth-century political history, scholars had not progressed far beyond the Progressive synthesis's muscular partition of the American political universe into ideological camps pitting liberals against conservatives. The Progressive synthesis endured and was tweaked to illuminate the conservative alternative to liberalism, some of the key conservative protagonists that had been overlooked, and a new litany of key elections, beginning with Ronald Reagan's election in 1980. The Progressive synthesis morphed into the Progressive/conservative synthesis.[2]

Rather than positing political history as the clash of liberalism and conservatism, the essays here direct our attention to the ways in which Americans have braided public and private actions, state and voluntary-sector institutions, to achieve collective goals without undermining citizens' essential belief in individual freedom. This is a perspective capable of capturing moments when "liberals" employed the market to achieve key objectives, and illuminating instances in which "conservatives" financed their ends through the public purse. It is a framework that weighs the manner in which interests are organized, including those interests organized around identity, as heavily as the interests' rhetorical embrace of liberalism or conservatism. It is hospitable to the powerful influence of spatial factors that scholars have deployed recently. And it takes seriously the changing material conditions that influence public policy as well as the social relationships and processes that often determine those conditions, from communications to scientific and technological advances. It is an approach that values the history that occurs *between* purportedly key elections as highly as the history that unwinds in the immediate wake of November 1932, 1964, or 1980. It is a framework that captures the crucial political development that occurs between the so-called cycles of reform.[3]

I have labeled this approach to political history the "associational synthesis." It displaces discourse with behavior as the formal currency of the political realm and decenters critical elections, replacing them with the dynamic ways in which public officials—both elected and appointed—engaged their constituents. It considers, for instance, the ways in which political conflict was shoehorned into the narrow channels of interest-group politics in the first half of the twentieth century, and the implications for public policies that could be targeted at more narrowly drawn groups of citizens as a result. It acknowledges the ever-changing authority of professional knowledge and the organizational resources and political autonomy that the professions brought to politics. And it weighs heavily the evolving technology of mass communications, from the impact of the first wire service on party structure to the ways in which ubiquitous public opinion polling displaced interest groups and political parties as the sole sources of information about voters. This associational framework evaluates "the rhetoric of 'anti-government' and 'free enterprise' conservatism as a political and cultural construct, a discursive fiction," to quote the historian Matthew D. Lassiter, rather than as a blueprint for the programs actually carried out by those conservatives. It compares the anti–big business language of Progressive Era icons like Gifford Pinchot to his corporate-friendly actions.[4]

Intense conflicts have characterized twentieth-century politics in the United States. For instance, Americans have battled over the balance between individual and collective action or the proper mix of individual, market, voluntary-sector, and state responsibility. The associational synthesis encourages scholars and informed citizens alike to understand these struggles by considering a more capacious range of motivating factors than ideology and to dig beneath rhetorical representations in order to assess their outcomes. It takes seriously interests, the material factors that shape worldviews—from occupation to suburban homeownership—along with ideology. And it contends that the outcome of these struggles is best understood through a perspective that analyzes the capacity of each advocate's ability to adapt public policy prescriptions to prevailing conceptions of the proper balance between collective ends and individual opportunity. One of the keys to getting that balance right is connecting citizens and the state through a politically palatable mix of intermediary institutions—be they church, university, voluntary agency, corporation, or local or national government. Examining the history of these associational relationships lies at the core of the approach to historical understanding developed in these essays.

External threats to the nation's security often changed the rules of engagement, as did economic crises at times. Yet even at the height of the Great Depression and World War II, the associational synthesis explains a great deal—from the use of interest groups rather than the state to administer the nation's key response to the crisis in agriculture, to the ways in which private public relations firms were tapped to mobilize Americans during wartime.

I am hardly the first historian to call attention to associational patterns of political development. As the historian Ellis Hawley put it almost fifty years ago:

> America's associational sector had continued in the twentieth century to assume or be assigned governmental duties. In a land that had retained strong constraints on the growth of administrative statism, the desire for economic and social management had produced an expanded system of extra-governmental governance operating through business corporations and associations, labor, farm, and professional organizations, philanthropic orders and foundations, private-sector think tanks, and other agencies justifying their exercise of private power as essential to the maintenance of public order and progress.[5]

Yet Hawley's prescient work on the first three decades of the twentieth century was pigeonholed between a historiographical view of the nineteenth century that positioned associations as the antidote to an energetic state and Herbert Hoover's embrace of associational techniques culminating in the spectacular failure of the National Industrial Recovery Administration during the early New Deal.

Understanding how and why the relationships among citizens, intermediary institutions in the private and voluntary sectors of society, and the variegated branches of the state are associated is essential to understanding the nation's political history. Using that knowledge to assess how these partners performed can also provide insight into politics today and offer some clues about the nation's future.

The associational balance is constantly changing. The continuum of possibilities ranges from government capture by private interests to state overreach. However frustrating the condition of today's associational landscape may be to advocates of liberty on the one hand or collective action on the other, understanding the contours of politics through a historical perspective that connects citizens to the state through a range of intermediary institutions and is sensitive to the material factors that constantly rearrange that balance illuminates America's centuries-old tension between liberty and the commonweal. Scholars are poised to decode the history of the institutional arrangements that have mediated between citizen and state. The rest of this introduction outlines how they arrived at this point.

Bringing the State Back In and Leaving Associations Out

Thirty years ago, political scientists and sociologists joined forces with several historians who had forged the organizational synthesis. This disparate group crafted a historical framework that was relatively free of ideological markers and that privileged the institutional capacity of the American state. This is not to say that these scholars were any less ideologically driven in their personal views than the historians working in the Progressive tradition. They were, however, focused on the ways in which the state—usually the central state—carved out autonomy from a society that, at best, distrusted centralized government authority and, at worst, left the state underdeveloped (in their assessment) compared to other industrialized nations. These scholars "brought the state back in." Regardless of professional discipline, most identified their field as American Political Development (APD), which was represented by the new journal *Studies in American Political Development*. They coined phrases like "state capacity" and "bureaucratic autonomy." They cared deeply about administrative agencies' discretion and the power that came with the executive branch's authority to implement programs. They were soon joined by policy historians, who founded the *Journal of Policy History*.[6]

APD scholars underscored the importance of professional competence and reputation in crafting politically viable public policy. They tended to downplay the electoral connection and focus on policy outcomes. They paid special attention to the institutional and constitutional constraints that stacked the odds in favor of past patterns of governance through mechanisms like "intercurrence" and "path dependence." Change was possible, but only during "critical junctures" that offered rare opportunities to revise the rules of the game. And the catalysts for change reached far beyond the older political science conception of "critical elections" that correlated so conveniently with the Progressive synthesis's emphasis on waves of reform.[7]

War complicated easy assumptions between critical elections and policy reform. The economist Robert Higgs offered a powerful thesis regarding the "ratchet effect" of war and economic crisis, arguing that government expansion in response to these extraordinary circumstances persisted even as the crises subsided. Other historical developments extended the reach of government as well: inflation, technological breakthroughs, changes in political communication, social and cultural trends, the ways in which large segments of Americans conceived of their identities, not to mention America's engagement in a world that did not necessarily conform to the latest election results in Washington, DC.

Examining the relationship between citizen and state altered the traditional narrative. As the political scientists Suzanne Mettler and Andrew Milstein observed, "When the role and presence of the state is viewed from citizens' perspective . . . a different periodization becomes apparent and eras that have received relatively little attention from scholars appear to be pivotal." It was not the left-leaning Reconstruction Congress or Progressive Era reformers that created a "prodigious" benefits regime for Civil War veterans, for instance. Rather, pensions expanded during the 1890s. The pathbreaking reforms embodied in the New Deal's Social Security Act reached relatively few Americans during that era. Rather, eligibility for social insurance ballooned during the Eisenhower years, powered by bipartisan support. Techniques like cost of living adjustments, begun during the Nixon administration, provided record-breaking benefit increases to the elderly. APD scholars exposed "hidden" regimes of tax expenditures and legal mandates that expanded America's pension and health care benefits at government expense and incarcerated Americans at unparalleled rates—all during periods dominated by the rhetoric (and votes) of "small government" conservatives.[8]

Even though APD scholarship took explicit aim at the Progressive synthesis, the first generation of this scholarship shared a crucial unexamined conceptual premise with Progressive historiography. Both schools of history were based on the belief that there was an impermeable boundary between state and society. At their most fundamental level, both frameworks credited the rise of a powerful, effective, centralized state with breaking the grip of pluralist congeries of power that overrepresented social elites.

For those who subscribed to the Progressive synthesis, that broker state was adequately harnessed only when forced to serve the will of the entire citizenry, a phenomenon that occurred when liberal reform administrations were empowered. This was especially true when effective Progressive presidents like Teddy Roosevelt, Franklin Roosevelt, and Lyndon Johnson were able to transcend the clutter of interest and partisanship to carry out the will of the people. The vision of effective governance was far less egalitarian in the original APD model, but the implications for state-society relations were the same. Autonomous state actors acquired the wherewithal to govern effectively precisely by freeing themselves from the parochial, partisan, and often petty constraints levied by various spokespersons who claimed to represent fragments of the public.[9] Neither approach considered the possibility that the public might actually communicate rather effectively through the interests. Nor did Progressive historiography or the founders of APD initially take seriously the crucial role that the private sector, trade associations, and professional organizations played in actually implementing public policies. Progressive historiography and much of the original APD scholarship shared the assumption that civil society was independent of the state and that the voluntary institutions and interest groups that made up civil society failed to represent the public will effectively.

For the pioneers of APD, the very essence of the scholarly endeavor was to carve out a space for a state that was independent from the day-to-day tug of interest-based politics. Stating the agenda succinctly in a section headed "The Autonomy and Capacity of States," the political scientist Theda Skocpol insisted that "states conceived as organizations claiming control over territories and people may formulate and pursue goals that are not simply reflective of the demands or interests of social groups, classes, or society." "One may then explore the 'capacities' of states to implement official goals," Skocpol continued, "especially over the actual or potential opposition of powerful social groups or in the face of recalcitrant socioeconomic circumstances."

APD provided a way to break out of the structural-functionalist straitjacket that dominated social science in the post–World War II years. The price, however, was a clean break with institutions embedded in a society that threatened to undermine the bold national purpose that European states were perceived to possess.[10]

Stephen Skowronek's *Building a New American State: The Expansion of National Administrative Capacities, 1877–1920* concentrated on the structural restraints to state autonomy. In spite of the Herculean efforts of reformers and the hospitable environment for such measures that the Progressive Era offered, the Constitution, the extra-constitutional machinations of political parties, and the statutory interpretations of courts encumbered the early twentieth-century administrative state with the centrifugal mechanisms and inept practices of an earlier "state of courts and parties." Indeed, these roadblocks were built into the very foundation of the newly reconstructed twentieth-century state. Enduring structures (such as the Constitution) and practices (nurtured by political parties) crippled the state's autonomy despite decades of seemingly successful reform.[11]

Skowronek's protagonists were experts who moved in and out of the state and constituted an intellectual vanguard. They used their knack for political learning to craft solutions that liberated the state from the grip of parochial interests, bolstering the autonomy of administrators wherever possible. Yet, Skowronek continued, in spite of the Progressive reforms that these men achieved in the military command structure, railroad regulation, and systematic budgeting and accounting, "The incremental struggle simultaneously to break with the governing arrangements articulated over the course of a century and to build a whole new range of governing capacities ultimately produced a state in disarray." Reform and augmented state capacity marched hand in hand, yet the edifice they produced had been compromised at the very core in America's decentralized and porous polity.[12]

Despite these limitations, identifying those who successfully built state capacity as independent causal agents and highlighting that capacity as the crucial prerequisite to reform offered a powerful alternative to Progressive historiography's ideologically driven interpretation. Among political historians, it emerged as the leading alternative to the Progressive synthesis. As I wrote in *Social Science History* upon the twentieth anniversary of the publication of *Building a New American State*, "Structure—of the Constitution, of the party system, of the judiciary, of a bureaucracy carved out from these materials—not ideology is what powers Skowronek's analysis."[13]

If state builders did not achieve all they set out to accomplish, scholars who charted state capacity did succeed in building a sturdy cottage industry, if not a state. As a first-year graduate student in 1983, I wrote a master's thesis that was eventually published under the title "Securing Support: The Emergence of the Social Security Board as a Political Actor." As I breathlessly proclaimed, "With acronyms replacing surnames as history's protagonists, it will not suffice to treat these complex organizations merely as politically passive vehicles. We must chart their political development and attempt to measure the breadth of their influence on the policies they administer," concluding that the agency I studied was a crucial political actor that developed skills essential to ensuring its programs' lasting impact. I need not have worried. Scholars far more seasoned than I were on the case.[14]

Treating the sources of state capacity as an analytical question to be examined more systematically than those who originally sought to bring the state back in, a younger generation of scholars like Dan Carpenter identified key variables, such as reputation, that allowed mezzo-level administrators to act independently. Like Skowronek and Skocpol, Carpenter had to look hard to find autonomy: Indeed, it appeared to be a relatively scarce commodity in the American state. But where it did exist, it was autonomous bureaucrats who initiated and shaped public policy that differed "materially from the designs of elected officials." Bureaucratic autonomy was sustained in agencies like the Food and Drug Administration or the Department of Agriculture's Forest Service by "reputational coalitions" that were "neither partisan, nor ideological, nor sections, nor reducible to one organized interest."[15]

By 2003, Skowronek declared that what previously had served as an agenda had become "common wisdom." History was crucial to the way in which the state developed. And the way the state developed affected all that it touched. Politics was about state building and, more important, politics was the "centerpiece of the social problem, not a mere epiphenomenon." In short, the state was "back in" and the key to understanding politics and broader trends in American history lay *inside* the day-to-day workings of the state.[16]

Recent work suggests that the relationship between state and civil society is far more fluid than either Progressive historiography or the early APD literature envisioned. Indeed, scholars like William Novak have insisted that civil society itself is shaped by law and public policy. Skocpol has argued that the history of voluntary organizations in America cannot be understood without considering the ways in which the polity has influenced their development. In *A Government Out of Sight* I drew on the insights of those who chronicled associational patterns of governance to argue that the intermediary institutions used to craft and administer national policy enjoyed broad public support in the nineteenth century, compared to the alternative: direct administration by the government, especially the national government.[17]

Bringing Associations Back In

Even though Skocpol warned against simply turning the theoretical emphases on their head, cautioning that "state-determinist" explanations should not simply replace those grounded in society-centered accounts, our quest to put the state back into the conversation soon overshot the mark, threatening to do just what Skocpol and others cautioned against. In fact, the cacophony created by carpenters eager to build this state-centered account inadvertently reinforced a deep affinity with the very Progressive historiography that the APD construction crew had set out to demolish.[18]

The conclusion shared by both progressive historiography and the founders of APD was that civil society, the murky territory that lay somewhere between citizen and state, could not be trusted with any of the responsibilities or duties integral to governing. The interests that populated civil society, whether voluntary or profit seeking, were especially suspect. Indeed, what distinguished the state from society was government's plenary power and the ability to wield that power directly in order to fulfill the will of citizens—a mandate that was often thwarted precisely because of the self-serving machinations of interest groups, political parties, and market-driven incentives that skewed the common weal.[19]

No sooner had the intellectual concept of the autonomous state been articulated than many of its architects began renovating it. They were encouraged by a host of other scholars who pushed the state back out—not only meeting civil society half way but noting the manner in which interest groups, voluntary organizations, the professions, and even corporate practices and ideas were shaped by the state. State authority, it turned out, could be enhanced through private and voluntary mediation, consultation and the creative tension spawned through this associational approach.

Once the state was back in, even those who charted state capacity and bureaucratic autonomy readily acknowledged the intercourse that occurred regularly between state builders and the institutions of civil society. Carpenter, for instance, who sought explicitly to isolate those factors that allowed administrators to act independently, stressed the importance of coalitions built in conjunction with key elements of civil society. Granted, the public administrator's value added was his ability to survey the landscape, mobilize professional expertise, and discern the political climate in order to forge such alliances. Nevertheless, successful bureaucrats got their hands dirty. In the words of Carpenter, "they engage in coalition politics. They assemble broad-based alliances behind their new programs, coalitions wrought from the multiple networks in which these unique bureaucrats travel." Autonomous, in the sense that they ultimately pulled the policy strings, these officials hardly did it alone. Indeed, it was their ability to draw upon and mobilize resources in civil society, especially opinion leaders and interest groups, that connected policy makers to broader constituencies, sustaining bureaucratic autonomy.[20]

Although "state capacity" dominated the APD literature in its early years, social scientists soon broadened their questions. Two powerful initiatives cut against the fortified border that separated state and civil society constructed by the original APD generation. Citizenship studies, or, more specifically, studies of those who were excluded from citizenship and their struggle to procure full citizenship, drew upon social history that took seriously race, class, and gender and recognized that the political aspirations of many of the nation's historically marginalized residents were often better served outside of the kind of formal politics that many in APD leaned toward. Rogers Smith, for instance, illuminated the constellation of practices, legal and extra-legal, that hedged citizenship based upon the values ascribed to Americans with racial, ethnic, and gendered identities. These ascriptive rights and restrictions formed a powerful order of their own that often trumped liberal ideals and constitutional protections. Smith connected this important world of social identity to the more formal array of rights and privileges allocated by the state, pulling APD outward toward practices deeply rooted in civil society. Along the way, the APD citizenship scholarship exposed the vast realm of politics that existed beyond the confines of the state and chronicled how historical patterns of exclusion and bias were inscribed into state-society relations.[21]

Somewhere between scholars who brought the state back in and those who examined Americans that the state left out, a third group of APD scholars deployed the concept of governing "regimes" to explore the connections between ideology, state capacity, and voter demands. Scholars such as David Plotke and Steven Skowronek, in *The Politics That Presidents Make*, searched for patterns of policy making that crossed functional boundaries and defied simple partisan explanations. For Samuel Kernell, or historians Paul Milazzo and Julian Zelizer, Congress was ground zero—at least as the lens that provided the best perspective on the ways in which these factors came together. It was also an institution, they noted, that left its own distinctive imprint on the patterns that emerged.[22]

Scholarship that explored the relationship between the state and private-sector corporations also eroded conceptions of state autonomy. Cathie Jo Martin documented that in the early twentieth century, the powerful National Association of Manufacturers (NAM) sought a charter establishing NAM as the formal intermediary between the federal government and a large section of the business community—an ideal similar to corporatist models established in European industrialized democracies. Partisan opposition, federalism, and the local nature of business-government relations thwarted these plans, however. As NAM's quest for a federal charter suggests, it was no advocate of free market ideology in its early years. Rather, it was the nature of the political regime that NAM encountered that forced its leaders to reconsider their strategy, including their attitude toward the state. Although limited state capacity surely explained part of this story, NAM's experience navigating uncharted shoals between industrial clients and a political regime that was sensitive to partisan competition explained far more. Citizenship studies, regime studies, and historical analysis of business-government relations demanded that APD scholars engage with key institutions and behaviors that were deeply embedded in civil society and the market in order to account for political outcomes. Ideology alone did not suffice.[23]

Long-standing assumptions regarding the nineteenth-century American political economy were also challenged. Recent APD scholarship has recovered the state's active role in that economy, challenging assumptions about a "stateless" past. For Richard Bensel, regional and partisan agendas combined to propel active state intervention in the political economy, including the management of the currency, crucial tariff decisions, and in the North, active state–private sector collaboration during the Civil War. The Confederate States of America, Bensel argued, was forced to rely more heavily on naked state power because the institutions of its civil society were *less* developed than those of the Union. Richard John mapped the extensive reach of state-subsidized and -directed communications systems. Robin Einhorn demonstrated both the power of local governments and the way in which tax policy reinforced crucial social predispositions in early America. Bill Novak documented the extensive reach of both social and economic regulation at the state and local level as well as the ways in which the law shaped the very institutions that composed civil society.[24]

I drew on their work to synthesize a narrative of nineteenth-century political development that stressed the persistent demand for governance, even governance orchestrated by the distant national state. That authority, however, had to be exercised in ways that diminished its visibility. This entailed mobilizing compatible resources in the private and voluntary sectors, which often proved more effective than applying unilateral state power. While my insights were gleaned from the theoretical perspective of scholars like Michael Mann, historically, this is exactly what Americans preferred. Where no intermediate institutions stood between citizen and national government, Americans consistently advocated energetic governance when it came to trade, security, and economic development. Where local and state government was up to the task, or where voluntary and private groups might fulfill public purposes, Americans preferred that the national government enable rather than command.[25]

If some APD scholars who focused on the state were pushing outward into civil society to explain enduring patterns of governance, others worked the opposite end of the block and met the state builders half way. More often than not, that ground was occupied by professional organizations, trade associations, voluntary organizations, and, on occasion, corporate headquarters. Rather than simply discussing how the groups that inhabited civil society warded off the state, wary of its encroachment, or how the state replaced or brought to heel these key institutions of civil society, APD scholars were increasingly inclined to consider the possibility that the state could govern *through* these institutions. Associational relationships enhanced state authority without provoking charges of "big government" and, on occasion, even made public spending more palatable, or at least politically acceptable.

Once again Theda Skocpol took the lead. Examining the public policy that has consistently drawn resistance from a majority of Americans—welfare—and noting the welfare-like expansion of benefits that occurred in the case of Civil War pensions, Skocpol grounded American support for benefits in a maternalist perspective that was deeply rooted in the federated structure of women's organizations, just as Civil War pensions were part and parcel of the federated nexus of veterans' organizations and the Republican Party. Identifying the key causal relationships as reciprocal, Skocpol noted the ways in which the American polity encouraged groups to organize. These patterns mirrored the structural outlines of federalism embodied in the Constitution.

As she subsequently argued in *Diminished Democracy*, "Civil society and government thus worked hand in hand to fashion and sustain America's version of the modern welfare state." Signaling what would soon become a frontal assault on notions that civil society constituted a demilitarized zone safely removed from the impulses of the meddling hand of government, Skocpol moved beyond the structural influences on the shape of voluntary groups to argue that such groups both pressed for and were the beneficiaries of government largesse.[26]

With the advent of federal payroll deductions for social security and income tax (begun during World War II), even charitable organizations that feared competition from the government, such as local community chests, were pleased to take advantage of this technique to fund their operations. As historian Andy Morris has noted, this "not only demonstrates the voluntary sector's entrepreneurial ability to take advantage of the shift in governance, but it also suggests the ways in which the public and private aspects of the welfare state became increasingly blurred in the postwar era."[27] In her current project, titled *Civic Gifts: Benevolence and the Making of the American Nation-State*, Elisabeth Clemens argues that American governance and politics were largely based on associationalism and sustained by practices of "charitable citizenship." "As federal spending programs increasingly recognized non-profit organizations—whether social welfare agencies, community hospitals, or research universities—as legitimate recipients of public funds," she suggests, "the ingredients were in place for the distinctive brew of public and private efforts that has come to characterize American governance in the second half of the twentieth century."[28]

In his 2001 article, "The American Law of Association: The Legal-Political Construction of Civil Society," Bill Novak challenged the tendency to romanticize the civil sphere. He noted that many strains of the revived interest in civil society shared one trait—a belief in the autonomy of the social sphere of civil society and its insulation from the political economy. This distorted emphasis, Novak argued, often led directly to utopian assumptions, not unlike those held by advocates who insisted that the hidden hand of the market could most equitably resolve conflicts. In this case, it was civil society that was artificially removed from the contestations of power and control. For Novak and several other APD scholars, exposing the legal and political battles that shaped civil society was the foremost challenge facing students of political history.[29]

Eldon Eisenach also explored the boundary between state and civil society. While Skocpol and Novak underscored the way in which the state shaped civil society, Eisenach reminded us that associations, ranging from loosely organized movements for women's rights during the Progressive Era to professional organizations and the universities, were essential partners in virtually every effort to extend national authority for much of the twentieth century. He labeled such intermediaries "parastates." As Eisenach put it, "agents of . . . liberal nationalism are national 'establishments' in the form of universities, professional associations, charitable foundations, the national media, the public school establishment, and the hosts of national reform movements, support groups, and think tanks that have waxed and waned throughout our history. National 'liberalism' in this positive sense of reform projects has always been an alliance of national institutions." The analytical key to understanding governance and reform in the American setting lay at the intersection of state and society rather than exclusively in either one.[30]

It is in the realm of political economy that a heuristic approach that weighs the reciprocal relationship between the state and society has produced the most dramatic revision to the Progressive synthesis. The foil was an oversimplified dichotomy that separated state and market into discrete spheres. State "intervention" into the market was only notable when the state "interfered" in what was presumed to be an organically functioning market. As Marc Eisner has noted, this construction diverted attention from "the role of public policy in *constituting* (italics added) markets and shaping economic activity more generally." A rigid approach to state-market relations limited our thinking about the mutually constitutive nature of markets and the state. Charles Lindbloom argued that this perspective prevented consideration of the market as a variable, rather than a "fixed element around which policy must be fashioned."[31]

Law was the key mechanism by which the state constituted the market and other elements of the economy. It was crucial to the components of the market—corporations, unions, and trade associations, for instance—and to the rules and expectations of the market itself. "Rather than existing as a self-constituting and self-regulating realm of human action," Eisner insisted, "markets are in a real sense an expression—both intended and unintended—of public policies and institutions." From this perspective, the market was simply another sphere in which the state organized social transactions, rather than a safe haven from the state. For scholars like Eisner, "[a]ny references to state intervention in the market ignore the basic fact that the market itself is constituted by public policy." Dan Carpenter not only agreed; he noted that approval of new regulation often created new and superior markets. Such was the case in the pharmaceutical industry. To argue otherwise assumed that societies could generate markets in the absence of supporting institutions. Regulation did not interfere with or disrupt the market. Rather, it constituted the market.[32]

The professional arena provided equally fertile ground for exploring the ways in which the state laundered its authority through non-state actors. Gerald Berk documented a "third way" that directed the course of industrialization over the first third of the twentieth century. Eschewing calls to break up large corporations or regulate them, Berk chronicled the ways in which Louis Brandeis and Herbert Hoover embraced the techniques crafted by professions like cost accountants and engineers. This "regulated competition" was guided by agencies like the Federal Trade Commission, which sanctioned the techniques of these professionals and cooperated with the business community to create "developmental associations" in industries like printing. Their objective was to tame ruinous competition without creating monopoly control. The technique and the professional autonomy to ensure that these practices were effectively carried out loomed large in Berk's story. But the creation and maintenance of the larger economic and political environment in which these professionals operated would not have been possible without state supervision.[33]

Policy entrepreneurs "reached across historical, institutional, and cultural boundaries," Berk argued, "to find resources, which they creatively recombined in experiments in business regulation, public administration, accounting, and trade associations." The administrative epicenter of this experiment was the often discredited Federal Trade Commission. There, "creative commissioners," Berk suggested, "recomposed resources from civil society to create a network of business and professional associations devoted to upgrading competition through deliberation and cost accounting." They formed a network of deliberative forums that merged experience with technique to create a "usable model of developmental association." While NAM may have altered its vision of formal corporatist arrangements in the first decade of the twentieth century, by the 1920s, business interests and professionals had forged relationships with state agencies that managed competition through key professional intermediaries rather than formally chartered trade associations.[34]

Why the Associational Turn?

Why has it taken so long for APD scholarship to catch up with Ellis Hawley? Because Hawley wrote *The New Deal and the Problem of Monopoly* at the height of the prominstrative state's power, his clear-sighted vision of the past crashed head-on into powerful contemporary evidence that announced the triumph of an autonomous state. One only had to read the headlines proclaiming the unprecedented domestic reach of the Great Society or a warfare state that flexed its muscles in Vietnam to glean the national government's intrusion into civil society and market relations (not to mention Cambodia). And if this was not enough evidence of an autonomous state, these extensions were pursued against the larger contours of a seemingly unending Cold War that continued to demand the ultimate sacrifice by citizens.

APD scholarship belatedly embraced Hawley's fundamental insight as both the domestic and global context in which the state operated shifted dramatically. The ideological roots of this reorientation, for instance, reached back to the 1970s and the rise of "neoliberal" thought, which redirected the spotlight away from government action toward the market. That intellectual movement, in turn, was energized by the economic shocks of the 1970s and the political demands articulated by the "Reagan Revolution." Bill Novak has noted the ways in which the velvet revolutions of Eastern Europe focused attention on the yawning gap between union-based, society-centered organizations like Solidarity, on the one hand, and one-party states that leaders like Lech Walesa sought to reform. With the consolidation of conservative political gains, the unprecedented terrorist attacks on America's "homeland," and the prosecution of two wars, scholars and public intellectuals began to notice that conservative governance often produced big government and bigger deficits. They examined more closely the state's contractual relationships with private corporations like

Blackwater and public intervention into areas of life that previously were considered to be private, family, or religious preserves.[35]

Further from the headlines, a robust challenge to the long-reigning conception of the American political economy forged by Alfred Chandler also altered scholars' perception of the relationship between key industries and the state. Chandler famously eschewed a place for public affairs in his vision of the core sector of the economy. Galambos and Pratt challenged the notion that these "core industries" could operate without regard to their political environment. More recently, Phil Scranton questioned the very shape of the American political economy in the first half of the twentieth century. [36]

In *Endless Novelty* Scranton argued for the significance of specialty manufacturing such as jewelry or decentralized clusters of manufacturers who produced machines and tools for the mass production sector of the economy. These specialty industries often shared information and techniques across company lines. They were linked to each other through contracts and geographically centered institutions that promoted technical education, like the Franklin Institute in Philadelphia. The economy that Scranton described was far more diverse than the one chronicled by Chandler, and more open to inter-firm collaboration. The significance of these kinds of industries to the economy in the second half of the nineteenth century and the cooperative fashion in which they shared information challenged Chandler's "throughput"-oriented model of industrial efficiency. It also resonated with twenty-first-century headlines about the power of networks in the new economic juggernaut of the economy—the dot.com "revolution."[37]

The new business history paints a portrait of private-sector organizations that are far more amenable to state intervention than once thought, but it also stresses the collaborative, cooperative networks that cut across firms. While zero-sum efforts by state bureaucrats to dictate to the private sector in the first third of the twentieth century—through trust busting or rigid regulation—still drew strong resistance, less intrusive initiatives that emphasized data collection, professionally sanctioned standards, reinforcing compliance, and collaborative learning—in short, the core qualities of an associational approach—fit neatly with this revised conception of business.

Gerald Berk's *Louis D. Brandeis and the Making of Regulated Competition, 1900–1932* encapsulates many of the recent insights of the APD literature and applies them to a political economy that resembles the one characterized by Scranton. It serves as a useful guide to scholars who seek to revise our understanding of the relationship between state and society in the twentieth century. Berk is explicit about the implications of his study, stating that the search for bureaucratic hierarchy and autonomy led many scholars to overlook the "cultivational" approach to administration pursued at the Federal Trade Commission. The FTC, he argues, valued a different set of features from those epitomized by state autonomy. Cultivational administrators valued deliberation among industries and between the private sector and the FTC; they sought to build up the "scientific and evaluative capacity in peak business, professional and trade associations through public/private collaboration." Rather than commanding industry, FTC commissioners and bureaucrats sought to reconfigure existing resources in civil society in order to create networks of professional and business associations. They tried to make competition more productive and creative, without dictating the outcome of that competition.[38]

This regulated competition included professionals who standardized information. It capitalized on the mutual desire by business and government to collaborate in stabilizing markets. Professionals devised classification schemes, measurements, and reporting mechanisms that allowed specialty manufacturers to standardize *information* rather than *products*. *Regulated Competition* criticized the older APD literature for missing the innovative relationship between the FTC and many elements of civil society. Those scholars, Berk argued, were looking for bureaucratic autonomy—agencies able to impose their will on the private sector, or corporatist counterparts in the private sector, able to discipline members and speak on behalf of an entire industry, sanctioned by the government. Berk offered an alternative template—one that relied heavily on professionals to systematize accounting for products that were *not* mass produced and industries that shared information across sectors.[39]

While professionals designed and staffed these systems, FTC commissioners and business leaders provided the institutional support, ensuring that this scientific learning was nurtured and disseminated through conferences, government reports, and trade associations. Most significantly, they promoted the kind of "reflection, deliberation and experimentation" that economists' models and judicial adherence to strict divisions between competitive and anticompetitive practices often precluded. From Berk's perspective, the law, reinforced by leading economists, used rigid classification schemes that divided the world into opposing camps: competition versus monopoly; public versus private. These classifications schemes failed to allow for the ways in which deliberation and private/public collaboration took place. While key judicial decisions limited the FTC's ability to command businesses and trade groups, it left open the path that the FTC ultimately took, one that cultivated the very collaborative practices that had taken place informally, offering a "third way" that defied the rigid boundaries established by the law.[40]

With growing consensus among APD scholars about the reciprocal relationship between state and society, and heightened interest by historians of all stripes in the state, the time is propitious to forge a perspective that can be translated into the nation's vernacular. That perspective can be summed up as follows. American political history has been a contest for access to resources that are often controlled or shaped by the state. Yet Americans have historically been ambivalent about the role of the state. For too long, liberals and conservatives, aided and abetted by a once powerful interpretation of political history, have eagerly embraced the notion that some Americans like the state, while others detest it. This bifurcation distorts the nation's history and is one of the sources of frustration with politics today.

Recent historical scholarship overwhelmingly supports a very different history of politics in the United States. The vast majority of Americans, not merely those advocating Progressive reform, have demanded a great deal from their state. Yet that same majority of Americans has distrusted the state to deliver these benefits directly. The result of this backhanded support for public intervention is that groups that have organized most effectively and engineered a politically acceptable alliance of institutions and professionals in civil society and the private sector to deliver these public benefits often prevail. While money, gender, race, and education have historically given some groups great advantages in effecting successful associations built around government resources, changing material conditions faced by the nation, the nation's role in international affairs, the prevailing modes of mass communication, changes in the political culture, demographic shifts, the relationship between society and the environment, and historically contingent events offer a never-ending opportunity for individuals previously excluded from successful associations that link citizens to the state to intervene in this dynamic contest and tilt the current beneficiaries of public largesse toward a different set of clients. It is precisely that kind of intervention, not an ideological predisposition against public benefits per se, that has empowered the Tea Party Patriots.

Even during times of crisis, and stretching back to the origins of the United States, citizens have benefited individually and collectively through strategic combinations of the state and intermediate institutions. Cutting through the false charges of statist overreach or neglect and assessing whether or not the allocation of resources and the manner in which they are delivered are just, fair, and benefit the nation as a whole should be the basis for determining whether any given associational settlement should be embraced or not. The United States is fortunate to have spawned a rich associational life. It squanders that advantage when it fails to recognize that this landscape is the product of an energetic state and active polity.

Chapter 1

The Enduring Legacy of Nineteenth-Century
Governance in the United States:
The Emergence of the Associational Order

That nineteenth-century Americans did not want the national government involved in their lives, that they preferred to leave things to state and local government and a free market unencumbered by government intervention and that they got their wish—a central government that did not do anything important—has informed popular interpretations of nineteenth-century U.S. history. It has influenced scholarly accounts of twentieth-century political development as well, and continues to frame twenty-first-century political debate, with partisans dividing over the battle to resurrect or bury America's *laissez-faire* tradition.

But what would our account of state building in the twentieth century look like if the fundamental historical premise upon which Progressives and conservatives have waged war for the past one hundred years is flawed? What if the battle between big and small government, and the sharp line often drawn between public and private, is grounded in a false historical premise?

I argued in *A Government Out of Sight: The Mystery of National Authority in Nineteenth-Century America* that although the United States did indeed govern differently than its industrialized counterparts, it did not govern *less*. Americans *did*, however, govern *less visibly*. The key feature that distinguished the United States in the nineteenth century was the preference among its citizens for national governance that was inconspicuous. Americans preferred to use the language of the law, the courts, trade policy, fiscal subsidies—supported by indirect taxes—and partnerships with non-governmental associations, instead of more overt, bureaucratic, and visible interventions into the political economy.[1]

These patterns of interaction between citizens and the national government established over the course of the nineteenth century are best described by a phrase coined by Ellis Hawley and applied to his interpretation of the middle third of twentieth-century American history. As Hawley saw it, an "associative state" emerged in the early twentieth century. By then, many of the private, voluntary, and federated state and local organizations that were born in the late nineteenth century had come of age. Some were corporations that were national, if not international, in scope. Others were professional organizations like the American Medical Association. Still grounded in its state chapters, it began to have a national impact through its federated structure. Voluntary organizations like the International Red Cross were full-throated advocates for and recipients of the national government's power to organize and coordinate public policy across state and local boundaries. National authority was exercised through these key intermediaries and in partnership with them, paving the way for public policies that were national in scope.[2]

The associative state overlaid the kinds of horizontal interlocking relationships between citizens and their localities and states that had evolved over the first 150 years of American history. These kinds of relationships were epitomized by the nested layers of jurisdictions that Americans called federalism. But an emerging associational order offered opportunities for citizens to break out of that older regime while avoiding the kind of central, hierarchical government that Americans had always feared and continue to resist today.

An organizational revolution, from the Gilded Age through the 1920s, powered reforms that were national in scope yet stopped short of building a powerful central state. Because the private and voluntary sectors of the civil sphere had outgrown local and regional constraints, many of the organizations that now inhabited these realms stood ready, willing, and able to work in conjunction with the national government, just as their more localized forerunners had partnered with state and local government as they strived to realize the commonwealth ideal of mixed enterprise for much of the nineteenth century. In the nineteenth century, these partnerships produced an impressive system of communications, starting with the U.S. Postal Service, and extending to roads, canals, and railroads. In the twentieth century, such partnerships ranged from farm supports to tax expenditures for so-called private health care provision.

By the twentieth century, the states themselves sought more systematic ways to coordinate their efforts in order to achieve national objectives, ultimately founding the National Governors Association in 1908. While it would take them a bit longer, cities, by the second half of the twentieth century, emerged along with the states as one of the nation's more powerful national lobbies by, in many instances, lobbying for more national funding. To ignore the long-standing pattern of cooperation across the public/private boundary, or to neglect the public impact of organizations and federations that served national constituencies just because they did not wield plenary state power, is to misunderstand one of the great turning points in American history.[3]

Standard accounts of American political development characterize the Progressive Era as the moment that the rise of the modern administrative state emerged, replete with the bully pulpit and newly found centralized authority. It was the dawn of the "administrative state" as scholars like Stephen Skowronek have called it. While instances of such expansions in unitary state power are surely part of the story, they are the least representative part of the quest to tackle the national challenges that Americans faced at the turn of the century.[4]

The kind of state that Progressives advocated was best articulated by Eldon Eisenach when he talks about "parastates." He defines them this way:

> Progressives deeply doubted that the presently constituted national government and, indeed, most state governments were capable of achieving "stateness"—and for good reason. They were equally skeptical—absent a changed legal and institutional framework—about the willingness of large financial and industrial trusts to institutionalize and embody a larger public good. What they did instead was to impute "stateness" only to those institutions and practices consciously devoted to an articulate conception of the common good regardless of their legal or constitutional status.[5]

Although the transition evolved slowly over the course of the nineteenth century, the remnants of authority that had resided in "the self-government of households, towns, counties," and the several states themselves were undermined by associations that cut across such little "republics," allowing citizens working through these national associations and organizations to engage directly with, or serve as a substitute for, the national government. Bolstered by the very Fourteenth Amendment that was intended to protect the rights of freedmen, corporations took full advantage of their due process protections when states sought to rein in their growing reach. To be sure, their first purpose was to turn a profit, which they did handsomely, and it often came at the expense of those workers who rarely shared fully in those profits. Yet many of these same corporations were the first to promote the very kinds of practices that ultimately subdued parochial and short-sighted practices, whether it was selling meat that had not been inspected or decimating forests that happened to be easily accessible to local populations.[6]

As Theda Skocpol and others have demonstrated, national associations from the American Association for Labor Legislation to the General Federation of Women's Clubs were as locally grounded as towns and counties. But properly organized and effectively mobilized, they offered citizens direct access to national policy decisions—from public health to civil service reform.[7]

This is not to say that national organizations displaced federalism. Powerful groups like the American Medical Association still relied heavily on state licensing laws to control entry into the profession. Ultimately, however, national associations did undermine the authority of political parties, which, until the late nineteenth century, had enjoyed the advantage of serving as one of the few nationally organized voluntary groups that could mobilize voters locally to address, or at least claim to address, national issues. By the 1920s, interest-group politics shaped both electoral preferences and policy outcomes that had once been the relatively exclusive domain of partisan politics.[8]

The emergence of partners in the private and voluntary sectors who were capable of operating on a national scale and the increased federated activities of states and even cities that on occasion partnered with the national government spurred Progressive Era development. Sometimes these associations served as catalysts toward national expansion and sometimes they were the deputized agents, distributing the national authority parceled out to them. This associational order addressed problems spawned by industrialization, international trade, and rapid urban expansion, arming reformers with a long-standing American approach to problem solving. It relied on the national government to serve as coordinator and facilitator.

Rather than command, national governance was more often hidden in plain sight. The organizational revolution that swept the nation from the Gilded Age through the Progressive Era meant that reformers now had the wherewithal to execute this associational approach to national problems, as corporations, trade associations, interest groups, professional organizations, and federations of state and local officials expanded to continental proportions. In the wake of the exceptional, and exceptionally unsuccessful, attempts to maintain a strict division between public and private action during the Gilded Age, Progressives embraced this associational order, addressing problems that ranged from labor relations to conservation.

Ellis Hawley's scholarship best captures these associational interactions, distilling the model in his article "Herbert Hoover, the Commerce Secretariat, and the Vision of an 'Associative State.'" Hoover believed that the way to reconcile individual initiative while harmonizing interests "lay in the development and proper use of cooperative institutions, particularly trade associations, professional societies, and similar organizations among farmers and laborers." Yet Hawley's work, though highly influential among a handful of policy-oriented historians, never fully captured the hearts and minds of political historians. Rather than acknowledge the associational nature of national power, scholars, even today, remain wedded to accounts that chart the rise and fall of liberalism—framed as the battle between big and small government.[9]

Indeed, shoehorned into the twentieth-century historiographic straitjacket of liberal, or Progressive, history, Hawley's insistence that Hoover sought to capitalize upon the malleable boundaries between the public sector and private sphere, mediated by interest groups and encouraged by a political culture hospitable to pluralism, serves as a footnote for the more sophisticated interpretations of a transition from nineteenth-century classical liberalism to the big government future embodied in the New Deal. Other interpretations simply consign Hoover to a reactionary fate.

Besides the long odds that any synthetic reinterpretation would face in challenging a powerful scholarly approach that reinforced more popular understandings of history, associational interpretations suffered an even more daunting challenge. They lacked range. Compared to the work of Charles Beard, Vernon Parrington, and Frederick Jackson Turner, who, between them, covered much of American history, an interpretative framework confined largely to twenty years stood little chance. It was hard to associate the associative state with much beyond Herbert Hoover's rise to power and some of FDR's early programs, like the National Industrial Recovery Act. Even the organizational synthesis, which embraced Hawley's interpretation, was grounded in the first half of the twentieth century and, infamously, used Robert Wiebe's "island communities" as its Gilded Age launching pad—a move that only reinforced notions of the "modern" state's laissez-faire precursors.[10]

Yet Hawley was on to something big. Indeed, he began to sketch an interpretation that offered a powerful alternative to the standard Progressive story of American political development. Hawley got the middle right. And Eisenach's conception of parastates illustrates the Progressive Era reliance upon the cooperative governance that the associational order was built upon. It now remains for scholars to apply that interpretive framework to the beginning of American political development and to its most recent twists and turns.

With some allowances for time and place, and greater attention to the law than Hawley and Eisenach devoted, many of the central patterns of governance forged in nineteenth-century America anticipated the kinds of associations among private, voluntary, and government actors that Hawley and Eisenach wrote about. What's more, the national government's role as coordinator, catalyst, and at times regulator endured for much of the twentieth century as well. Once the false dichotomies between laissez-faire and big government are exposed, and once the long history of mixing public and private authority in the nineteenth century is revealed, the pervasive nature of associational governance in America, and, perhaps more importantly, its enduring legacies, can serve as a powerful template for understanding two and a half centuries of American political development.

Five Enduring Patterns

Over the course of the nineteenth century, Americans eschewed visible, centralized, national administration by the central government. That citizens resisted a national bureaucratic state does not mean that they did not ask the national government to do a lot for them. Combining national resources and private initiative proved to be a consistent formula for political success in policies ranging from land distribution to internal improvements. Subsidizing a communications system that provided access to newspapers in remote locations stimulated national political debate in a polity that was highly decentralized. The general government was instrumental in constructing a national market—a contribution soon washed from memory in a torrent of congratulations for America's exceptional stature among supposedly far more statist industrialized nations. During the Gilded Age, the federal judiciary labored mightily to separate public from private action. It failed to do so, opening the door for the reintegration of public and private endeavors on a national scale in the twentieth century.

There were plenty of exceptions to this rule. Americans consistently supported a more energetic, even bureaucratically empowered state, whenever they perceived their security to be threatened—a second pattern that played out over the course of the nineteenth century. The Civil War was the most pronounced example of this pattern—especially the Confederacy's Leviathan-like intervention into the private sphere. The same phenomenon was evident with the War of Independence and, to a lesser degree, the wars of 1812 and with Mexico. Americans were willing to grant the federal government even more power when Indians threatened security and economic development. The Trail of Tears was forged by an extraordinary mobilization of federal resources and naked use of force.

A third pattern was the tendency to endorse unmediated national power when it was geographically removed from the locus of established authority. This was the case in the territories that eventually became states, which were governed directly by the national government, and for a short period, in the early twentieth century, in territories acquired during the Spanish-American War. It also was the pattern established through the programs aimed at western resource development, such as irrigation and forestry. It was no coincidence that the U.S. Army proved to be a crucial resource here too. Americans who would never have tolerated this threat to their autonomy back East supported it out West. It was used to subdue Indians and police national forests. Eventually, it was used to build dams and determine grazing rights.

The key variable was the availability of intermediary institutions. Once they existed, Americans preferred that they be used, rather than extending national authority directly. But the principle of empowering the central government at the periphery prevailed precisely because such intermediaries did not exist out West or abroad. Sustaining national authority in such remote regions required that intermediaries, starting with the basic building blocks of federalism, be nurtured to accommodate policies made in Washington, DC, to local needs.

A fourth pattern, closely related to the first, was resistance to visible forms of national taxation. This, of course, was one of the reasons that Americans went to war against Great Britain. The threat of British functionaries violating the civil liberties of British North Americans was as unnerving to the colonists as the financial consequences of such taxes. Unable to avoid national taxation entirely, Americans settled uncomfortably on the tariff. The discomfort, however, had more to do with the inequitable distribution of costs and benefits from the tariff than the manner in which this tax was imposed. Almost all Americans agreed that this indirect form of taxation was preferable to direct taxes such as excise taxes.

Use of judge-made law to shape the political economy constituted a fifth legacy of nineteenth-century governance. Like the tendency to rely on intermediary institutions in order to stave off centralized control, heavy reliance on courts allowed for national policy with little in the way of bureaucracy.

To sum up, Americans were willing to support powerful centralized institutions during crises that threatened their security or when these institutions operated far from population centers, where there were no intermediate institutions like states and localities to get the job done. For most day-to-day responsibilities, however, indirect taxes supported a national government that sought to coordinate rather than command and that depended upon judge-made law to pave the way for a national market. For the most part, the national government remained hidden in plain sight, as it operated through subsidies, diplomacy, and partnerships with intermediaries ranging from local governments to private corporations. As the number of organizations that operated on a national scale expanded during the Gilded Age, the possibilities for a national associational order expanded.

Relocating Twentieth-Century Governance

More effectively, albeit less boisterously than the high-profile battles fought between those who worked to expand the national bureaucratic state and their opponents who sought to impose an idealized conception of Gilded Age laissez-faire on state-society relations, nineteenth-century patterns of interaction between state and society were advanced during the twentieth century through national associations working in conjunction with the federal government. Some of these associations were public—states and local governments. Some were voluntary organizations like Blue Cross and Blue Shield. Some were religiously inspired: Even in the American Economics Association, almost half of the original members were ordained clergymen. And some were profit-making corporations that ranged from defense contractors to the trade associations that served corporate masters. While the American Red Cross was unique in that it was chartered by the U.S. government in 1900, formalizing what would grow into a powerful working relationship between government and the voluntary sector in foreign affairs, most of these associations engaged national public policy in ways that strengthened their ties to the central government over the course of the twentieth century.[11]

Working with the national government, these groups constituted an associational order. Consummated on a national scale at the end of the nineteenth century, this associational order operated within the contours of political patterns established over the course of the nineteenth century. State and local governments developed the capacity to act in concert on a national scale. Professions developed powerful national organizations, and universities emerged as national centers of expertise. Voluntary organizations adapted their agendas to national needs. Interest groups and trade associations flocked to Washington, DC. Corporate social policy competed with voluntary organizations and public agencies to promote welfare. By targeting their appeals through national organizations that worked with the national government and often administered its policies, both at home and abroad, Americans demanded support and services from the national government at the same time that many continued to rail against big government. Filtered through the associational order, such federal support seemed less threatening—even traditional.[12]

With this set of nationally organized associations serving as intermediaries between national government and the individual, Americans could preserve their sense of individual autonomy and personal control. The associational order capitalized on the collective impulse inherent in the commonwealth tradition without abandoning the classical liberal commitment to individual rights. Individually oriented rights and the preservation of individual initiative, both economically and politically, provided the essential link between classical and new liberalism. Yet associations served collective ends, even if those ends spread beyond local or state boundaries.

The new national associations did not eviscerate the federal forms of representation built into the core of the Constitution. But they did overlay that federal structure, thickening the opportunities for intercourse beyond town, state, and region, and ultimately changing the very shape of federalism itself. The associational order tapped public-sector resources, nationalized through the rich range of organizations that emerged by the early twentieth century. This provided the possibility of achieving, on a national scale, what proponents of the commonwealth ideal had hoped to accomplish locally in the mid-nineteenth century. Like the facades of nineteenth-century buildings that now grace modern office buildings in Washington, DC, federalism endured but now served as only one doorway—and often a symbolic one at that—to edifices built at a very different time, to serve far more national constituencies.[13]

A history of twentieth-century political development that is informed by our revised understanding of Americans' quest for governance out of sight alters the standard story. A number of scholars, many of them political scientists, have already begun to pull back the curtain and reveal the "hidden" welfare and carceral states, or the "contractual" national security state. Others have chronicled the powerful way in which the national government has responded to waves of moral impulses. Many of these scholars explore the deep historical roots of such policies. However, few have recognized the degree to which this tendency to delegate national authority, and, in some instances, to disburse huge sums of taxpayer dollars through intermediary institutions, accelerated a long-standing American tradition forged over the course of the nineteenth century.[14]

A quick review of a few of these "hidden" networks of twentieth-century national authority underscores the continuity of this aspect of nineteenth-century state-society relations. Framing twentieth-century development in this longer-term historical pattern also connects submerged and inconspicuous realms of national authority to a broader interpretation of the evolution of American politics. It offers an alternative to the reigning perspective that pits small government against big government. It confirms that Americans have always turned to the national government to solve certain kinds of problems and that they were most successful when they crafted solutions that did not rely exclusively on that national authority.[15]

Much of the Progressive Era's effort to shape the social environment should be viewed in the context of restoring some of the traffic across the artificial boundary that Gilded Age jurists, theorists, and some politicians sought to erect. While Progressives were eager to intervene in ways that reshaped the environment and leveled the playing field for individuals, they

feared that any bureaucratic structures developed by the national government would soon be captured by partisan or, even worse, corrupt field
marshals. They did not have to look far for examples, citing the U.S. Pension Bureau as exhibit A. Progressives hedged their bets, treating national
administrative capacity as merely one of many kinds of associative actions
required to solve the nation's problems.[16]

At first glance, the Progressive Era certainly appears to signal the rise of
the administrative state. The traditional story turns on impressive examples
of state building at the national level. To cite just a few, Teddy Roosevelt
and his chief forester, Gifford Pinchot, used the president's executive
authority to add tens of millions of acres to the forests managed by the
national government. By the time Pinchot left office in 1910, the federal
government managed two hundred million acres. The 1906 Pure Food and
Drug Act and Meat Inspection Act subjected food and other products to
testing by national inspectors for the first time. Each of these important
actions either increased the size of the national bureaucracy or significantly
expanded existing authority.[17]

Placing each of these federal interventions in a historical context that
accounts for the ways in which nineteenth-century Americans governed
and the national associational order that emerged at the end of that century
explains these developments more effectively than a sudden infatuation
with national state building. The national government acted far more
directly and powerfully at the margins of the nation. Many of Roosevelt's
and Taft's conservation programs could never have been imposed in the
East. That the national government remained the largest landholder in the
West was one crucial reason for its authority. Many Westerners demanded
a federal presence, for the same reasons that nineteenth-century Americans
had clamored for internal development and territorial governance: It was
crucial to their economic and political development.

While Gifford Pinchot lashed out at corporate greed, he worked closely
with the largest livestock associations to craft a grazing policy for the
national forests. The American National Live Stock Association shared Pinchot's vision of managed grazing in the national forests. Pinchot even
appointed a stalwart in the Arizona Wool Growers Association to head up
the Grazing Division. By insisting on managing the nation's forests "scientifically," Pinchot emulated the policies of the largest lumber interests, such
as Weyerhaeuser. That the Forest Service claimed to be self-financing from
selling lumber in the national forests was an important element of the

conservation program, often overlooked by historians. Taking millions of acres of forest out of circulation undoubtedly increased the value of forest held by large corporate interests, pushing up the price of lumber. Rather than displacing the market, federal intervention into forestry shored up that market on a national scale. It did so in conjunction with corporate partners in lumber and agribusiness and by blending public and private efforts.[18]

Newly empowered professionals were a key ingredient in this mixture. These experts supposedly could transcend partisan and parochial interests. Produced by graduate programs, like the Yale School of Forestry, these professionals stood as crucial intermediaries in the new associational order.[19]

The movement for pure food and drugs was another policy area where such experts were in evidence. Here, the key government official was Harvey Wiley, who was the chief chemist in the Chemistry Bureau. Wiley's initiative, Progressive muckraking journalism, the publication of Upton Sinclair's *The Jungle* (which described in graphic detail just what went into processed meats), and public furor over the safety and the quality of its food were all important components of the drive for action that resulted in federal legislation. But it was Wiley's ability to draw on a broad range of associations, ranging from the National Food and Drug Congress (which included professional groups, public health agencies, and grocers) to the American Medical Association and the General Federation of Women's Clubs, that provided the political staying power to push through the pure food and meat inspection acts. More importantly, the largest meatpackers were already inspecting. They had to do this in order to serve an international market that demanded as much.

National legislation imposed costs on smaller operators that were already being borne by the corporate first movers in the associational order, and shifted the responsibility and cost of coordinating this effort to the national government. As with forestry, the national government worked in tandem with large corporations to stabilize the market and ensure a continuous supply of quality product.[20]

The examples of "special" associational action—"special" because they *did* expand the administrative capacity of the national government—were a small fraction of the associational expansion in the first third of the twentieth century. Progressives turned to a range of nationally oriented organizations as *alternatives* to federal administration: Eisenach's "parastates." They ranged from loosely organized women's groups to hierarchically organized corporations. Their degree of federal involvement also varied from minimal to extensive. But the trajectory in all cases was similar—toward a more active federal role in coordination and financing.[21]

Women who organized around issues of special concern to their sisters constituted one such parastate. For decades, women were instrumental in forging voluntary networks that provided social services to the indigent, especially women and children. Even without the vote, these women soon turned to state and local governments and eventually the national government—lobbying for the Sheppard-Towner Act—to finance these efforts. Ultimately, the Women's Bureau established a beachhead in the national government for programs directed at women and children. Whether financed at the local or the national level, however, many of the actual services were delivered by a diverse array of voluntary groups, making these programs more palatable to a broad range of Americans.

Contrary to the scholarly truism that women were more powerful politically *before* they had the vote, women leveraged their votes to hold elected officials accountable. True to a tradition that preferred the national government to play a supporting role, many women demanded that services be delivered through the voluntary, state, and local outlets that constituted the associational order, not directly by the national government. Thus, funding for health services in the states actually increased after the Sheppard-Towner Act expired.[22]

Universities also constituted a crucial parastate. Perhaps their most important contribution to the associational order was to create and certify professionals. Universities helped professions, like medicine, establish control over an exclusive body of esoteric knowledge that increased its authority and stature. Of equal importance, universities limited access to the professions, reducing competition within the profession itself. Through state licensing, professionals were granted a remarkable degree of autonomy over their own practices. Delegating life-and-death decisions on health care to groups like the American Medical Association had important public policy implications. Like other parastates, the professions and universities soon dramatically increased the support that they received from all levels of government while retaining a great deal of their autonomy. Although state legislatures, on occasion, intervened in highly visible fashion, and even though the national government eventually demanded more accountability, for much of the twentieth century vast sums of taxpayer money, public authority, and crucial policy choices were delegated to the professions and the universities that created and renewed these professions.[23]

Universities also served as coordinating mechanisms for state and federally sponsored public programs. The best example of this is the farm experiment stations and the extension service that worked hand in hand with
them. The 1887 Hatch Act provided federal funding for agricultural
research at the state land-grant colleges created by the Morrill Land-Grant
College Act of 1862. These laboratories were established to generate new
knowledge and, more importantly, to apply that knowledge to the needs of
farmers. Land-grant colleges created, and the national government eventually subsidized, an extension service that translated science into productive
agricultural practice.

Even when Americans were forced to construct new national bureaucracies in response to the economic crisis of the 1930s, long-established
patterns prevailed. There is no better example of this tendency than the
legislation that many consider to be the crowning accomplishment of the
New Deal state: the Social Security Act. That social insurance program had
highly visible and even intrusive elements. Franklin D. Roosevelt, for
instance, worried that assigning numbers to working Americans would
smack of totalitarian government; he was concerned that these numbers
would be labeled "dog tags." Yet social insurance—which did assign social
security numbers—was the *only* title of this omnibus legislation that was
administered at the national level. Welfare, unemployment compensation,
and several other key social programs included in the act were administered
at the state and local levels. FDR was keen to spin off administration of
social insurance as well, but even his brain trust could not figure out a way,
in an age before computers, to keep track of Americans who were likely to
move between states over the course of a lifetime. Keeping track was essential because the Social Security Administration and the Democratic Party
claimed that retirement benefits were akin to personal savings accounts that
would be there when most needed.[24]

It was the contributory element of social insurance that Roosevelt liked
most—even if it did require national administration. The program's supporters labored to maintain the image that workers got back what they put
in, even as the program itself became an engine for fiscal redistribution
from younger generations to the elderly. It lifted several generations of the
elderly out of poverty at the expense of future generations of retirees. Three
quarters of a century later, social security remains one of the few nationally
administered income maintenance programs, and it is sharply distinguished
from locally administered "welfare" programs by the perception that those

collecting social security benefits are merely getting back what they contributed *individually*. The social insurance formula hit the trifecta in this regard: Individuals felt that they had their own private accounts; employers (and the individuals) contributed to a trust fund that specified what these revenues could be spent on; and the government—as inconspicuously as possible—subsidized several generations of beneficiaries.[25]

As in the past, Americans did empower the national government to expand its administrative reach (and suspend civil liberties) when national security was threatened. World War II and the ensuing Cold War leaps out as the most illustrative example, although the most sweeping reorganization of the executive branch of the national government since the Cold War era occurred in the wake of the attack on the World Trade Center and Pentagon on September 11, 2001. Like British North Americans, or Americans in 1861, mid-twentieth-century Americans jettisoned their concerns about standing armies and quickly embraced a central government with considerably enhanced powers. During the Cold War, they went even further, constructing what I have labeled a "proministrative" state that combined professional expertise with federal administrative capacity to wage this twilight struggle. Even during the Cold War, however, Americans avoided what Harold D. Lasswell labeled the "garrison state." They did so by constructing a "contract state," taking a page out of the nineteenth-century Post Office and the nineteenth-century Army procurement handbook. The military-industrial complex thrived in the American setting by outsourcing to the private sector and to academia some of its most vital functions, ranging from weapons development to psychological warfare.[26]

The classified, contractual, national security state is merely one of several vast regimes that remain hidden and, consequently, insulated from careful scrutiny. The others do not rely on security clearances. Rather, they are hidden in plain sight, obscured only by our failure to appreciate long-standing patterns of American governance. While the list of such regimes is long, the hidden elements of the welfare state, the carceral state, and the federally subsidized infrastructure for suburban growth epitomize America's ability to ignore the national government's influence when it is delivered in a manner that does not create visible national bureaucratic structures. The great irony is that this is precisely how Americans prefer their governance.

Management guru Peter Drucker, writing in the 1970s, referred to the proliferation of private pension plans that dotted the corporate landscape after World War II as an "unseen revolution." In Drucker's opinion, it was an "outstanding example of the efficacy of using the existing private, non-governmental institutions of our 'society of organizations' for the formulation and achievement of social goals and the satisfaction of social needs." Drucker got one thing wrong: the nongovernmental part (although he was correct to deny the presence of visible national institutions). As Jacob Hacker, one of the charter scholars of the "hidden welfare state" school, put it, "Quite the opposite: Private pensions have been encouraged by public policy both directly and indirectly—through tax and labor law, through targeted regulatory interventions, and through the structure and reach of Social Security itself." Health care provision has traveled the same path, being shaped by federal tax policy that subsidizes "private" health care benefits provided by employers. The taxes forgone (or expended) on pensions and health benefits neared $200 billion by 1999, approximating the cost of Medicare.[27]

Conclusion

The decision to delegate national treasure and administrative capacity to the associational order has had significant consequences. Pensions and health care delivered through private mechanisms, regardless of the billions of federal dollars that subsidize them, are skewed toward the middle class and upward. While the United States spends no less on social provisions than other industrialized nations, its benefits go disproportionately toward those who need them the least. No wonder that Progressives are wary of hidden states. No wonder that to the extent Progressives acknowledge these regimes hidden in plain sight, they call for alternatives.[28]

This is where I part ways with most Progressives. I do so for two reasons grounded in lessons drawn from my historical understanding of American political development. The first lesson is that history endures. In spite of a Herculean effort to distinguish sharply between public and private spheres in the Gilded Age, the long-standing pattern of melding these two spheres persisted in America. In fact, this amalgam of public and private soon thrived at the national level like never before—aided by the emergence of an associative order and connective institutions like the American Farm Bureau Federation and the American Medical Association. Second, governance out of sight "works" in the sense that Americans accept it. Indeed, they demand it.

Medicare may be the best example of this. It is an example that most Progressives still fail to appreciate. During the heat of the town hall meetings on President Obama's health care reform proposal, one outraged citizen warned conservative Congressman Robert Inglis (R-SC) to "keep your government hands off my Medicare." Inglis responded, "Actually, sir, your health care is being provided by the government." "But he wasn't having any of it," Inglis told the *Washington Post*. Progressive blogs were soon all over the story. *Slate*, for instance, noted similar confusion between public and private benefits among Medicare recipients during the Clinton campaign for health care reform, and it vowed to keep a running tally of people who encourage "such nonsense." Bill Maher likened the statement to "driving cross country to protest highways."[29]

The phenomenon that Representative Inglis addressed was not new. Americans have been forgetting about the state since the founding. Recognition of the role that the feds played is often the first casualty when historical narratives are constructed. The state has consistently been displaced by individual initiative and market mechanisms in personal and collective memory and, more often than not, in scholarly interpretations as well.

Reorienting the contemporary debate from big versus small government to a discussion about how best to solve pressing problems through means that Americans historically have embraced—means that *include* national governance—offers a great opportunity to break a stalemate that historically has only been resolved during times of crisis. Conservatives should concede that Americans have always turned to the national government to solve problems. In fact, conservatives—whether Gilded Age jurists or businessmen eager to establish national markets—have often been the first to advocate energetic national governance.

For their part, Progressives should break their lock-step assumption that cooperative partnerships between public and voluntary, or even private, organizations are inherently regressive. Progressives should also master the art of turning the legal and fiscal resources of the national government toward redistributive ends. In short, they should learn how to make government work toward Progressive ends through means that reinforce the powerful belief that the central government is merely coordinating individual initiative or a range of more trusted intermediaries. That is precisely what FDR achieved with social security legislation and what Lyndon B. Johnson achieved by building on the conception of "individual contributions" to Medicare. While this is no easy task, it is far more promising than reverse-engineering the mechanisms through which Americans have governed for much of their history.

Americans must reclaim the national government's critical role in enabling nineteenth-century American expansion, stimulating economic development, and managing international relations. This reclamation project will not get far if it fails to place the engagement of a twentieth-century associational order in the nineteenth-century tradition of governance that regularly blurred the line between public- and private-sector solutions. We must better understand the range of cooperative mechanisms that connected state and society. Governmental authority today, as it has for most of our history, relies on a series of compromises brokered between central authority and local administration; it continues to rely on a host of private and voluntary partners that blur the line between public and private spheres. Although instances can be found from the Gilded Age that correspond to the strict division between public and private spheres inherent in conservative ideologues' and Progressive pundits' views of the world, those who seek to ground America's future in that vision of the past should be aware of the extraordinarily narrow and precarious sliver of history upon which it stands.

Chapter 2

Scientific Forestry and the Roots of the Modern American State: Gifford Pinchot's Path to Progressive Reform

Gifford Pinchot was the Progressive Era's Forrest Gump. When it came to the politics of conservation, he was everywhere. Pinchot was the youngest member of the National Forest Commission in 1896. He directed the Division of Forestry (later the Forest Service) from 1898 through 1910. Pinchot engineered the transfer of the national forests from the Department of Interior to the Department of Agriculture, where his Forest Service was based. He actively managed those forests, even when this entailed fierce battles with Western interests. Pinchot battled Secretary of the Interior Richard A. Ballinger over the future of conservation in the Taft administration. He insisted that the nation's natural resources be used productively even at the expense of damming the Hetch Hetchy Valley to provide water to the City of San Francisco. No wonder that Pinchot is a central figure for environmental and political historians alike. Illuminating a powerful new current in environmental history that treats man as an essential part of nature, Char Miller's *Gifford Pinchot and the Making of Modern Environmentalism* portrays Pinchot at ease in both the "utilitarian" world as well as the world of trees, streams, and wildlife. Miller's work offers a promising route out of the conservation versus preservation dichotomy that once structured the work of environmental historians examining the Progressive Era.[1]

Complementing Miller's contributions to environmental history, this essay reconsiders the *political* ground that Pinchot stood on when he launched his career in the late nineteenth century. William Cronon has summed up Pinchot's current political profile best in a synthetic essay written for *The Oxford History of the American West*. Pinchot spearheaded a drive to convert public land policy from one that sought first and foremost to disperse public holdings to private interests to a policy that sought to retain, conserve, and manage the public land. To achieve this, Cronon writes, Pinchot turned to a new body of knowledge—scientific forestry— and a new cadre of experts who circumvented traditional democratic practices in order to make long-term decisions that better served the general public. Pinchot was able to instill in the young men who subscribed to this "gospel of efficiency," a remarkable esprit de corps. Progressive conservationists were suspicious of democratic institutions and preferred executive authority to legislative maneuvers. As Cronon puts it, they "saw the good of 'the whole' (by which they often meant well-to-do middle-class easterners like themselves) as being more important than the special concerns of individual constituencies." Neutral expertise, esprit de corps, solicitude for the general good over the grasping machinations of special interests, a preference for executive action, and centralized control over crucial elements of the economy previously left to the private sector: These are the central themes of the Pinchot story and of Progressive state building as we know them today.[2]

Whether one looks at reclamation, grazing, or forestry, the Progressive agenda in the field of conservation produced major repercussions at the national level. "What," Karen Merrill has asked, "could be more statist than to take property out of the marketplace and lodge it under permanent government administration?" The reaction of many Americans, particularly Westerners, underscores Merrill's point. One congressman described the newly minted regulators created by the Forest Reserve System as "goggle-eyed, bandy-legged dudes from the East." Senator Henry Teller (Colorado) characterized these bureaucrats as men "who had absolutely no acquaintance with the subject, who were too indolent to go over the country and examine its geography, who simply sat in their offices and made the laws, doing the utmost injustice to the people."[3]

Gifford Pinchot bore the brunt of such criticism. Born into a wealthy family in 1865, educated at Yale, trained as a forester abroad, Gifford Pinchot became the head of the Forestry Division of the Department of Agriculture in 1898. In his twelve years as the nation's chief forester, Pinchot transformed a sleepy office of ten that controlled no forests of its own into the U.S. Forest Service with a staff of more than 2,500. Many of these foresters were professionally trained—a disproportionate number at the Yale School of Forestry. The Forest Service actively managed an empire of reserves that, by the time Pinchot was forced out of office in 1910, consisted of approximately two hundred million acres. Pinchot also promoted the concept of conservation as Teddy Roosevelt's de facto adviser on this policy area and through numerous presidential commissions.

How did Pinchot achieve so much? This essay revises three crucial elements of the standard answer to this question as summed up in Cronon by looking the early career of Gifford Pinchot. I examine some of the personal networks that Pinchot developed at Yale. These proved to be remarkably enduring. Because Pinchot, like other Progressives, eschewed partisan patronage politics, he turned to a personal network reinforced by his private wealth to administer a program that spanned the nation. Personal and financial connections were the prerequisites for the much-vaunted esprit de corps that the Forest Service became famous for.

Next, I explore the process through which Pinchot was transformed into a professional. It was, to say the least, half-baked. Nevertheless, Pinchot emerged as a leading expert in the American context. He recognized the great political value of professional expertise and dedicated his energy and personal fortune to establishing his profession in America, eventually founding the Yale School of Forestry. Pinchot's expertise was a political tool that he honed more sharply than his woodsman's axe. Pinchot not only deployed expertise for political gain—he helped define expertise in ways that would yield political benefits.

By looking at Pinchot's initial foray into publicity while managing Biltmore Forest for George Vanderbilt, I also revise one of the most fundamental misconceptions in the scholarship on Progressivism. I recapture a Pinchot at odds with the centralizing command and control model generally associated with him and other Progressive state builders. It was at Biltmore that Pinchot learned the value of framing publicity to demonstrate that scientific forestry met market tests. Like other lessons from his early career, the rhetoric of the market would be deployed to garner support from a majority of Americans. When personal patronage is substituted for team spirit, expertise placed in its proper political context, and demands for extending federal control ameliorated by appeals to traditional nineteenth-century faith in the market, a different perspective on Pinchot emerges. Combined with the examples of Pinchot's reliance on special interests and dependence on the legislative process for the most important public policy achievement of his career—the transfer of the national forests from the Department of the Interior to Pinchot's control in the Department of

Agriculture—I portray Pinchot as extraordinarily sensitive to the democratic give and take of early twentieth-century politics.[4]

Before examining Pinchot's use of personal and financial ties, his meta-
morphosis from novice forester to American expert, and his turn toward
market models in order to demonstrate that forestry paid, it is useful to
examine Gifford Pinchot's personal motivations and how he reconciled
these with the demands of career, religion, and class. Pinchot's personal
resolution, it turned out, resonated with millions of Americans precisely
because it resolved some of the tensions between consumption and utility
(categorized later by scholars as preservation and conservation). Pinchot
was no theorist. More than anything else, he was a guy who wanted to get
out into the woods. But there was no escaping the upper-class background,
religious upbringing, and parental demands that enveloped him. It was out
of these pressures that Pinchot forged a career in forestry. Nor did there
seem to be any way to manage a forest successfully, save through the federal
government. The solutions that Pinchot crafted to these pressures ultimately did help him get out into the woods, at least when he was not
behind his federal desk.

Working Out of Doors

Gifford was born at his grandfather's summer house in Connecticut on
August 11, 1865, to James and Mary Jane Pinchot. James, the son of a
wealthy Pennsylvania landowner, engaged in land speculation himself and
eventually established a company in New York that sold interior furnish-
ings. Besides providing support for the arts, natural history, and improved
housing for the poor, James was an amateur student of forestry, which he
had observed in Europe, long before it was practiced in the United States.
Mary Jane Pinchot was the daughter of Amos Eno, one of the richest men
in the United States at the time. Gifford grew up in New York City and, by
adolescence, had traveled extensively in Europe.[5]

From the Pinchots' perspective, privilege did not mean a life of leisure.
Despite the family's wealth, James and Mary Pinchot were determined that
their children not be spoiled. Privilege carried with it a special obligation
to conserve the legacy that each Pinchot inherited and to add to it through
his or her labor. As Gifford explained to a friend in 1914, "My own money

came from unearned increment on land in New York held by my grandfather, who willed the money, not the land to me. Having got my wages in advance in that way, I am now trying to work them out."[6]

For men like Gifford Pinchot, Teddy Roosevelt, and William and Henry James, who did not work out of financial necessity and whose work yielded virtually no financial return (or in Pinchot's case drew heavily on the family's principal), why they worked, what they worked on, and whether they worked hard enough to retire the debt "advanced" to them were permanent concerns. Disciplined work did not come naturally to Gifford Pinchot. He was an energetic boy who from a very early age seemed drawn to action, not reflection. From the moment Pinchot left his parents' direct supervision through college, Pinchot battled parental demands that he work harder and more methodically. Sometimes Pinchot's parents approached the matter subtly, such as James's musings, drawn from a weekend's reading and passed on to his seventeen-year-old son Gifford. "On the Neck of a young man sparkles no gem so gracious as enterprise," James wrote his son. "A man accustomed to work is equal to any achievement he resolves on. More are made good by exercitation than by Nature," Gifford's dad continued. James, however, had no qualms about admonishing his son: "Education means discipline and from that standard you seem to get steadily further away." Mary Pinchot's concern with work and discipline was just as great; the rationale was more explicitly religious. Her letters kept alive the legacy of Puritanism as described by Max Weber, demanding not only that individuals embrace the calling to do God's work on earth, but insisting that men work regularly, conscientiously, and diligently.[7]

Enrolling at Phillips Academy, in Exeter, in 1882, Pinchot began with high hopes. These were dashed by the following year. "I have been thinking over the state of affairs lately," he wrote his mother, "and I have almost come to the conclusion that I had better take a year out of my school life and go into business." Informally, Pinchot had been working in a manly way for a long time by throwing himself into any outdoor activity that required great physical vigor. Outdoor recreation was the only boyhood activity that Gifford pursued assiduously and without prompting from his parents.[8]

As Pinchot began to contemplate careers, the problem of utility began to circumscribe his options. Nor could the question of social status be ignored. It was fine to prove that one could mix it up with the lower sorts. It was quite another thing to become one of them. Utility and social status complicated the challenge that to date the youthful Pinchot had shrugged off with the most cursory solutions. Teddy Roosevelt was about the same age when he traded in his vivarium for interests in law, politics, and public affairs.[9]

Perceived through the filigree of late nineteenth-century career options, working productively required that one derive the maximum utility from work. Utility was even more important than hard work. Like the pressure to work hard, utility fused religious and economic strains in American thought. What animated these long-standing predispositions in late nineteenth-century Protestant culture was the religious revival that swept the Anglo-American community in the 1880s. Both Mary and her son were exposed to the teachings of the social gospel. While in England, Gifford was caught up in a great revival led by Reverend Aitken. Pinchot attended just about every night. The social gospel that Gifford most likely heard at this revival and that framed his religious beliefs in subsequent years taught that regardless of how hard the individual toiled, salvation lay in collective good works: Nobody could be saved until all had been saved. As one of the leading lights in the American version of this religious revival, Washington Gladden, put it, we first discern God "in the common life of man." This powerful strain of millennial thought redirected religious campaigns from efforts to improve the moral values of individuals toward measures designed to improve man's environment. The social gospel revitalized many Americans' sense of collective mission, energizing the Progressive movement. It directed hard work toward practical, productive social endeavors.[10]

Though the work ethic was still powerful in nineteenth-century America, it was not simply the Protestant ethic in modern dress. The term "calling" faded from common usage, replaced by a concern with "usefulness." The religious roots of useful work were reinforced by economists and essayists. Victorians concerned with scarcity emphasized the economic necessity of constant doing.[11]

Even without direct exposure to the social gospel, it would have been difficult for any man born in 1865 to overlook America's growing obsession with useful, productive activities. The United States was moving from an extensive economy to an intensive economy. Hard work was no longer a substitute for technique—both social and mechanical—to squeeze the maximum productivity out of America's natural resources. By the twentieth century, Frederick Winslow Taylor codified some of the principles of this quest in the private sector under the rubric of scientific management. The quest for efficiency soon became a highly publicized affair. Caricatured by the media, so-called efficiency experts captured the imagination of millions of Americans by the first decade of the twentieth century in what some have called the "efficiency craze."[12]

From the perspective of young men in Pinchot's position, the professions offered the best opportunity to fuse the productive and moral elements in the quest for social efficiency. The professions also preserved status. Thus, Pinchot's first mature career inclinations were divided between medicine and the ministry. Professional training met the requirements for hard work, suggested a degree of utility not easily found outside of business, provided a calling, and conferred status. Children of wealth from Pinchot's generation, like William and Henry James, paid the interest and then some on inherited "advances" through intellectual heavy lifting. Strenuous activity that took place in professionally sanctioned gymnasia was perceived to be useful, morally uplifting, and prestigious.[13]

Pinchot crafted a similar solution to his own dilemma: If the professions would not move out of doors, perhaps he could professionalize outdoor activities. The campaign took place at universities like Columbia and Yale. Pinchot's first love, like Frederick Winslow Taylor's, did not fall neatly into an existing professional domain. Like Taylor, Pinchot created a profession that fused his love, his obligation to preserve his gentlemanly status, and his efficient stewardship of God's resources in a world that demanded social utility. By the time Gifford was twenty-five his quest to establish himself as the nation's first professional forester had synthesized his love of the outdoors and sense of duty to God, class, family, and nation. Forestry promised the possibility of resolving some of the most pressing tensions in Pinchot's life. Whether defined as a calling, work, career, or profession, forestry, in Pinchot's case, wedded each to personal pleasure. "Just what a forester did . . . was beyond my ken," Pinchot recalled many years later. "But at least a forester worked in the woods and with the woods—and I loved the woods and everything about them."[14]

Pinchot's synthesis, forged in forestry, did more than resolve conflicting personal pressures: It reconciled work and pleasure at the very time in American history that the two had begun to compete vigorously for the moral and social high ground. Pinchot succeeded at the federal level precisely because his personal compromise, once transformed into a public agenda, carried so much cultural currency. By the last third of the nineteenth century, even the religious strain in American culture was suspended between worshiping a stern god who demanded constant work and a God who presided over a more bountiful kingdom—a God-as-friend who insisted that his flock take a vacation every now and then. The latter vision accompanied the rise of consumption and the promotion of leisure that by the 1880s had begun to take root among the upper and middle classes in the United States. By 1882, even Herbert Spencer could remark, "We have had somewhat too much of the 'gospel of work.' It is time to preach the gospel of relaxation." No wonder that department-store mogul John Wana-maker's Bethany Presbyterian Church in Philadelphia contained ushers that subscribed to the same spirit of service as his sales staff, featured an orchestra at worship services, and served its public around the clock. The broad appeal of Pinchot's personal compromise lay in its catholic embrace of the romantic elements historically associated with the preservation of nature and in its utilitarian appeal to employ God's resources in the most useful and productive fashion available.[15]

The Yale Machine

Embracing the compromise was cathartic for Pinchot. Realizing it was another matter. Technique—and a profession grounded in science that could mass-produce technicians—was the ideal vessel to contain the disparate elements of nature and utility. Enrolling at Yale, Gifford soon found out just how little forestry technique there was in the United States and how far from a profession forestry was in his native land. Gifford had literally to create a profession. There was some good news in this. As Gifford excitedly reported home, Professor Brewer told him, "I shall have not only no compeditors [sic], but even a science to found for he says there is no such science as Forestry in this country. This is certainly as good an opening as a man could have." Nevertheless, the task must have seemed daunting to a twenty-year-old who was admitted to Yale by the skin of his teeth and expected to be thrown out of the first division of his class.[16]

Although colleges like Yale became the breeding ground for specialization and the emergence of the new professions, the primary goal of universities in the 1880s remained the formation of character, not technical skills. When Pinchot entered college in the fall of 1885 there were no programs for the systematic study of forestry anywhere in the United States. Pinchot tapped other resources at Yale. Chief among these were the men that would serve at his side after his rise to national power. Not only were they Yalies, most were also brothers in the secret society Skull and Bones. The Forestry Division under Pinchot quickly became known as the Yale Club and for good reason. Counting Gifford, five of the Forestry Division's employees (out of an original staff of eleven) were Pinchot's friends from Yale. They held all of the key positions. The ratio did not change as the division expanded, although Pinchot's personal bonds were replaced by his family's bequest to Yale that helped create the School of Forestry. Out of fifty-five successful civil service examinees in 1905, twenty-four were Yale men.[17]

"At the end of the course at Yale I had a little new knowledge, many friends who were to last through life, and associations worth more than any riches," Pinchot concluded. Skull and Bones provided the skeleton for those associations. It was in clubs and fraternities that lifelong bonds were formed. As Pinchot wrote to his brothers from Paris a year after graduating, he could now appreciate Bones more than ever. "Bones has been one of my strongest reasons for wanting to get home."[18]

Bound by honor, tradition, and secrecy, Bones men formed ties thicker than blood. Members of Skull and Bones met twice a week in "the Tomb," a mausoleum-like windowless block of a building on New Haven's High Street, to discuss their most intimate affairs. Each member ultimately presented an LH—a life history. At his LH, for instance, George Herbert Walker Bush, Bones '42, told of his harrowing brush with death as a pilot during World War II. Members built up to the LH by revealing their romantic and sexual histories in a talk called the CB (short for "connubial bliss"). Years after graduating from Yale, Pinchot and his brothers continued to update their CBs. Describing in graphic detail his revulsion toward the French students he met at the Forestry school at Nancy, Pinchot wrote that he did not get on well with them "for they are not interested in any thing in this world but chippies." According to Pinchot, French students couldn't have fun without chippies, and these harlots boarded where the students did. "Any student who has no mistress is considered an ass." At social gatherings, "People sat in other people's laps and got squeezed and slobbered over . . . and the whole business simply downed booze for keeps."[19]

Virtually all of Gifford's close friendships with buddies from Yale who would go on to serve under him in the federal government traversed the broad chasm of social class. This cut against the trend at Yale in the 1880s. Secret societies claimed to be a bulwark against the new plutocratic domination. Ostensibly choosing its members based on merit, Bones judged men by their contributions to life at Yale. Pinchot seems unwittingly to have reinforced the ideal. As one contemporary commentator observed, an archetypal story for this period was the poor Westerner who meets a rich prep school boy at Yale and goes into his father's business. Pinchot personally mass-produced this ideal, selecting candidates from the ranks of his Bones brothers and ultimately inviting poor boys to join Uncle Sam's burgeoning operations, rather than his father's.[20]

A good example was George Woodruff. Woodruff was part of Pinchot's circle at Yale. Pinchot and Woodruff discussed life and romance, or shared sophomoric humor. Woodruff corresponded with Pinchot and even went to visit him in Paris after Gifford graduated in 1889. As both men matured, the correspondence was increasingly filled by accounts of Woodruff's deteriorating finances and search for a career. Pinchot assisted with both. When Woodruff's plans to market an automatic pea sheller fell through in 1902 (Woodruff belatedly discovered to his horror that restaurants used canned peas even in the summer!), Pinchot loaned Woodruff $7,500—twice the amount of Gifford's annual salary as the nation's forester—so that his friend could buy into a plumbing and heating business in Chicago. At the same time, Pinchot lobbied Philippines civil governor William Howard Taft to consider Woodruff for service. Pinchot's letter to Taft emphasized Woodruff's self-made character. Woodruff prepared for college in a Pennsylvania mining district, Pinchot noted. He earned the money to do so by teaching at a night school for miners. Woodruff's case was not made solely on appeals to Taft's sympathy: George graduated among the top five in his class, Pinchot underscored. He was also a team player, carrying the ball for the Yale eleven and pulling his own weight on the crew for four years. All this,to graduate facing staggering debt from his tuition. Woodruff accepted a job coaching football at Penn in order to pay off his debts. Obtaining a law degree while coaching, Woodruff ultimately broke with Penn because it adopted practices that he considered morally contemptible.[21]

Within a year, however, Woodruff appealed to Pinchot again. He wanted to get out of the plumbing business. Woodruff's dilemma was far different than the one Pinchot faced ten years earlier. Lack of funds, not the legacy of wealth, plagued the struggling attorney. Woodruff had a profession. He was not, like Pinchot, looking for one. Woodruff was not particularly drawn to the out of doors, although he did not care much for indoor plumbing. Yet for all the differences in their situations, forestry seemingly offered an ideal solution to both. "If I could take care of myself for a year of hard study in and out of the woods," Woodruff inquired of Pinchot in November 1902, "[do] you believe there would be a living of around $2,000 in such work for me?" Pinchot needed to hear little more; he hired Woodruff to head up Forestry's legal division. Woodruff went on to serve Pinchot ably and loyally. Pinchot was instrumental in promoting Woodruff to U.S assistant attorney general. Later, when Pinchot was elected governor of Pennsylvania, he tapped Woodruff as his attorney general. Woodruff, according to one Pinchot biographer, was probably Gifford's "closest and dearest" lifelong friend. Their college and secret society ties and Pinchot's emotional, moral, and financial support undoubtedly contributed to a bond closer than blood, class, or partisan ties. Such bonds would be crucial as Pinchot sought to administer a far-flung national bureaucracy in a decentralized nonpartisan fashion. As Woodruff wrote his friend in January 1903, "You may count on me always for any service to any extent and need not feel need to explain the why and wherefore." He proved to be a man of his word. Woodruff became Pinchot's and ultimately the Roosevelt administration's point man on law and the land.[22]

Henry Graves was another Yale undergraduate and Bones man on whom Pinchot came to rely heavily. After Graves completed a year of graduate study at Harvard, Pinchot guided his friend through the same course that Gifford had followed after Yale—including a year of study in Europe. The son of a prep-school teacher, Graves, like Woodruff, worried constantly about finances. Henry was teaching Latin and coaching athletic teams at a private school in Stamford, Connecticut, hoping to earn enough money to pursue graduate training in chemistry when Pinchot convinced him to consider professional forestry. Graves traveled to Europe for professional training but wondered if he would be able to afford it. "Forestry at home is in such a transitory stage that work is scanty as yet, and I really don't feel like running behind 550 or 600 dollars more than I have already," he wrote Pinchot in 1895. Graves insisted that he didn't go into forestry for money, but, given his ominous financial situation, it was a matter of "bread and butter." Their Bones mate Horace Walker opposed Graves's entry into this field. "It's not that he isn't fitted for it," Walker wrote Pinchot. "But what chance to ever amount to anything has a fellow got who possesses no independent means for travel, observation and foreign study? Wouldn't it be poor business for him on that account?" Graves's father cautioned his son that he had "a living to make, as well as a mission. [Y]ou can't afford to give your services free to the Education of the public." In an obvious reference to his son's mentor, the elder Graves added, "Let the millionaires do that." Pinchot's response was personally to employ Graves after he completed his European training. Pinchot remained Graves's sole source of financial support until the newly appointed forester hired Graves in 1898 to serve as his principal assistant in the Division of Forestry.[23]

School ties, fraternity, close personal friendship, and Pinchot's financial wherewithal converged in Pinchot's project to develop Graves. From his early work at Biltmore Forest, Pinchot learned that social class, though it had its advantages, did not bind men as firmly as financial dependence might. Pinchot had hoped to develop a young friend of the family as his sidekick, perhaps grooming him to take over Biltmore when Pinchot moved on to larger projects. Much to Gifford's chagrin, this man soon quit his apprenticeship in forestry. Perhaps it was to be expected: Post was a Harvard man. True to form, Pinchot spent little time reflecting upon this "mistake." He soon was writing to his boss, George Vanderbilt, asking his permission to train an entirely different sort of man—Henry Graves. "My long and rather curious experience with Post as a forester has come to an end," Pinchot informed Vanderbilt. Gifford then introduced his new protégé, assuring Vanderbilt that it was far more likely to succeed. "This time I have chosen a Yale man whom I have known for six or seven years, with whom I have already worked considerably, and who both needs to work in order to support himself, and has already had some experience in doing so. Furthermore," Pinchot continued, "he is a worker and a stayer by nature, and I hope therefore to make something of him." A brother in Skull and Bones and, like Pinchot, a class deacon, active in the YMCA, and a vigorous member of the Yale football squad, Graves met all of Pinchot's criteria.[24]

Graves emerged as one of the nation's leading foresters at the same time that he consistently toed the Pinchot line. Just as corporations had begun to develop key personnel and move them to sensitive positions around the nation (and the world), Pinchot used Graves to forge new ground in forestry. Forestry was a possibility in the Adirondacks? Send Graves. The U.S. Geological Survey needed men to do boundary work? Pinchot sent Graves, even though his assistant found the pay to be a little low and complained about having to advance his own funds for his travel expenses. Always solicitous, Graves concluded that he would go if Pinchot thought it was best. Then it was back to Washington in October 1898 to assume the post of superintendent of working plans, as Pinchot's right-hand man in the Division of Forestry. Graves not only worked closely with Pinchot, he was his houseguest for two years as well. In early 1900 Pinchot tapped Graves to become the first dean of the Yale School of Forestry. Graves would be missed in the Division of Forestry, Pinchot confided, but he would be of the "most use to forestry" at Yale. For Graves's part, this was the opportunity of a lifetime. Shortly after the appointment he wrote Pinchot to express his gratitude. "If I can ever, even in a slight measure, make any return for all your kindness to me, I shall be a happy man indeed," Graves closed.[25]

Pinchot's system produced impressive results. Loyalty meant little if the men chosen failed to perform adequately. Woodruff far exceeded that standard, crafting interpretations of forestry law that withstood Supreme Court scrutiny all eleven times that they were reviewed. Graves reached the pinnacle of his profession, succeeding Pinchot as the nation's forester. Yale men like Graves, Woodruff, and a host of others were instrumental in helping Pinchot manage a large national operation. Even at the cutting edge of professionalization, that abstract force often credited with eroding machine politics and partisan advantage, social ties and personal finances were instrumental in commanding the kind of loyalty that party bosses hoped to mobilize and professional paradigms would soon demand. In Pinchot's case, deference built on social ties and gratitude bred on financial largesse bound key members of his administrative cadre to their chief as it forged an alternative to partisan patronage. Pinchot's was an agency yearning to enhance its reach and its capacity. To do that in an environment pockmarked with patronage in an age before professional specialization, Gifford built his organization by relying on his personal appeal and the power of his message. But he also took full advantage of the kind of material and social lubricants that were designed to bind key elements in that national organization to their leader, and to do so over the long haul. Pinchot replaced partisan patronage with his own personal machine.[26]

A Better-Informed Amateur

Virtually everybody Pinchot talked to after graduating stressed the importance of European training. Only study abroad could provide the kind of expertise that Pinchot sought. Pinchot turned down an opportunity to work under Bernhard Fernow, head of the Forestry Division in Washington, and sailed for England in October 1889 with no clear plans beyond buying a few books on forestry and visiting a special exhibit on waters and forests at the Paris Universal Exposition.[27]

In London, Pinchot ran into a high official in the Indian administration who discussed Indian forestry with him and, more importantly, guided Pinchot to the leading authority in the world on forestry—Sir Dietrich Brandis. A German who had been knighted by the British for his pathbreaking work in Burma, Brandis was originally a botanist who introduced forest management in Burma and India in the 1850s. Although Brandis formally retired in 1883, he remained active and influential in forestry through his publications and teaching.[28]

Not less than two months after beginning his studies, Pinchot was thinking about the day he would begin to apply them in America. Pinchot expected to return in the fall, less than a year after sailing for Europe. Brandis had a different conception of professional training. "One thing that Dr. Brandis says that is not so pleasant," Gifford reported home, "is that I cannot possibly learn enough in one year to be able to take charge of a forest on my own responsibility." On this point, Brandis never budged. For years he reminded Pinchot that his training had been cut far too short. "Nothing whatsoever can make up for imperfect professional training," Brandis lectured. More pointedly, Sir Dietrich continued, "Social influence and personal status are excellent aids in public matters, but perfect competence in your own profession is an infinitely more powerful level. This I have endeavored to put before you repeatedly, but it is the one point in which I have always felt, that I failed to gain your complete adherence."[29]

Brandis understood well that Gifford was highly influenced by his family's wishes. Thus Brandis wrote to James, warning that if Gifford interrupted his studies to return in the fall, "he will have learnt something, but he will not be master of his profession. Though he will know a great deal more than most of those who at present seem to waste their time in America in talking and writing about good forest management, he will after all only be a better informed amateur than the others."[30]

Gifford did not budge either. "I am going to try and show him some Yankee push," Pinchot told his parents. Pinchot was convinced that conditions were so different in America as to make extensive training unnecessary. "I see no reason why our Forestry system should not be as unlike and as superior in the end to the European as our Agricultural methods are," Pinchot wrote his mother.[31]

An accurate reading of the basis for professional status also propelled Pinchot. Brandis was technically correct. Pinchot, by dint of training, was no more than a "better informed amateur." But Gifford understood that this was training enough in a nation that had no schools of professional forestry and a great hunger for expert guidance. Upon returning to the United States in December 1890, Pinchot was treated as an authority on forestry. He was asked to deliver a paper at the American Forestry Association. He was commended by the *New York Tribune* for his work in forestry, and he was hired as an expert consultant by Phelps, Dodge & Co., which owned extensive timberlands. Even Pinchot was surprised by the ease with which he was accepted as a leading authority. "No talks about forestry, which was a relief," Gifford reported to his diary upon his return. "For people seem to think I have distinguished myself. Which is nonsense."[32]

Pinchot's tutelage with Brandis, if not his classroom work, taught him a number of important lessons. The most important was the conceptual approach to forestry that guided Pinchot's entire career. Pinchot learned scientific forestry from Brandis. For Brandis, forests were not only a source of beauty, they were also a crop. That crop could be nurtured, just as any other. In fact, the more regular the annual yield, the more effective the management. Regularizing the production of lumber, while simultaneously enhancing the condition of the whole forest, was known as "sustained yield." Pinchot described annual sustained yield in an article he wrote for *Garden and Forest* in August 1890. The first objective, Pinchot wrote, "is the cutting each year of an amount of timber equal to the total annual increase over the whole area, and no more. It is further desirable in any long settled community that the forests be so managed as to yield a measurably constant return in material. Otherwise difficulties in the supply of labor and the disposal of the produce make themselves felt, and the value of the forest to its owner tends to decrease." As Pinchot explained to his parents, Brandis preached and practiced the belief that you can't look at forestry from a standpoint of "mere preservation of forests." Rather, you had to approach the matter "with the distinct idea of making them pay at the same time that they are preserved and improved."[33]

The Brandis market-oriented conception of forestry required several elements that guided Pinchot's approach throughout his career. The authority and ability to plan were essential if such a systematic approach was to be successful. In Germany, France, and Switzerland, the public sector was vested with this authority. In India, it was Brandis's signal accomplishment to revise the prescriptive rights of forest users in a manner that allowed for greater state management of forests. Expertise was another crucial component. Without trained foresters to mark the trees that should be cut, oversee the cutting, and develop plans to protect forests from fires and pilfering, sustained yield and preservation were impossible. A seemingly contradictory component was politics. Forestry would not work if it was unpalatable to those who used and lived near the forest. Brandis overcame this problem in India by employing natives to do much of the work and proving to those who lived near the forest that systematic forest management paid dividends. Finally, for Brandis, the key to successful politics was demonstration. Only when foresters could demonstrate practical results would their theory, economics, and political prescriptions be taken seriously.

Pinchot distilled these lessons and got his start in the politics of American forestry by delivering a paper to the American Forestry Association in 1890. The topic was forestry abroad. Focusing on European forestry and the Brandis experiment in India, Pinchot accepted without question the premise that lay at the heart of systematic forest management. As he concluded, "The forests which are most profitably used are the forests which are best preserved." Expertise was required to properly manage forests and state authority was required to ensure the integrity of long-term planning. Pinchot stressed these aspects in his explicit comparison to America's nonexistent forest policy. Pinchot was also explicit about the reasons that Americans opposed systematic forest management. Two facts learned in India, Pinchot insisted, carried

> special significance to us as citizens of a country where any interference by the Government with private rights would be so vigorously resented, and where private enterprise must consequently play so conspicuous a part: First, a body of efficient and experienced officers of all grades has gradually been formed in the state forests whose services are available for the management of the private forests . . . ; secondly, the example set by the well-managed state forests and the steadily increasing revenue which they yield have induced native and other forest-proprietors to imitate the state.

Progress, in Pinchot's view, began with state control. "From the first . . . forest-property is safest under the supervision of some imperishable guardian, or, in other words, of the state." Expertise applied in state-managed forests could demonstrate the practical financial value of systematic forest management. Once demonstrated, the private sector would not only accept state forestry, it would mimic it. It would do so because forestry produced profits.[34]

As far as private funds went, Brandis had a very specific funding source in mind: Pinchot's grandfather, Amos Eno. Brandis approached the topic gently in his letter to James. After reiterating that "there seems very little prospect at present of action being taken . . . by the Governments of the States or by the Union Government," Brandis predicted that regular forest management would be started by private individuals "as soon as they see that it will pay in the end. The thing would be for 2 or 3 families of means to join in an investment of this sort." "Something like that," Brandis concluded, "would be a business for your Son to undertake." Sir Dietrich was obviously more direct with the younger Pinchot. Brandis advised Gifford that he was better off managing a forest than accepting the position that Bernhard Fernow was holding for him at the Division of Forestry. The problem was finding a forest. As Gifford wrote his mother, "I see no prospect of getting such a forest unless grandpa was willing to make an investment in forest lands on a large scale." "Do you think grandpa could be counted on to invest half a million in timber lands and let me take charge of it? It scarcely strikes me as likely." Pinchot knew his grandfather. But he and Brandis were persistent. "Dr. B is still anxious as ever for Grandpa to buy me about $500,000 worth of forest," Pinchot wrote his mother in September. Eno's answer remained the same.[35]

Armed with a conceptual framework for systematic forestry, clothed in a newly minted armor of expertise, and eager to use his considerable social capital, Pinchot returned to put into practice some of the lessons he learned in Europe. The first lesson he applied was the importance of demonstrating results. Once demonstrated, systematic forest management would melt opposition, Pinchot believed, just as it had in India. Demonstrating success, political spadework, an overarching conception of forestry, and cashing in on social ties were all stepping-stones toward achieving Pinchot's ultimate objective: strengthening public authority so that forests could be systematically managed by the national government. Just as Gifford believed he could learn in less than a year what German foresters took seven years to master, he was convinced that national forestry, which seasoned veterans like Fernow felt would not prevail for decades in antistatist America, could be launched quite soon. That he sought to realize this vision by demonstrating results in the private and voluntary sectors confirmed that Gifford was beginning to understand American politics well. Perhaps national forestry could convince the private sector in Europe and its colonies. In the United States, however, Pinchot correctly perceived that there never would be national forestry until forestry could demonstrate its advantages in the private market.

Marketing Forestry

George Washington Vanderbilt, a grandson of "Commodore" Cornelius Vanderbilt, the railroad magnate, provided Pinchot with a more permanent platform for forestry. In October 1891, Vanderbilt invited Pinchot to Biltmore, North Carolina, to discuss the possibility of forest management there. The proposal was finalized in early December when Pinchot paid a call on Vanderbilt. Vanderbilt engaged Pinchot to prepare a working plan for systematic management of the forest. Vanderbilt was very specific about the purpose. "The object," as Pinchot noted in his diary, was "to get opinion about feasibility of handling big tract profitably."[36]

This was Pinchot's opportunity to demonstrate to businessmen and possibly political leaders as well that forestry was a paying practical proposition. Not everybody agreed with Pinchot's decision to work for Vanderbilt. Fernow, who still expected Pinchot to join him at the Division of Forestry, was incensed. Fernow had no doubt that Pinchot's connections and skills were best employed in public service: Vanderbilt's assignment was a costly detour. "If we had a man like you now devoting all his time and energy," Fernow wrote Pinchot in February 1892, "to informing & arousing a large public & to influence a broad policy for a large country, we would in less than a year establish a dozen beginnings of Government Reserves & forest administration by the side of which your little private effort will vanish, if indeed you can show more than how to spend money on an impracticable fad!" When Fernow visited Biltmore later that year, his prognosis was even more pessimistic. "I found the opportunity for carrying out such a program as you outlined to me, even less than I had anticipated," the forester wrote Pinchot in September 1892. "If you make forestry profitable in the next ten years, your [sic] [the] wisest forester/financier of the age."[37]

Gifford disagreed. "More I see of the timber," Pinchot wrote in his diary on October 15, 1891, "more sure I am f. man. [forest management] will be a success." That is how he described the Biltmore Forest that he would soon be managing. His enthusiasm continued into his second day on the job: "Work well started & with good progress." Undaunted by the assessment of more experienced foresters like Fernow, Gifford was delighted to be managing any forest. This was his opportunity to fulfill a dream and act on his mentor's advice about the practical value of demonstration. Pinchot soon recognized, however, that making the Biltmore Forest profitable was not going to be easy. Working the forest daily, Pinchot's rosy assessment ebbed.[38]

Had Pinchot's future success depended on his ability to accurately assess the value of forest lands, or manage them, it is not likely many would ever have heard of him. Fortunately for Pinchot, he was far better at selling than at seeding or sawing. At the very time that even the optimistic Pinchot was beginning to realize that forestry in Biltmore Forest would probably not pay, publicity from the experiment at Biltmore convinced some that forestry could turn a profit. Sir Dietrich, who understood that forestry in Biltmore Forest would never pay, continued to press for demonstration on some tract that might. "The successful management of a large forest area in your own hands will, as far as I can see, make you master of the position in the U.S," Brandis wrote Pinchot in January 1895, "much more than any amount of talking and writing. Real success in that line will convince those who doubt and hesitate at present. Words alone will not convince them." Once again, Brandis was right about forestry but wrong about American politics. While the seeds that Gifford planted in his first year at Biltmore failed due to the weather, the seeds of publicity from Biltmore prospered. The roots of the modern American state might indeed be built on talk, not results.[39]

For all of Pinchot's determination to demonstrate successful forestry in America, publicizing forestry before anybody could possibly determine its success proved to be more valuable than demonstration. After Pinchot's initial flurry of publicity when he returned from Europe, a volley produced primarily by tethering Pinchot's newfound expertise to family social ties, capturing the ear of the nation had proven frustrating. Pinchot was having trouble drumming up interest in Biltmore, even in North Carolina. He had sent editorials to all the state's newspapers, but few had published them. The Chicago Exposition of 1893 and a pamphlet that Pinchot produced for his forestry display there changed Gifford's publicity fortunes.[40]

Pinchot's display was the principal American exhibit on the science of forestry. Amid the marble of the "White City," the forestry building was marked by its open veranda lined by 270 tree trunks displaying every imaginable kind of bark. The display promoted forestry in North Carolina by comparing the work at Biltmore to sophisticated examples of European forestry. The impetus came from Vanderbilt but Pinchot seemed as excited about it as he was about managing Vanderbilt's forest. Four months after taking charge of Biltmore Forest, Pinchot departed for Europe to collect suggestions and materials for the display. Initially, Pinchot had planned quite a traditional exhibit—slices of lumber and trees from various parts of Europe and Biltmore. He quickly bogged down in logistics.[41]

The decision to build the exhibit around photographs of forestry from Europe and Biltmore saved the day. Photographs were widely used at the Exposition, where the public's thirst for vicarious pleasure seemed insatiable. As Smithsonian assistant secretary, G. Brown Goode, the man in charge of classifying exhibits, put it, "The exhibition of the future will be an exhibition of ideas rather than of objects." Photographs helped in the transition from objects to ideas.[42]

Pinchot was particularly excited about the display's potential for capturing press coverage. Photographs were also a crucial element in the pamphlet that Gifford distributed at the Exposition in the winter of 1893. Entitled "Biltmore Forest: An Account of Its Treatment, and the Results of the First Year's Work," the pamphlet contained images that graphically displayed the condition of Biltmore's forest and the work being done to improve it. The pamphlet reported on the methods used by Pinchot and the financial results of the first year's efforts.

In Chicago, Pinchot grafted two seemingly contradictory strains to craft a market for his conception of scientific forestry. He insisted on divorcing forestry from the romantic roots that attracted many of its advocates in the American Forestry Association. Forestry was a hardheaded, money-making proposition that had the added advantage of leaving America's forests in better condition than foresters had found them in. As a *Garden and Forest* editorial put it, "Mr. Pinchot's scheme . . . proposes three general objects—a profitable production which will give the forest direct utility, a nearly uniform annual yield which will give steady employment to a trained force of foresters, and a gradual improvement in the present unsatisfactory condition of the forest." Ostensibly the ultimate proof of this was in its demonstration at sites like Biltmore Forest. "A great deal has been written during the last ten years in the United States," *Garden and Forest* continued, "about the importance of preserving the forests of the country. . . . But example is better than precept, and it has been left to Mr. George W. Vanderbilt to set an example in forest management which is likely, as the years roll by, to have a momentous influence on the prosperity of this country."[43]

As Pinchot well knew, really demonstrating the results of a process that relied on sustained yield would take a generation or more. He and his compatriots, Pinchot shrewdly discerned, were in no mood to wait that long. Just as Pinchot had hurdled through a smattering of training in Europe, he bolted after a few months of hands-on management at Biltmore to the more malleable world of exposition and publicity. Photographs connected visitors with distant places and practices, neatly replicating, in the case of wilderness protection, the relationship between East and the West.

In the process, image replaced concrete results; photographs replaced timber. As Pinchot pushed the rationale for scientific forestry to its utilitarian extreme, he substituted the camera for the saw or the cash register as the legitimate instrument of measurement. Like his assessment of the threshold for professional status, Pinchot correctly gauged the public pulse. The official history of the Exposition described Pinchot's exhibit as "the principal American exhibit on the science of forestry." Pinchot's photographs delivered a sense of immediacy that the slow-paced techniques he advocated in the woods could never compete with. His gigantic prints were perceived as real, as tangible; the lumber and the woods they represented, distant and ephemeral. It was now the rationale that was utilitarian—the medium for conveying it romantic. The profession Pinchot hoped to found in America promised to meld both. Just as the painted and photographic landscapes of the West implied that "the natural and technological sublime were compatible," systematic forestry insisted that the wilderness could be converted to economic use. Nancy Anderson's assessment of Western landscapes painted after the Civil War might well be applied to Pinchot's quest: "Carefully composed and skillfully executed, such paintings minimized the conflict that accompanied development by suggesting that the natural sublimity of the land and the technological achievements of man could harmoniously coexist."[44]

The exhibit at Chicago and the pamphlet produced a dramatic turnabout in Pinchot's publicity fortunes. Just months after the pamphlet was published, New York Superintendent of State Forests William F. Fox wrote Pinchot, inviting him to a forestry meeting in New York. "It will help boom our little convention, as your name has been very prominent lately in the newspaper articles throughout the country. You would have been surprised if you could have seen the newspaper clippings which we receive here in which editorials were devoted to your operations at Biltmore." All of the articles stressed that Biltmore was the first American experiment in scientific or practical forest management and that Pinchot sought to make the forest pay healthy returns. A *Buffalo Express* article of February 23, 1894, was typical. It reported that "Mr. Vanderbilt has given the first exhibition on a large scale, of the results of managing forest property on scientific principles in such a way as to stop waste and yet make forestry profitable."[45]

Correspondence to Pinchot suggests that news accounts and editorials, not the forest, the exhibit, or even the pamphlet itself, were the decisive media for reaching his intended audience. As the clerk of forestry for Ontario wrote Pinchot, "I am not aware that you have issued any report of your operations in Biltmore Forest except the first one . . . yet I have read somewhere that you had got the account with a balance on the right side of the ledger." The forester requested more information to support his plan that Ontario reserve and manage wooded lands. Reports that Pinchot had profitably managed Biltmore were politically crucial, the Canadian inferred, because "one of the arguments that will be urged against the plan will be the financial one. . . . I would like some American experience to support my opinion."[46]

Garden and Forest published an editorial in February 1894, noting that "the appearance of the short report . . . marks what must be considered a most important step in the progress of American civilization, as it records the results of the first attempt that has been made on a large scale in America to manage a piece of forest property on the scientific principles which prevail in France, Germany and other European countries." Although Pinchot's pamphlet stated that "the pecuniary results of this first year have not been unsatisfactory," the details revealed a net operating deficit of $392.40 for the first year of operations. *Garden and Forest* quickly dismissed that lackluster figure. Pointing to more recent data provided by Pinchot, it exclaimed "this deficit became a surplus of more than $1,200— certainly a remarkable result."[47]

Practical landowners had reason to conclude after a casual glance at the Biltmore pamphlet, reinforced by the *Garden and Forest* editorial, that systematic forest management might pay. As Pinchot correctly noted, the existing management could well have supported a forest far larger than the four thousand acres actually supervised.

A closer examination of the numbers, however, undermines any semblance of profitability. More than a third of the assets reported by Pinchot came from "Stock on Hand." Pinchot, however, learned almost immediately that there was no local market for Biltmore's products and that their quality was too poor to make shipping beyond the local market feasible. Thus the majority of Biltmore Forest's revenues came from sales to the Biltmore Estate itself, and more than one-third of the wood products harvested in the first year had not yet been used by the time Pinchot published his pamphlet. The expense side of the ledger fared even more poorly under close scrutiny. Pinchot had not charged any of his $2,500 salary to the forestry operations at Biltmore—his primary responsibility. Although he scrupulously recorded interest and deterioration of capital improvements—the sawmill, for instance, depreciated at the rate of $27.70 in 1892—no cost for land or taxes was included in the budget. These items were the major expenses.[48]

Accurate figures on Biltmore expenses and revenues were not produced until the German forester Carl Alvin Schenck took over the day-to-day management of the forest. Even then, Pinchot remained his nominal superior, and the financial condition of Biltmore remained murky. To this very day, historians have accepted Pinchot's version of the story. Pinchot, however, understood that it would be a long time before Biltmore could even hope to break even—one of the main reasons he moved on.[49]

Moving on, however, did not change the combination of market rhetoric and questionable accounting that put Pinchot and Biltmore on the map in the first place. Indeed, Robert E. Wolf has documented this pattern throughout Pinchot's career as the nation's chief forester. Pinchot's promise to Congress that he could make the national forest reserves pay was a crucial part of his successful campaign to gain control over these reserves. It was in the three-year period between this transfer and the end of Teddy Roosevelt's administration that the Forest Service witnessed its greatest growth. In testimony before the House Committee on Expenditures of the Department of Agriculture in 1907, Pinchot forecast a cumulative profit of more than $5 million for the federal government by 1917. As Wolf documents, this entailed a remarkable degree of "creative" accounting. In Wolf's assessment, the Forest Service never showed a profit, with losses increasing as the size of the service grew.[50]

Conclusion

By personally grappling with one of his generation's central dilemmas—the relationship between social utility and the growing allure of consumption and pleasure—Gifford Pinchot constructed his argument for conservation in terms that resonated with a broader public. The public valued local, accountable government. But that is not all they valued. Pinchot enhanced the Forest Service's cultural capacity and in doing so, managed to reduce its perceived political distance. This hardly silenced critics, particularly those in the West who felt their immediate material interest to be threatened by big government. But Pinchot's effort, in conjunction with narrower interest-group support, proved to be formidable in neutralizing and at times vanquishing antistatism.

In administering the domain that he helped to create, Pinchot turned to networks of school ties reinforced with financial incentives from his own private wealth. Though scholars have been quick to note the Progressives' disdain for administrative mechanisms laced with political patronage, a closer examination of Pinchot's experience reveals that the techniques he used mixed private resources with public purpose—a pattern that fits neither the laissez-faire nor the autonomous state model.

Establishing expertise in his field was crucial to Pinchot's success. However, he was content to rely on public validation of that expertise, not the judgment of the profession itself. His year of travel around Europe and meetings with Brandis were "good enough for government," as the saying goes. The benefits that Pinchot accrued by being acknowledged as an American expert, however, were not lost on him. He founded the Yale School of Forestry, which again mixed private money with public purpose as it turned out generations of foresters who would staff the programs that Pinchot helped to found in the national government.

Finally, Pinchot forged, from the beginning of his career, a nexus between market-driven tests and selling expanded government programs. That Pinchot was a master at publicity is well known by scholars. That his first foray into the genre was based on misinformation and that what he sought to publicize was often the supposed profitability of public-spirited endeavors is less appreciated. Pinchot was hardly the first or the last public official to claim more than he could deliver. Far more significant from our perspective is the "social language" that Pinchot used, first, to gain national notoriety and, later, to enact his vision of scientific forestry. Pinchot forged, from the beginning of his career, a nexus between market-driven tests and expanded government programs.[51]

Though I might quibble with Pinchot's accounting, these observations are not intended as a criticism. Rather, they are offered in the spirit of recognizing just how difficult and compromised the state-building project was in America in the absence of external threat or internal crisis. That Pinchot was able to establish a formidable national program in forestry is a tribute to his energy and creativity. That he achieved this goal by relying on private and voluntary resources wherever possible is just American.

The greatest gap between the standard Pinchot story and the revised account that I have offered in this essay lies in each interpretation's conception of the proper mechanism for promoting social harmony. Pinchot and Progressives, according to standard interpretations, sought to interpose administrative discretion, in place of the market, in order to achieve socially beneficial outcomes. Yet one of the crucial lessons that Pinchot learned before he ever set foot in a federal office building was the significance of framing his programs in the rhetoric of the market. It is *this* social language that must be incorporated into our understanding of Pinchot and Progressivism more generally. Deploying the rhetoric of profitability was perhaps the best way to ensure that one's message was not lost in the translation. This is a language that historians have ignored in their attempts to recapture the Progressives' appeal, but it, along with a more politicized understanding of expertise and the makeshift mechanisms that administrators employed as they sought to move beyond a state of "courts and parties," holds great promise for unearthing the tangled roots of the modern administrative state.

Chapter 3

"Mirrors of Desires": Interest Groups, Elections, and the Targeted Style in Twentieth-Century America

The template used by elected officials to discern the preferences of their constituents is fundamental to democratic governance. This template shifted in the first third of the twentieth century. The way in which elected officials conceptualized voters evolved from one that employed reliable partisan cues about voters' wishes to one that relied upon far more specialized profiles of voters and that delivered policy-prone information to elected officials. The dynamic relationship between interest groups, rapidly changing conceptions of consumers, and electoral politics, combined with the declining ability of political parties to convey voter preferences, accounts for this fundamental shift. Conceptualizing the electorate as a congeries of group preferences best discerned through the platforms and policy agendas of interest groups constituted a distinct period in American political development that shaped the political system from roughly 1900 through 1970.

Interest groups played a key role in linking voters to public officials in the first half of the twentieth century. A pronounced feature of the political landscape since the founding, they began to replace political parties as the most reliable media both for ascertaining and responding to the views of segments of voters by the twentieth century. In that regard, they anticipated the daily tracking polls that emerged by the 1970s as the most reliable link between public officials and key constituencies. Indeed, the emergence of regularized and reliable public opinion polling signaled the end of a distinct period in American democracy that ranged roughly from 1900 through 1970 during which interest groups served as crucial conduits of the democratic will.

During this period, political parties, the nineteenth-century mechanism used by public officials to take the pulse of the electorate, proved less adept at fulfilling this task. The reasons for this are varied. Voter participation fell off dramatically. While some scholars have argued that this was the result of elite reforms that self-consciously sought to restrict poor and uneducated citizens from voting, others have suggested that broader social trends contributed to activities that, in effect, competed for voters' attention in a world filled with mass-produced entertainment. With the rise of civil service requirements and professional administration at the state and local levels, parties lost control of some of the tangible benefits they had once had at their disposal to reward voters.[1]

In response to the declining electoral hold of political parties, presidential candidates experimented with new techniques of campaigning and with "going public" as a strategy for governing from William McKinley in 1896, and forward. Public officials, by the 1920s, operated in a broader social and cultural environment characterized by the emergence of mass marketing and the celebration of consumer choice. This market model of mass consumption also explained why public officials turned to interest groups for political intelligence.[2]

The shift in the medium through which day-to-day exchanges between citizens and their representatives took place was not dramatic or sudden. Nor did the proliferation of interest groups eliminate political parties. But it did reshape the connection between democratic choice and policy outcomes. Recognizing a shift in the nineteenth-century party system, scholars have focused much of their attention on the relationship between presidents and the mass public, emphasizing the growing role played by an independent news media and the emergence of personality as an important factor. The role of interest groups in the electoral process, however, has largely been neglected in this literature.

This essay examines one campaign for the presidency—Herbert Hoover's in 1928. Hoover did not invent a new role for interest groups. As Gerald Gamm and Renee M. Smith demonstrate, McKinley delivered policy-related speeches to groups such as the National Association of Manufacturers as early as 1898. Hoover, however, did integrate interest groups into his campaign more fully than had previously been the case. He was the first modern president who rose to power outside of the party structure and who was more beholden to interest-group cues rather than partisan intelligence for his connection to the voters. This essay also focuses on the

1928 campaign because of the extraordinary documentation contained in the Hoover Presidential Library. These rich sources have allowed me to capture the role played by interest groups at a level of detail rarely glimpsed by historians. Hoover sought to tap the votes of a variety of interests by adapting some of the same techniques used by savvy marketers who appealed to a variety of consumption communities.[3]

Understanding the way in which consumer choice drove electoral politics provides a framework through which scholars can reexamine the links between electoral behavior and public policy outcomes. Hoover candidates, like General Motors, appealed to diverse "markets" by targeting specific messages toward discrete groups of "consumers," seeking their votes, rather than their money. A rapidly nationalizing communications system made it more difficult to do this along sectional and regional lines—the most basic fault lines reinforced by partisan competition. Nevertheless, the powerful networks established by interest groups and their mastery of communications made it easier for candidates to distinguish between voters by class, occupation, and policy preference, and for voters to reflect their wishes back through these same channels.

The portrait of the political system that emerges from this case study is one in which elected officials and administrators alike differentiated between voters in far greater detail, just as marketers in the 1920s and 1930s began to distinguish the subtle differences in communities of consumption. The ability to distinguish among one's constituents in a more selective fashion (rather than Republican or Democrat, Pole or German, Southerner or Northerner) laid the groundwork for crafting public policies that expanded the scope of government to serve select (and powerful) constituencies while avoiding the always dangerous charge in America of contributing to the growth of big government. Because the business sector and professionals were often "first movers" in this pattern of politics and often maintained a healthy advantage when it came to organizational resources, many of the areas in which the government expanded in the first half of the century served the needs of these interests.[4]

Interest groups broke down the heterogeneous mass electorate along class, business, occupational, professional, and, eventually, gender lines, complementing the long-standing racial, ethnic, and regional ties that supported partisan conceptions of the electorate. As the federal government expanded, interests that were organized around beneficiaries of public "entitlements" (as contrasted to partisan patronage) played an even greater role.

Often left out of scholarly discussions of interest groups, however, is the electoral connection. Since the days of Mark Hanna and the growing reliance of political parties on contributions from corporations and interest groups, it has been assumed that interest groups influence electoral politics through campaign contributions. While the recurring efforts to reform campaign finance law over the twentieth century pay ample tribute to this straightforward means of influencing electoral outcomes and the policies pursued by winning candidates, these efforts ignore a far more important role played by organized interests. Interest groups traded valuable electoral intelligence for commitments to public policies ostensibly endorsed by their members. Politicians could increase their "market share" of the vote by listening to these cues and delivering the policy goods.

In bringing the state "back in," we have left elections, and the democratic politics that elections represent, out. Recent gendered interpretations of social provision in the early twentieth century epitomize the disconnect that has transpired between scholars' treatment of interest politics and electoral clout. The reigning paradigm in this field has reinvigorated interest in interest groups by painstaking and pathbreaking studies of the ways in which women organized and the public policies that these interests crafted. However, the paradigm emphasizes the advantages that accrued to middle-class women *because* they were denied the vote, arguing that the vote made women less politically effective. Hoover, my evidence suggests, took the votes of women quite seriously and his campaign went to great efforts to treat independent and Democratic women as a nascent interest group.[5]

I approach this topic through the lens of institutions, broadly defined to include values, patterns of behavior, and, most significantly, historical context. The interest group is the central institution that I examine here. I employ David Truman's classic definition of interest group to mean groups that share attitudes and make claims upon society based on these attitudes. The ways in which interest groups mobilize range from small-group initiatives by economically or professionally integrated associations, to coalitions that emerge out of broad social movements.[6]

The conceptual model that frames my evidence was crafted by the political scientist John Mark Hansen. Interest groups, Hansen argues, interpreted voter demand for politicians. Ultimately, they were able to do this, in some instances, even more effectively than political parties. Hansen's work has been augmented recently by the scholarship of the political sociologist

Elisabeth Clemens, who, like Hansen, grounds the emergence of interest-group politics in the first two decades of the twentieth century. Like Clemens, I hope to show the significance of interest groups, without assuming that their triumph was foreordained. This distinguishes my perspective from the organizational synthesis, which assumed that modern institutions required the kind of "continuous management" provided by interest groups, and from advocates of corporate liberalism, who assumed that interest politics would inevitably serve corporate America. Like Clemens, I hope to construct a framework that encompasses "the people" without overdetermining their eventual triumph or oppression. Interest-group politics did not automatically appear as an alternative to partisan politics. Rather, it was nurtured and developed by innovators who often had tried a number of alternatives first—some quite radical by American standards. Americans learned, and eventually naturalized, the language of group interest. Although prominent political scientists found the nation awash in it by the 1920s, its roots lay in state and local activities reaching back three or four decades, Clemens argues. Over that period, popular movements learned how to narrow their claims. While falling short of the social democracy envisioned by some populists, the organizational repertoire from which activists drew broadened the range of options available to interest groups. Thus women's groups, though using some of the same techniques as business lobbies, turned far more readily to state intervention than business did.[7]

Besides seeking to restore the electoral basis for interest-group clout, I also pose an important—and underappreciated—corollary to the interest-groups-shape-public-policy model. Hoover the administrator crafted techniques based on his experiences as secretary of commerce that energized, mobilized, and, in some cases, organized interests in the hope of shoring up firmer bases of electoral support. This aspect of "policy feedback" directly affected the electoral base from which public officials sought cues about voter preferences. As the federal government increased its range of day-to-day dealings with organized interests, politicians seized on the pattern of transactions that occurred in the administrative realm to shape not only policy outcomes, but electoral preferences as well. Public policy, in other words, reconfigured the key medium for influencing elections.[8]

Interest groups, like political parties, proved to be less than perfect engines for transmitting the will of the people. But like political parties, they managed to get the job done some of the time, indeed, far more often than the scathing attacks on interest groups launched in the mid-1960s, and glorified in today's headlines, might suggest. With the emergence of reliable public opinion polling data, public officials began to explore a third mechanism for intuiting the will of the people (along with political parties and interest groups). By the 1970s the daily tracking poll had begun to gain the kind of allegiance among public officials that information about voters conveyed through political parties in the nineteenth century, then interest groups in the twentieth century, had once enjoyed. With this ability to target voter preference more specifically and more regularly, another era in the evolving relationship between democratic choice and public policy emerged. And just as political parties were maligned by Progressive reformers for their corrupt distortion of the people's will, today's reformers rail against the vested interests for their failure to represent accurately the opinion of all Americans. Indeed, with the information-transmitting function of interest groups dwarfed by public opinion polling, the constructive role once played by interest groups was eclipsed, leaving behind only a residue of financial influence in increasingly expensive campaigns driven by interest-group contributions.[9]

From Soda Pop to Targeting Independent Voters

The political basis for targeting voters was built upon pervasive trends in the emerging mass consumption economy. In business, the original thrust toward national markets tended to homogenize consumers into a one-size-fits-all mentality epitomized by the rise of brand names. Both mass production and the national scope of markets encouraged the kind of standardization and homogenization epitomized by Henry Ford's Model T automobile. However, homogeneous consumers were soon replaced by segmented consumption communities. Marketing strategies that imbued products like Coca-Cola and the Model T Ford with a "changeless quality" were soon displaced by the strategy pioneered by General Motors in the 1920s. GM viewed its consumers through a far more specialized lens than Ford. Its slogan—a "car for every purse and purpose"—helped inaugurate market segmentation.[10]

The trajectory was identical in politics. Nationalizing trends quickly gave way to segmentation. As with corporate consolidation and mass-produced standardized goods, the twentieth century gave birth to a distinctly national polity. A national citizenry that transcended party and regional boundaries was one of the Progressives' core beliefs.[11]

Standing between individuals and their potential contribution to a national electorate in the nineteenth century were political parties. Progressives prepared to fill the role served by political parties by reaching "independent" voters through new techniques. The *New Republic*, for instance, praised the political introduction of radio: "It has found a way to dispense with political middlemen," this Progressive mouthpiece swooned. Just as business moguls had originally hoped to sell one brand of biscuit or soda to a homogeneous national market, Progressives envisioned a newly nationalized citizenry, reached through national communication networks, ready to break the bonds of section, ethnicity, and party.[12]

Like the commercial techniques it was modeled on, commodified politics was perceived to be homogenizing and standardizing. The earliest and most incisive commentator on the trend was Walter Lippmann. In *Public Opinion* (1922), Lippmann recognized that with communications carried on at greater distances and at a faster pace, citizens—even well-informed citizens—were forced to rely on stereotypes and images to arrive at decisions. Lippmann pointed explicitly to politicians as the most sophisticated observers and practitioners of this process. Politicians relied on vague symbols to bring disparate groups together. The apparent consensus that elections created was not a product of rational agreement. Instead, it reflected the ability of successful politicians to use effective symbols to disguise disagreement. The "politics of personality" forged a bond that appeared to be intimate but that in fact was ephemeral. It leveled and consolidated constituencies, reducing the masses to the lowest common denominator, mesmerized by personality and celebrity.[13]

While homogenization certainly took place, in politics, as in business, standardization was only part of the story. Interest groups in the twentieth century learned how to harness mass communications so as to build support among constituencies. The old-style interest-group lobbying turned inward toward the political center and was usually linked to one political party; the new style continued to mount political pressure along traditional lines but was far more adept at molding public opinion to support legislative ends. It cut against the grain of partisan attachment. It sought broad-based support for policies by appealing directly to the electorate. It identified and mobilized segments of a given politician's constituency around specific policy ends. From the interest groups' perspective, this created a more permanent base, ensuring continued legislative and administrative support. Interest groups and politicians seeking their members' votes used the new techniques of publicity, including advertising. They beamed their message at a narrower spectrum, thereby crafting the "targeted style."

As advertisers scrambled to understand newly segmented markets, politicians sought any assistance they could find in reconceptualizing constituencies. No savvy politician would turn down support from his or her party or miss an opportunity to pick off votes through the politics of personality. But most politicians also embraced ubiquitous interest groups as sources of information. Harwood Childs, a leading student of interest-group politics in the 1920s, summed up his detailed study of the Chamber of Commerce and American Federation of Labor in this way: "The Chamber and the Federation . . . play an important role in the policy-determining activities of the state. They are at the same time reservoirs of ideas, mirrors of desires, sifters of major from minor policies, agencies for leading and directing the legislative activities of the government."[14]

The discovery of political transformations wrought by interest groups was a growth industry for political scientists in the twentieth century. Arthur Bentley's *The Process of Government* (1908) led the way. Bentley wanted political scientists to dig beneath the calm surface of politics constructed of rhetoric, formal rules, constitutional division of power, and party platforms. There they would discover that most citizens were members of a number of cross-cutting groups. Public opinion was equally driven by group preference, according to Bentley. "There is no public opinion that is not activity reflecting or representing the activity of a group or of a set of groups," Bentley wrote in his chapter on public opinion and leadership. Political success required reading group interests.[15]

The tendencies toward a new kind of segmentation observed by Bentley in 1908 became increasingly apparent to a generation of political scientists writing in the first two decades of the twentieth century. Summing up the major developments of the past thirty years in *Recent Social Trends* (1933), Charles Merriam, arguably the nation's preeminent political scientist at the time, declared, "The upward thrust of organized social groupings and their intimate and often dominating relation to traditional government are one of the most striking of all governmental trends, and perhaps the most profoundly significant." Merriam readily acknowledged that the pressure of organized interests was as old as the state. But the greater size and power of many groups now active, and their ability to engage the modern techniques of "propaganda," made their activities a formidable new development. While estimates of the actual number of interest groups at work during the first third of the twentieth century vary, it is clear that Bentley and Merriam were reacting to significant growth. One estimate placed the number of lobbyists in Washington, DC, at the end of the Civil War at about fifty. By 1929, E. Pendleton Herring estimated the number at five hundred.[16]

Beneath the Progressive vision of national opinion, a far more variegated picture emerged. In their rhetoric, Progressives stood by "the people" in opposition to "the interests." In the world of practical politics, however, Progressives, as well as their opponents, turned to interest groups to divine illusive public opinion. Politicians, like marketers during the first two decades of the twentieth century, thrilled to the possibility of national constituencies, only to discover that these national markets could often be reached most successfully by identifying and targeting fragments of the whole—whether defined by gradations in income, functional group representation, or gender. By 1920 Progressives such as Herbert Hoover subscribed to the belief that the only way to make the national government democratic was to insert group participation directly into the policy-making process.[17]

Polishing the Mirrors of Desires:
Hoover as Secretary of Commerce

When war broke out in 1914, Hoover acted on his commitment to public service, creating the Commission for Belgian Relief. After the United States entered World War I, Hoover returned to accept the position of U.S. food administrator. Hoover's wartime experience taught him a great deal about reaching mass markets. Public relations and advertising were key factors in the success of his public ventures. As the U.S. food administrator, Hoover mastered the techniques of well-publicized slogans and stunts such as pledge cards or "meatless" and "wheatless" days. As a result, Secretary of Commerce Hoover was able to call on a network of influential newspapermen, publicists, and public relations experts unequaled by any cabinet member or, for that matter, president.[18]

Hoover understood that although markets were national in scope, a one-size-fits-all approach would not suffice. At Commerce, he spearheaded an effort to conduct a census of distribution. It would provide the kind of detailed information on consumption that the Bureau of the Census had for some time been collecting on production. The endeavor, stimulated by government, cofunded by the Chamber of Commerce, and promoted by trade associations, epitomized the cooperative approach to planning embodied in Hoover's vision of the "associative state." The associative state would not rely on government coercion. Rather, it would depend on voluntary cooperation. This vision could only function if trade associations and interest groups accurately conveyed the preferences of each sector of the economy to the president, collected data for national distribution, and disseminated policy directives back out to the grass roots. The crucial vessel for uniting disparate individuals toward associative ends was the interest group.[19]

The Department of Commerce under Hoover was a veritable incubator and magnet for business, functional, occupational, consumer, and charitable interests. Frederick Feiker, who ran the Associated Business Papers after consulting for Hoover at Commerce, seemed almost to caricature the associative state when he reported that "Camp Co-operation, annual conference of the electrical leagues sponsored by this Society, has been in session all week at Association Island, New York." Addressing businessmen on November 25, 1928, about what to expect from the president-elect, Feiker predicted that "business may expect to see plans and methods further set up whereby all groups in our community may take collective action in their relationships to the Federal government." At Commerce, Hoover established more than 350 advisory committees staffed with representatives from business. "Once appointed the members or their successors form a connecting link with the work of the Government and make collaboration easy and constant," Feiker concluded.[20]

Herbert Hoover thus entered the presidential race of 1928 after having spent the last fifteen years of his life grappling with markets and encouraging the articulation of interest groups. Hoover understood that America's electoral markets were as segmented as they were vast. Fearful of state control and the waste of competition, Hoover built his vision of America's future on the bedrock of interest-group politics. He was a novice at electoral politics and had weak ties to his political party. He detested the "politics of personality." The situation was ripe for a campaign that balanced the chimera of personality with appeals made through channels of ubiquitous interests.[21]

Master of Reflections: Hoover and the Election of 1928

The standard political histories of the 1928 campaign suggest that politics proceeded as usual. There is ample evidence in the campaign files to support this interpretation. The independent Hoover for President organization indulged in the kinds of appeals that had been the staple of Republican campaigns for well over a half a century: appeals to ethnicity, race, and patronage. There is even reason to believe that Hoover served as the bag man for cash contributions funneled to the New York headquarters of Hoover for President.[22]

Examples of the campaign's determination to use Hoover's personality to its advantage also abound. Indeed, at times it appears that finding a personality to display was the greatest challenge faced by Hoover's handlers. Hoover viewed public displays of his family life and publicity about his past accomplishments as unprincipled appeals to base emotions. When Will Irwin turned his flattering biography of Hoover into an even more emotionally charged campaign film entitled *Master of Emergencies*, Hoover bristled. "I remember that the night you saw it," Irwin wrote Hoover in September 1928, "you said that it would get votes only from the morons." Hoover's qualms aside, the film was political gold. "We had to repeat it and re-repeat it," Irwin reported. The crowd went wild over it. "By the end," Irwin reported to Hoover, "they were sobbing all over the house. And when they cry, you've got 'em. Those tears mean votes." As for Hoover's misgivings? "At least three-fourths of the voters, in my opinion," Irwin assured Hoover, "are moronic enough to be persuaded by their eyes and their emotions."[23]

Over the course of the campaign, Hoover succumbed to more intrusive forays into his personal life. Although he refused to part with his collection of mining photographs, he could do little but throw a tantrum when a campaign aide, George Barr Baker, "lifted" them—frames and all—from Hoover's house and put them to use in the campaign. The campaign could easily purchase photos of Hoover from the wire service, another staffer noted. But "the ones we were after were more personal."[24]

Historians, however, have failed to grasp the way in which human interest stories and the elaboration of Hoover's personality were targeted at specific constituencies. Hoover also deployed past policy achievements in the service of these policy and electoral appeals. Although scholars have taken it as axiomatic that women did not vote as a bloc in the 1920s, the Hoover campaign made women the centerpiece of its targeted efforts. Recently enfranchised, women exemplified the potential vote that Republicans hoped to garner through the elaboration of personality. In an appeal that urged women to display their support for Hoover publicly, Marie M. Maloney telegrammed the essence of the Hoover campaign's strategy vis-à-vis women. "If Mr. Hoover is to be elected against Tammany Organization . . . it will be largely due to the votes of great numbers of women who have never taken part in politics. Political counselors agree on this. Possible to get votes of home women if they can be reached in time and in right way. Churches and women's magazines are most direct contact."[25]

Hardened political professionals like Kansas Senator Arthur Capper agreed that women would be a crucial factor in the election. Capper predicted that the percentage of women in the midwestern farm states voting for Hoover would top 80 percent. When asked to assess the key factors in Hoover's victory, William H. Hill, the head of the campaign for the state of New York and editor of the *Binghamton Sun*, was unambiguous: "The women were the big factor to my way of thinking." The Republican state headquarters in Texas came to a similar conclusion. In an analysis of national election returns published in the *New York Times*, the Yale economist Irving Fisher named increased registration and the women's vote as the top two entries in his list of factors that led to Hoover's victory.[26]

After the election, transition adviser Lawrence Richey employed the Republican National Committee (RNC) Research Bureau to poll knowledgeable party operatives about the nature of Hoover's victory. Richey wanted to know "just how the various voters did align themselves— whether into racial, religious or just what sort of groups." Undoubtedly, Richey's December 15 deadline reflected his desire to incorporate the detailed analysis of voting patterns into the Hoover administration's program planning. The RNC was particularly eager to learn how Hoover had fared among women. J. Bennett Gordon summed up the answer in a report back to Richey: "Most conspicuous and important was the tremendous support given President-elect Hoover by the women. No matter how variant were other influences, or how the support from other groups of voters fluctuated, according to local conditions and political cross-currents, the militant support of Mr. Hoover by America's womenhood was constant in every state."[27]

Public policy played a crucial role in attracting the female vote. Hoover's support of prohibition undoubtedly excited women and motivated them to participate actively in the campaign. Gordon's report notes that "the general testimony of the reports is to the effect that the prohibition issue more than any other *issue* accounted for the outpouring of women and their activity in support of Hoover." Building on this appeal, Republicans made kitchens the focal point of their appeal to women. The "kitchen" campaign capitalized upon Hoover's record as food administrator. The campaign also publicized the fact that Hoover was the first secretary of commerce to list "homemaking" as an occupation in the Census.[28]

Important as they remained, traditional partisan techniques and linking the politics of personality to policy did not begin to exhaust the ways in which the Hoover campaign mobilized voters. A framework that takes seriously Hoover's conception of government, considers the mechanisms that he employed to govern, and examines the ways in which these influenced his campaign reveals impressive evidence documenting the campaign's acute awareness of the role to be played by independent voters. It demonstrates the promise that the "targeted" style held for capturing voters who had been loosened from the grip of partisan ties.[29]

Tension over how best to pursue the independent vote and allegiance to Hoover (as opposed to allegiance to the party) at times threatened to tear the campaign apart. The Hoover for President organization was often at odds with the RNC. Frustrated by the internecine fighting that continued as patronage was handed out after the election, Hoover dashed off a brusque note to the RNC's leader, Hubert Work. "I greatly regret your attitude toward practically every one of my loyal friends. . . . They all want to work with you but they have so many rebuffs that it is a matter of common gossip." The problem was structural, not just a question of personalities. It was particularly acute in the South where white voters, eager to support Hoover, were not keen about sharing resources with African Americans who had long since established a beachhead in the Republican Party.[30]

Political parties had always been the central mechanism for determining which way the wind was blowing. Strongest at the local level, the organizations could report up the chain of command just how "their" voters were thinking. As the link between party and voter loosened, candidates resorted to alternative techniques to determine voter preference. Freed from the organizational base of parties when it came to surveying voter attitudes, campaigns began to perceive segments that had not been transparent during the heyday of partisan politics.

Hoover was in an ideal position to do this, having worked extensively with both interest and trade groups during his tenure as secretary of commerce. Hoover, by 1928, was knowledgeable about the growing body of social science that had begun to encourage product differentiation. He supported further development of that knowledge and threw the government's data-gathering facilities behind it. The endeavor, stimulated by government, cofunded by the Chamber of Commerce, and promoted by trade associations, epitomized the cooperative approach to planning embodied in Hoover's vision of the associative state. If producers, wholesalers, retailers, and the consumers could pool data, and if the Department of Commerce could collect and publicize that data, inefficiencies could be wrung out of the system, reducing costs and increasing profits for all parties involved. The associative state would not rely on government coercion. Rather it touted voluntary cooperation.[31]

Hoover's vision of interest groups was clearest when directed toward his own profession, engineering. Hoover believed that, acting as a profession, engineers could draw on science to negotiate between the individual and society. As he told the American Engineering Council in 1924, "There is somewhere to be found a plan of individualism and associational activities that will preserve the initiative, the inventiveness, the individual, the character of man and yet will enable us to socially and economically synchronize this gigantic machine that we have built out of applied sciences. Now, there is no one who could make a better contribution to this than the engineer.." One did not have to be a professional to participate in this vision. As Hoover told the American Wholesale Grocers' Convention in 1923, "We have come to appreciate a new value in trade associations. There may be some acts which may seem contrary to the public welfare but the great majority of associations and their work are distinctly helpful and in the public interest."[32]

In the absence of reliable sampling techniques, Hoover's aides developed a targeted style built around some of the very interest groups and trade associations that had worked with the Hoover administration while he was at Commerce. The point man for this strategy was Nathan MacChesney. MacChesney presided over an empire of Hoover organizations that claimed to have captured five million voters. The Hoover organization was best distinguished by the degree to which it eschewed partisan rhetoric and thrived in sectors of the electorate where party ties were weakest. A fellow graduate of Stanford in the early 1920s, MacChesney served as general counsel to the National Association Real Estate Board and was appointed by Hoover to chair the Committee on Uniform Law and Regulation of Hoover's National Conference of Street and Highway Safety. As head of the Hoover-Curtis Organization Bureau, MacChesney viewed it as his mission to attach wayward independents to the Hoover slate. He summed up this approach in a final report on his campaign activities to the RNC: "In a campaign like the present one, when party lines are broken down and hundreds of thousands of voters are dropping old partisan ties, they can make the change to another political party through the medium of a volunteer organization with less violence to their former partisan prejudices than would be the case if they were approached by the regular Republican organization." A volunteer campaign that was in harmony with the state party apparatus, MacChesney wrote Hubert Work, "can lay hold of voters who are breaking away from former party ties; or who are without party affiliations; and bring them into the Republican party."[33]

MacChesney's Organization Bureau spearheaded the targeted style. In some cases, the bureau simply added a touch of coherence to groups that were already well entrenched and highly mobilized. But the bureau also reached all the way down to the grass roots, bringing together voters who had little in common except their gender, or the college they attended, or the fact that they were first-time voters. Those reached at the amorphous end of the continuum hardly constituted organized interests. The framework through which the Hoover campaign approached these individuals, however, was forged through the "Chief's" vast experience with highly organized interests.

MacChesney swung into action in mid-July. He was highly sensitive to the potential threat to party functionaries that this new style of organization represented. Although it was time-consuming, MacChesney's bureau cleared the names of state and congressional district chairs through state RNC channels. Drawing on a technique used by Hoover during the war, all of the volunteer organizations collected signed pledge cards, accumulating millions of names. This undoubtedly unnerved Republican regulars. To facilitate the Election Day get-out-the-vote drive and assuage the fears of party loyalists, the cards were handed over to party workers. "This produced the results election day," MacChesney reported, and also avoided the fear in some quarters of a "continuing rival organization."[34]

MacChesney established three broad categories of volunteer organizations at the state and county levels. The Hoover-Curtis business and professional leagues paralleled the associative relationships already established by Hoover's service at Commerce and drew on the strength of well-established economic interests. For these business and professional groups, past policy positions and future policy opportunities loomed largest. A second order of groups, built around the Hoover-Curtis Civic Volunteers, sought to mobilize support through existing channels of fraternal, charitable, and educational organizations. Although less tied to specific policies, these groups were attuned to Hoover's general vision of an associative state. Like the economically based groups, these interests predated the Hoover campaign. Last, there were the broad-based Hoover-Curtis Volunteer groups that encompassed voters previously unattached or only loosely attached to business or voluntary organizations. Included in this category were the Hoover-Curtis Women's Activities Division, Hostesses for Hoover, college campus volunteer clubs, First Voters for Hoover, and (the most generic) Volunteers for Hoover.

A brief review of groups at either end of the organizational spectrum illustrates the way in which Hoover's targeted style earmarked segments of the population. The more highly organized the group, the greater the role of policy in the campaign's appeal. The Hoover Waterways Clubs, for instance, distributed a pamphlet titled "What One Man's Vision and Efforts Have Accomplished for the Northwest." At the other end of the spectrum, Hoover-Curtis Volunteer Clubs sought the least common denominator at the grass roots, urging members to arrange radio parties to listen to RNC broadcasts, to hand out literature, to display posters in their homes, to wear buttons, and to post Hoover stickers on auto windshields.[35]

Many of these groups appealed directly to their members' self-interest, reminding them that Hoover's past policies had proven beneficial and noting that a spirited campaign on their part could hardly fail to pay policy dividends should Hoover win. Realtors were the most outspoken in this regard. Harry Culver, president of the National Realtors' Association, organized Hoover clubs in five hundred cities, personally paying the expense of setting them up. "He went a little farther than I suggested," a sheepish Hoover wrote Hubert Work, "but I do not believe these informal organizations can do any harm." W. I. Hollingsworth, the national vice chair of the Real Estate Men's League for Hoover, left little room for imagination when he wrote realtors, urging them to set up clubs. "Get the boys together so that we can put you on record as not only being for Hoover, but having a live organization for him. We want your City recorded as having a League for Hoover. There is no telling—later on this work on your part may become invaluable to the National administration and we pledge you in advance Secretary Hoover's appreciation." As Hollingsworth reminded the boys, "If any organization in the United States needs a direct representation in Washington, it is the real estate fraternity."[36]

Hoover Waterways Club pursued a similar angle. The Minneapolis branch of the Hoover Waterways Club called upon the citizens of the Mississippi Valley: "No matter to what parties they belong, . . . unite on Mr. Hoover in the coming election as the one man in all of this country who understands best the economic needs of the Mississippi Valley and the one man in the United States who can bring to us real and genuine measures of relief. After all, the thing in which we are most interested is our economic pocketbook. The maximum development of inland waterways transportation in the Mississippi Valley will go a long ways toward filling our economic pocketbooks."[37]

Phil Brockman, writing on behalf of the Hoover-Curtis Automobile Dealers Sales League, urged his fellow car dealers to join up because Hoover had supported them in the past, organizing the Hoover conference that Brockman claimed was held "for our sole benefit, so to speak, as we are the ones who will profit in a way by having good laws governing the operation of automobiles. . . . Also, the safer the streets and highways, the more automobiles we will sell." Not to be outdone, the director of the Western division of the Hoover-Curtis Fruit and Vegetable League—a potato distributor—wrote fellow distributors urging them to join up. "I have often heard the thought expressed," he concluded, "that our industry was not given the consideration which it should receive. Perhaps this has not been our fault in the past, but if we neglect to bend every effort to elect the first President whom, I may say has had any understanding of the functions and importance of our industry the fault will certainly not lie with us."[38]

Many of the business and professional leagues went out of their way to state their appeals in nonpartisan terms. "Not knowing your politics, I am somewhat hesitant in calling upon you," a letter from the president of the De Luxe automobile company began. Fred Voiland, whose letterhead advised recipients to "dress well and succeed," urged fellow clothiers to "lay aside party affiliation, and do this great work for the United States of America. We are, after all," Voiland philosophized, "Americans first, and after that, retailers."[39]

At the other end of the spectrum lay blocs of voters who did not necessarily share business or professional ties. From the perspective of the Hoover campaign, they formed a bloc precisely because their members were more likely than other voters to cross party lines in support of Hoover. If these individuals could be identified, targeted, and cultivated, if they themselves came to perceive a shared interest, they might make the difference in a close election. No group better matched these criteria than women. Both political parties had cultivated women as a distinct voting group since the late 1910s. The political scientist Anna Harvey has documented the extensive campaign to enroll women by establishing women's committees in both parties and by campaign organizations such as "parlor meetings" and "Home and Harding" groups, or the Democratic "Victory Clubs" of women. The National League of Women Voters took the lead in forming the Women's Joint Congressional Committee in November 1920 to represent the legislative proposals of a number of other women's groups as well. About the same time, the American Federation of Labor spearheaded a campaign to attract working women to the Democratic Party. No doubt, the clear divide between Hoover's and Alfred E. Smith's positions on prohibition in 1928, and Smith's association with Tammany Hall politics, motivated women more than other issues. What is impressive nonetheless is the degree to which the Hoover campaign reconceptualized the electorate, identifying the "women's vote" as a crucial factor. Hoover forged an organizational path to capture this segment of his constituency.[40]

Like the savvy political aide she was, Mrs. Martin Kent Northam, the assistant director of women's activities at the Hoover-Curtis Organization Bureau, attributed the strong interest of women to the candidate. The body of the report that Northam submitted outlined the ways in which the campaign had been organized to tap this resource. The women's division sprang to life on July 26 when it established Hoover-Curtis Women's Volunteer Clubs at the precinct and township levels. The clubs secured the written pledges of women to vote for Hoover. To do this, they handed out literature, buttons, and automobile stickers. In all, more than one million pledge cards were received. These cards were in turn used to get out the vote on Election Day.[41]

One of the clubs' most significant activities entailed voter education. Here, the object was not the usual instruction in how to vote the straight-party ticket: quite the opposite. As Mrs. Northam reported, the clubs "conducted lessons in correct voting in order that those women of opposite party affiliations could learn how to split their ballot without disqualifying it." Indeed, the value of the organization, as Northam saw it, was to give "women with no definite party affiliations and also Democratic women, who did not wish to be considered as Republicans, an opportunity to unite with the Hoover-Curtis Organization for the head of the ticket, as the organization was understood to be only for the duration of the campaign." Splitting votes like this allowed women to vote with their party for the local candidate and Hoover for president. This approach, Northam argued, aroused the "civic consciousness" of women.[42]

In the final weeks of the campaign the Organization Bureau intensified its activities, establishing the "Hoover Hostesses." Mrs. Silas H. Strawn directed the program. The objective of this program was "to have interested groups in every home in the country listening in to Republican campaign speakers over the radio." Contacted through a gigantic chain-letter operation, hostesses created a nationwide network. At the high point, these meetings produced three thousand new pledges a day, according to Strawn's report. As the program grew in size, the campaign targeted radio broadcasts for this specialized audience. As Strawn put it, "It is the first time that women who cannot leave their homes, who cannot give money—old and young, rich and poor, shut-in, incapacitated, in any walk of life—can become active workers in a political campaign. In many cases, where a woman did not own a radio, she went to her neighbor, interested her and made her a radio hostess."[43]

Samples of hostess correspondence reveals the breadth of the program. There was, for instance, a special mailing aimed at recruiting "Colored" hostesses. The program also signed up Billy Sunday's wife and Mrs. Thomas Edison. Mrs. Strawn considered her program to be nothing short of a contribution to the "civic intelligence" of the nation. In revealing her plans for the future, Strawn embraced the associative spirit spawned by the Hoover campaign. "With more time and sufficient funds in subsequent campaigns," Mrs. Strawn concluded in her final report, "the plan could be enlarged upon by emphasizing the organization of industrial workers, welfare groups, churches, hospitals, business women's and social clubs, farmers' organizations and fraternal bodies. This would be in addition to the radio parties in private homes. An organization embracing *every activity in life*, both men and women, can be developed."[44]

Hoover Hostesses made great use of *Master of Emergencies*. MacChesney broadcast the results of the first public showing in New York, quoting the president of the local Hoover League, Mrs. Clarence Hancock: "Picture tremendous success. Made wonderful impression on our women." Mac-Chesney also quoted the woman who was vice chair of the Massachusetts committee. "Throughout the last fifteen or twenty minutes of the showing a great many people were in tears and the applause in each case was emotional, spontaneous and very heartfelt. [A]s a vote-getter," she continued, "it was far superior to any speaker whom we had heard and could undoubtedly be made very effective in reaching many voters who would never come to a regular Republican gathering." Some of the attributes most associated with the rise of personality in twentieth-century campaigning were evident in the reactions to this film. Yet in thousands of meetings "hosted" by women, the Organization Bureau targeted its message at the very voters thought to be most receptive to its message, and sought to connect Hoover the humanitarian portrayed in the film the public policies of Hoover the secretary of commerce and candidate for president.[45]

Hoover won the election handily. He racked up 444 electoral votes to Smith's 87. He outpaced Smith in the popular vote by almost six and a half million of the thirty-six and a half million votes cast. Hoover made deep inroads into the border South, carrying North Carolina, Virginia, Tennessee, Texas, and Florida. He won every non-southern state with the exception of Massachusetts. Although scholars continue to debate the nature of the female vote in 1928, Alan Lichtman has argued persuasively that women constituted a disproportionate number of the newly registered voters, swelling the electorate in 1928.[46]

Conclusion

Placing the Hoover campaign of 1928 in the context of market segmentation and examining the election through the lens of interest-group politics revises the prevailing framework used to understand politics during this period. Issue-oriented politics were deployed interchangeably with the politics of personality. The image that Hoover projected to the electorate was one drawn from his accomplishments and his stance on the issues. Alongside the politics of personality, the campaign waged a war for business and professional groups almost exclusively designed to appeal to their self-interest. Even when it came to the politics of personality, the campaign sought to target specific groups that it felt would be more receptive to its message. Women were the most prominent of these and they were singled out because they were thought to be the most likely to confound party loyalty. Although it is beyond the scope of this study to examine the ways in which electoral clout translated into policy influence, it is clear that policy making prior to the campaign influenced the shape of that campaign. Hoover's vision of the associative state was replicated in MacChesney's Organization Bureau. Even a cursory review of correspondence following the election reveals a strong expectation of policy rewards by the organized groups that lined up behind Hoover in the campaign. As W. I. Hollingsworth reminded his buddies: "There is nothing of more importance to the realtor than taxation and legislation and we need an intelligent, unbiased sympathetic friend in Washington." Electoral mobilization might ensure that an "unbiased" president would be both friendly and sympathetic.[47]

As some women found out in 1929 when Hoover failed to endorse legislation that would have restored women and children's health programs to the Children's Bureau, electoral influence did not automatically translate into policy victory. For advocates of gendered interpretations of politics, this failure is often seen as evidence that women were more influential before they had the vote than after. Anna Harvey, who examines the ways in which past gender bias influenced the structural barriers to female political participation in the 1920s, argues that "the severely diminished efficacy of women's organizations after 1925 was to last for approximately forty-five years, until 1970." For Lichtman, "Women became neither an independent force in American politics nor an interest group within the parties whose loyalty had to be preserved."[48]

If I am correct in asserting that the most fundamental shift in the political system between 1900 and 1970 was the emergence of interest groups as indicators of voter preference—and if we accept Childs's characterization of them as "mirrors of desires"—then gender, rather than forming a fault line around which all politics revolved, should be viewed as just another interest around which groups could and did organize. As such, women, like funeral directors, realtors, and osteopaths, would win their share of battles and lose their share of battles as they tried to convert their electoral clout into public policy. The degree to which the Hoover campaign sought to capitalize on the votes of women, however, should leave little doubt that practical politicians took the connection between elections and public policy seriously. This is not to say that women constituted an interest group. Women, however, did share certain broad sets of preferences that both politicians and corporate marketers sought to discern and cater to. Nor is it to argue that the influence of gender was limited to the interest-group model. However, to ignore the ways in which women's votes were sought through mechanisms that discerned policy cues from groups that shared attitudes and advanced claims based on these shared attitudes, to paraphrase David Truman's words, is to deny a large part of the history of politics and gender in the first two-thirds of the twentieth century.

By the 1930s Franklin D. Roosevelt had mastered the use of radio, perfecting the "politics of personality." The election of 1932 witnessed a dramatic shift in partisan alignment—a realignment that continues to shape politics even today. Both of these developments have been examined by political historians in great detail. More subtle, less conspicuous, but perhaps of equal significance, by 1928 candidates targeted campaign appeals to interest groups in an effort to reach newly segmented political markets. This too was part of a much larger trend that shaped the twentieth-century polity.

Given the vibrant scholarship on the culture of consumption, now is the time for scholars to revise their conception of how market models informed political development. Had markets remained the homogeneous aggregates that Ford hoped to reach with the Model T, there would be little reason to look for the roots of our complex and variegated public policies in political equivalents of the market. Electoral politics would continue to occlude, not illuminate. Had segments of that market remained exclusively the ethnic, cultural, and sectional groups that dominated nineteenth-century politics, there would be little cause to seek in them the origins of the complex policies of the twentieth-century state. That politicians identified markets, using interest groups and voting blocs as markers, and that policy was seen as the equivalent to merchandising—a way to attach interest groups to political coalitions—connects the study of elections to the evolution of governance. It also explains, in part, how the central government expanded in a political culture wary of big government. The targeted style laid the democratic framework for public policies that favored incremental growth powered by interest-group pressure.

Filling out the framework that I have sketched in this essay will revise political history in several ways. First, it reperiodizes political history, eschewing "cycles of history" and regimes defined by the degree to which

they advance liberalism. Rather, periods should be defined by the mechanisms used by public officials to discern the public will. From Reconstruction through the end of the nineteenth century, partisan intelligence
remained the staple of voter-public official relations. From 1900 through
the early 1970s, public officials used interest groups as surrogates for specialized intelligence about the electorate. This was eclipsed by the use of
daily tracking polls, which remain the staple of today's public official–
constituent relationship. A framework built on the mechanisms for interpreting voter preferences would illuminate the connection between election
campaigns, the public policies that emerge from these campaigns, and the
ways in which these public policies in turn reshaped the new electoral landscape. This approach restores agency to the world of politics by focusing
on key actors, like Hoover, who adapted the political system to their electoral needs and policy ends.

Most significantly, concentrating on the ways in which public officials
conceptualize their constituencies offers political historians the opportunity
to integrate their work into the broader contours of their profession. Ultimately, it was long-term structural changes in the economy, in the relationship between marketers and consumers, and in the cultural construction of
public opinion and consumer that underlay the symbiotic relationship
forged between public officials and interest groups in the twentieth century.
It is up to historians of politics, culture, business, and communications to
fill out a framework that, to date, is but partially glimpsed. I hope that
they will take as their central question the ways in which public officials
conceptualized their constituency, for it is by answering, more definitively,
this question that scholars can tackle some of the most fundamental issues
that undergird the problems and promise of democracy in twentieth-
century America.

Chapter 4

Reorganizing the Organizational Synthesis:
Federal-Professional Relations
in Modern America

Twenty years after Louis Galambos published "The Emerging Organizational Synthesis in Modern American History," the organizational strand
of revisionist history has become a mainstay of scholarly interpretation.[1]
One hallmark of its maturity is that today the organizational synthesis is
itself a subject undergoing revision by charter members and critics alike.
High priests like Galambos have underscored the wealth of scholarship
spawned by the organizational approach and have discerned broad new
trends and tensions in that scholarship. Galambos recently blessed three
denominations that have embellished and elaborated upon the founders'
abiding faith in the forces of modernization to reshape state-society relations: technology, as mediated through large-scale corporate development;
the administrative state, as it has developed over the twentieth century to
embrace a new, corporatist form of liberalism; and the pervasive professionalization of society.[2] Yet many leading historians remain outside of the
organizational flock. Alan Brinkley, one of the agnostics, has criticized organizational historians for pushing "vast segments of society to the periphery
of historical analysis."[3] Michael McGerr, an outright heretic, has questioned
the whole endeavor, doubting whether there "really was an 'organizational
society' in the early twentieth century (or even now)" and charging the
historians who invented that society with the sin of "presentism."[4]

Despite such accusations, organizational scholarship has rarely made it
past the New Deal.[5] For the most part, the organizational synthesis remains
rooted in the Progressive Era. One reason is quite prosaic. Many historians
don't consider events less than fifty years old to be history. Consequently,

the event that had the greatest impact on organizational development in the twentieth century—World War II—remains relatively unexamined. Another problem, this one endemic to the organizational synthesis, also explains that approach's stunted chronological growth. Having chronicled the most significant developments that separated nineteenth- from twentieth-century life and having explicated the ironclad laws that governed organizational development, the synthesizers did not bother to fill out the century. We were in for more of the same—perhaps a little bigger, maybe a little faster, certainly a lot more complex. Brinkley captured it best when he referred to organizational historians' description of the world conveying "an unmistakable aura of inevitability."[6]

Happily, the more recent work by organizational scholars not only expands and fills out the topics they originally explored through that synthesis, it has begun to build tension and indeterminacy into the organizational synthesis. The aura of inevitability is breaking down. Considered collectively, a dynamic element can be discerned in recent monographs that recaptures the contingencies of the state-society relationship. This dynamic element is the result of two important developments, each of which must be accelerated if the organizational synthesis is to remain a useful analytical tool with which to generalize about twentieth-century American history.

The first development is the product of a healthy ferment within the discipline of history itself—the eclipse of intellectual and political history by social and cultural history in the 1970s and 1980s. Even historians primarily concerned with the emergence of large-scale organizations and scientific modes of thought have begun to recognize that groups and ideas attuned to far different norms may have forced compromises not originally envisioned by bureaucratizers and professionalizers. At a minimum, in a decentralized, pluralist society like America, there was room for a number of attitudes toward state-society relations to flourish simultaneously. Historians cannot hope to capture the entire nation's history, or even a significant portion of it, by limiting their attention exclusively to the pattern of development advocated by just the latest participants in that long-standing debate. How each party adapted its thinking and political actions tells us far more. Scholars are just beginning to place bureaucratic/professional development in its social and cultural context by examining groups previously considered to be on the periphery of "organizational society" and ideas that professionals and bureaucrats continued to share with their fellow Americans.

Crucial advances within the social sciences, the second revitalizing development, have also helped build contingency back into an ossifying organizational synthesis. Organizational scholars originally constructed their interpretation upon a theoretical foundation grounded in the behavioral sciences of the 1950s—particularly sociology. That foundation has shifted, and with it the thrust of organizational scholarship has shifted as well. Much as particle physics shattered scientists' notions of what constituted the building blocks of nature, the revolt against Parsonian structure-functionalism in the social sciences challenged historians' lockstep conceptualization of bureaucratization, professionalization, technological advance, and evolution from entrepreneurial to corporate capitalism.

This essay analyzes the intellectual catalysts and the new empirical research that, in my opinion, hold the key to reorganizing the organizational synthesis. It demonstrates how these revisions can alter historical understanding, by considering one of the most fundamental relationships in twentieth-century politics: the coevolution of federal institutions and the experts who eventually staffed them. While the original organizational synthesis cemented a powerful alliance between experts and the federal government in the Progressive Era (a "truism" that few scholars have challenged, whatever their misgivings about other aspects of the organizational approach) I argue that the partnership had just barely begun at that time. A closer look at the history suggests that it could not have, because both federal administrative capacity and professionalization were in their infancy. The foremost concern among advocates for each was autonomy, not a potentially suffocating liaison. Exchanges between experts and the federal government evolved from what might be characterized as a coy but chaste Progressive Era courtship, to a triumphant marriage during the early years of the Cold War.

Relations have continued to evolve. I conclude my reexamination by surveying the politics of the prominstrative state, as I call the post–World War II union. Armed with unprecedented organizational resources, the federal government emerged from World War II as a formidable political actor in its own right. It not only responded to well-organized interest groups, it now had the capacity to create them. It not only had access to vast networks of expertise, it helped to create them and to define the research agendas of a host of professional disciplines. The evolutionary nature of its organizational base, however, ultimately undermined this relatively stable situation. As publicly funded experts proliferated, so did differing organizational and disciplinary perspectives. This created a never-ending series of policy disputes. When threatened with defeat in the insulated forums where much of the debate initially occurred, likely losers took their case to more public arenas. At the same time, a host of political actors initially excluded from the insulated corridors of administrative decision making—ranging from legislators to grass-roots "public interest" groups—demanded greater access to the organizational resources that they recognized were crucial to political success. These twin movements collided in the late 1960s and were an important structural precondition to the turmoil that swept through American policy making for the next fifteen years. Thus the contemporary relationship between professionals and the federal government, like its historical antecedents, remains contingent and open ended.

Part I

Building the Organizational Synthesis

It has been almost thirty years since scholars like Samuel P. Hays and Robert Wiebe launched what a decade later was labeled the organizational synthesis.[7] The organizational historians joined a field already crowded with "revisionists."[8] What united all revisionists was a common target: the Progressive synthesis.[9] The revisionists, none of whom would launch a frontal assault, sailed around the well-fortified core of the Progressive synthesis—which took its protagonists' words at face value—and exposed startling contradictions between the Progressives' rhetoric and their behavior. Measured by words or actions, the Progressive program contained some glaring inconsistencies.

The Progressive Paradox

Two central Progressive tenets seemed antithetical. The first—a commitment to open up politics to more democratic participation—was driven by a millennial belief in progress. While progress was no longer certain to occur without a conscious effort toward reform, it could occur, given proper human intervention. A better future, according to the Progressives' "philosopher," Herbert Croly, would "have to be planned and constructed rather than fulfilled of its own momentum."[10] Only a collective effort, leading Progressives argued, would bring on the millennium: It was as a community that America would ultimately arrive in the promised land. The millennial spirit that challenged Americans to respond collectively reached back to America's Protestant ideology.[11] But by the end of the nineteenth century, it competed with a worldview that increasingly emphasized technical prowess and specialization.[12] Remarkably, as John Higham put it, "Instead of continuing to retreat as technical relations expanded, the old ideological framework was temporarily revitalized." It was that revitalized sense of millennial collective mission that powered the passion often neglected by organizational explanations.[13]

Progressives believed that by putting their ideas into action, and by educating the people about these ideas, Americans collectively could manufacture progress. The movement proved its commitment to democratic participation through the electoral reforms that instituted the primary election, the initiative, and the referendum.[14] The rights of individuals remained dear to Progressive thinkers, but these rights were best fulfilled through participation, as opposed to rigidly defined autonomy. It was not "the absence of legal restraint," Higham concluded, "but the capacity to share as widely as possible in the common good of the whole society" that made Americans free and equal.[15]

The other tenet in progressive thought was the commitment to decision making by experts housed in expanded administrative mechanisms capable of managing complex problems. Experts solved problems by specializing; proper administrative control ensured that the specialized responses were aggregated to provide comprehensive solutions. Regulatory bodies such as the Interstate Commerce Commission (ICC) or the Federal Trade Commission (FTC) epitomized this approach to politics. The complexity of the problems addressed required esoteric knowledge, and as mechanisms for tapping that knowledge were established, they conveyed considerable power. In 1913 the Progressive Era's "political economist," Walter Lippmann, summed up the spirit that would inform the new institutions that Croly called for: "We shall use all science as a tool and a weapon."[16] Reliance on expertise and continuous management, however, was antithetical to collective millennial pursuits.

A critique of "the interests" was crucial to reconciling the Progressives' reliance on an expert elite, on the one hand, and its commitment to democratic participation, on the other. Theoretically, at least, both the masses and specialists had a stake in securing the political system against plundering well-organized, well-financed interests for which the Gilded Age had become infamous. Giant trusts that seemed to be overwhelming both consumer and government in all areas of life were the most dramatic examples of such interests. These kinds of concerns were a staple in American history. What distinguished Progressive Era "antimonopolism" from its antecedents was its unique grip on the middle classes.[17] Rising urban professionals were for the first time just as concerned about monopoly as rural populists had been for some time.

Progressive Era antimonopolism also differed because it targeted many other interests besides corporations. The culprits ranged from corrupt political parties to lobbyists employed by pressure groups.[18] Attacking these "evil" interests was as crucial to Progressives as their belief in direct participation or their reliance on expertise. Even more than the millennial spirit that pervaded Progressivism, this critique of political corruption through organization run amok mobilized the masses behind the Progressive cause.[19] As Richard McCormick observed, "This concept of a 'process' of corruption was central to the new understanding."[20] It was the catalyst for a burst of progressive legislation at the local and state levels in the first decade of the twentieth century.[21]

The Organizational Critique and Prescription

Organizational scholars first distinguished themselves from other revisionists by selecting the Progressives' attack on the "interests" as an object of critical investigation. From Hays, in the cases of conservation and school reform, to Wiebe and Kolko in the case of railroads, scholars writing in the late 1950s and early 1960s demonstrated that the Progressives' actions, as measured by their legislation and administration, were often far more responsive to some of the nation's most powerful interests than to the people.[22] The most influential individual work in this synthesis was Robert Wiebe's *The Search for Order*.[23] Like a literary aircraft carrier, *The Search for Order* dwarfed smaller vessels that had helped chart its course and provided a platform for new exploratory sorties.

Wiebe identified the sea change that Americans living at the turn of the century, and the scholars who subsequently studied them, had to ride out. It was the quickened pace of interdependence. Identifying the major causal agent in altered state-society relations was a necessary condition to launching a synthesis, but it was not sufficient. Wiebe added the missing link when he generalized about the way many middle-class Americans responded to the problems that buffeted their lives. Specialization lay at the heart of that response. Specialization, in turn, could only produce systemwide solutions if the isolated parts were linked together through administrative mechanisms capable of planning and coordination. Wiebe referred to this integrative process as "continuous management" and described the construction of structures to facilitate it as "bureaucratization." Wiebe's flagship proved such an important launching pad because it not only carried a powerful critique of society's problems, but also offered a powerful hypothesis about the prescription that Americans increasingly turned to.

The discovery that well-organized interest groups supported some major Progressive reforms, and the corollary recognition that public participation increasingly flowed through interest groups rather than through direct electoral participation, dramatically altered the prospects for reconciling the two antithetical strains of Progressive thought in an alliance held together by antipathy toward organized interests. Rather than targeting the corrupting interests, as Progressive historians had, organizational scholars underscored the rapid rise of interdependence as the source of society's problems. Specialization—a process that only generated more interest groups—was the answer, not the Mugwumps' call for virtue or even the Progressives' rhetoric about democratic participation.[24]

Organizational scholars argued that Progressive state builders and professionals eventually recognized this. The complicated social factors caused by interdependence, which created the problems associated with industrialization, urbanization, and immigration were met by Progressive reformers who embraced expertise and bureaucratization. Recognizing interdependence as the agent that caused many of society's and the state's problems— not attacking well-organized interests was the distinctive element in the Progressives' critique. Calling for continuous management, not direct democracy, was what distinguished their prescription (particularly from the Populists).

Organizational scholars thus subtly but decisively turned the relationship between Progressives and organized interests on its head, sapping the Progressive synthesis of its most powerful and dramatic causal agent. Substituting interest-group representation for the direct participation of the masses was the way Americans at the turn of the century ultimately reconciled democracy and expertise in this new interdependent world, organizational scholars argued. Progressives, as interpreted by the organizational synthesis, believed that both the people and even the largest corporations

could best be represented through the medium of interest groups competing within a new administrative state. Experts and bureaucrats would
resolve political disputes by selecting the scientifically correct solution, or,
where none existed, weighing competing sets of interests.

Demonstrating that Progressives recognized the stake that interest
groups shared in a society governed through "continuous management"
gave organizational scholars more than a powerful critique of progressive
historiography: It provided the basis for a compelling alternative synthesis.
Twentieth-century struggles could not simply be reduced to pitched battles
between the people and the interests. The history of the twentieth century,
as seen through the lens used by organizational scholars, was a series of
guerrilla skirmishes between competing interest groups. Conflict might
start in the legislative branch, but that is hardly where it ended. Hand-to-
hand battles inevitably carried combatants into the vastly expanded administrative forum and, by the end of the century, increasingly, into the courts.
As Wiebe astutely pointed out in a chapter labeled "The Illusion of Fulfillment," Progressives "carried an approach rather than a solution to their
labors, and in the end they constructed just an approach to reform, mistak-
ing it for a finished product."[25] Though Progressives ultimately may have
been disappointed by the product, scholars had much to gain from exploring how it worked. Understanding that approach—which encompassed
continuous management, professionalization, and bureaucratic thought—
could illuminate many of the mysteries of twentieth-century political and
social development. The organizational approach offered a way to navigate
through some of the major political and social debates of the twentieth
century. It beaconed to scholars seeking to identify key causal agents and to
generalize about the way Americans responded. Organizational historians
would eschew rhetoric or class cleavage as guiding lights. Instead, they
would pay close attention to interest-group politics, take stock of changing
organizational resources, and, most significantly, chart the changing forums
in which crucial political decisions were made.

The Organizational Paradox

Had the experts and administrators who staffed the mechanisms of continuous management been the apolitical, passive coordinators and technical
problem solvers envisioned by Progressive rhetoric, there would be little
reason to reconsider the original historiographic framework constructed

by the organizational synthesis. Progressive rhetoric about expertise and administration, however, has only recently been compared to Progressive behavior. The first generation of organizational scholars brilliantly reexamined the Progressives' relationship to the interests, discovering, despite the rhetoric, numerous alliances, but they largely accepted the Progressive view of bureaucrats and professionals as apolitical, while Progressive rhetoric about the apolitical nature of expertise and administration remained unexamined. In fact, the original organizational scholars built their synthesis in part on that rhetoric.

This oversight was not entirely accidental. It was the product of the social science literature that informed organizational scholars.[26] The hidden hands of Weber, Parsons, and Truman gave the original organizational synthesis a distinctly structure-functionalist cast. The very models derived from political science, for instance, which allowed historians to move beyond Progressive rhetoric on some topics and to analyze selected aspects of the movement's behavior, colored portrayals of state-interest group relations.[27] Until recently that literature envisioned two possibilities: Agencies could balance the views of a number of competing interest groups, or they would be captured by one interest group.[28] While obviously leading to contradictory conclusions about the functioning of pluralist democracy, these two alternatives shared one important feature: They assumed that the agency played a passive role in its relationship to interest groups. It was the interest groups that carried policy initiatives to the agency.

Sociology influenced organizational scholars even more than political science. Implicitly, the organizational synthesis was built on Weberian sociology, which treated organizations as rational and efficient actors, and Parsonian sociology, which treated professionals as independent and objective experts who brought unique skills to the problems they faced. Whether political science or sociology, the theoretical perspectives that informed the first generation of organizational scholars placed experts and administrators at the core of political development but discounted the possibility that these actors might harbor or be capable of pursuing political agendas of their own.

Recent Scholarship and the State

Since the mid-1960s, the theoretical currents that had directed the organizational synthesis's description of the administrative state have shifted dramatically.[29] The calm seas that structure-functionalists forecast were becoming choppy even as the new synthesis set sail. Relying upon a Weberian perspective, Wiebe's description of bureaucracy was hardly sensitive to the indigenous political agendas pursued by administrators.[30] Post-Weberians, however, "bounded" the supposed rationality of bureaucratic decision making: Politics and administration, they argued, were integrally related parts of the broader process of an agency's adaptation to changing conditions and needs.[31] They shifted the debate from description to an exploration of the sources of power. As Theda Skocpol observed, "When pluralists focused on the determinants of particular public policy decisions, they often found that governmental leaders took initiatives well beyond the demands of social groups or electorates; or they found that government agencies were the most prominent participants in the making of particular policy decisions."[32]

Among organizational historians, Samuel P. Hays was one of the first to recognize the significance of these developments. He called on his colleagues to pay closer attention to the relationship between administrative choice and politics.[33] Recent scholarship in sociology and political science has done just that, by bringing the state "back in."[34]

At the same time that changing theoretical currents were altering the course of organizational research, recruits returned from sorties with a wealth of empirical data that hastened the shift in course. While exploring how the state was constructed, many scholars discovered that large portions of its foundation were jerry-built. Stephen Skowronek's detailed account of state building in the Progressive Era put it best: "National administrative capacities expanded through cracks in an edifice of rules of action and internal governmental controls articulated by courts and parties."[35] Where administrative structures were established, the legacy of "courts and parties" was simply built into the new administrative structure.[36] America's federal system encouraged state or local jurisdiction whenever feasible.

Other historians, like Ellis Hawley, were influenced by the rising tide of cultural history. American political culture, they noticed, was distinctly antistatist. A rapidly modernizing society had to work around these constraints. "A weak administrative sector," Hawley noted, "sought to enhance its capacity by bringing private administrative resources into 'public service.'"[37] In other words, American policy makers hoped to use professional structures as an alternative to an expanded central state, and they turned to professional organizations and a host of other voluntary institutions to execute that vision.[38]

Combining post-Weberian sociology, political science that posited a more assertive role for federal administrators, greater sensitivity to the political power of America's antistatist culture, and new empirical research into Progressive administrative structures, recent organizational accounts significantly revise our understanding of state building. It was anything but inevitable and, even where most developed, hardly complete. State building required that administrators resourcefully mobilize political support: They were far more active and far more political in agency-group relations than originally envisioned. When a perspective that considers the constraints on state building faced by American administrators and the limited resources available to them is used to examine the complete continuum of agency relations with the public—from relatively unformulated mass opinion to tightly organized pressure groups—it becomes clear that, despite Progressive rhetoric, administrators from the very start of the Progressive Era sought to create group support in a variety of ways. To establish centralized administrative capacity in a pluralist, federal political system with strong antistatist biases, state builders were forced to seek political resources outside of the formal institutions that they labored to build. Influencing public opinion and converting that sentiment into the hard currency of interest-group politics was often the only way to accomplish that end.

Experts, of course, were a valuable weapon in the battle to obtain administrative autonomy as well as a prerequisite to solving complex problems. They could, however, prove to be a fifth column—a threat in and of itself to administrative discretion. It did not take long for even the most ardent proponents of expert discretion to realize that professional autonomy inside administrative agencies could trample years of political spadework. Federal administrators worked with professional expertise housed in voluntary or professional organizations wherever possible so as to distance the central government from charges of meddling.

Recent Scholarship and the Professions

At the same time that scholars reexamined organizational theory, sociologists revised their views on the sources of professional autonomy. Increasingly, sociologists rejected structure-functionalist descriptions of professionals.[39] Experts existed and were granted authority because a complex and interdependent society required it, the early organizational interpretations argued. Relatively little attention was paid to how the professions themselves developed and why they followed divergent courses.[40] To the extent that the pioneers of the original organizational synthesis added a historical gloss to this otherwise relatively static picture of expertise, they concentrated on tracing the historical developments that led to this social need: industrialization, urbanization, and so on. All causal paths led to interdependence.

Increasingly, sociologists rejected structure-functionalist descriptions of professionals, asking instead how these experts achieved their power.[41] As Burton Bledstein recently pointed out, Parsons had hermetically sealed the professions.[42] The original organizational synthesis entombed at its core that functionalist stasis. The thrust of recent scholarship, however, has been to analyze professional development in the same terms used to analyze other groups. Interdependence and the professionals' specialized response to it, for instance, is now the starting point, not the conclusion, of historical studies. From there, scholars have gone on to ask how professionals used these forces to reshape social, political, and cultural relations.[43] Once again, Samuel P. Hays led the way toward this more dynamic view of professionalization. In his introduction to *Building the New Organizational Society*, published in 1972, Hays observed that "while the agents of science and technology have professed to themselves and to the world at large that they were neutral instruments rather than goal-makers, they, in fact, were deeply preoccupied with shaping and ordering the lives of other men."[44]

To achieve the power they sought, the professions had to reconstitute themselves, replacing traditional bonds of deference to authority with a new science-based body of esoteric knowledge. Magali Sarfatti Larson has labeled this new base of knowledge "cognitive exclusiveness."[45] Professionalization, viewed from this perspective, was an attempt to "translate one order of scarce resources—special knowledge and skills—into another—social and economic rewards."[46] Professionalization was hardly automatic: Rather, it was a fierce struggle. The ability to establish "cognitive exclusiveness" often determined the outcome.

As with revised accounts of state building, recent accounts of professionalization have been more sensitive to America's unique culture. Scholars have asked how professional values have been influenced by broader American culture. The first generation of organizational scholars avoided this question, preferring to rely on Parsonian ideals instead. Professional ideals—particularly the service ideal, they argued—was a crucial distinguishing feature of the professions.[47] While the service ideal characterized the external relations of professions, an even more basic belief, the structure-functionalists argued, was reflected in the professionals' commitment to rational discourse, science, and efficiency. These were the core values, Wiebe argued, that held together the newly formed professional middle class—the source of Progressive reform.[48] Cultural historians in the past twenty years, on the other hand, have stressed the interplay between values championed by the rising professions and more deeply rooted cultural beliefs.[49]

When professionalization is treated as the product of a fierce struggle for autonomy—as opposed to a functionalist fait accompli—and then situated within an American political culture deeply distrustful of an enlarged state, we discover a significant problem that the early organizational scholarship avoided: the tremendous resistance by virtually all of the professions to central bureaucratic controls—particularly those of the federal government.[50] Unsure of their organizational and ideological solidarity, scientists, for instance, feared the corrupting influence of central government. In many instances they were prepared to forego its potential financial resources for what they hoped would be greater professional autonomy, secure in their belief that this was in fact the American way. Scientists and a host of other professionals did not actively seek federal aid to produce experts, sustain their research, and pursue professional policy agendas until after World War II.

While there can be no doubt that the Progressive Era served as a catalyst both for the growth of the federal government and for professionalization, it is their parallel development, not the merger of the two, that is most striking about the first half of the twentieth century in America. Shifting perceptions of organization and profession building, combined with a wealth of monographs that have begun to fill in the details of Wiebe's schematic portrait, leave the contemporary would-be synthesizer with a far less deterministic view of the relationship between experts and the state, and a far greater appreciation for the variety of mechanisms used to develop the state and the professions in the United States.

Thanks to recent organizational scholarship, we have a much better idea of how the professions and administrators achieved that end. It is a story that for its first fifty years yields two distinct chapters: one about building the professions, the other about building the state. It is only after 1950 that these two separate strands merge into one account about political power in the federal government.

Building the Professions

The recognition of cultural forces that constrained or competed with professional values and the realization that, as they specialized, the professions developed new agendas and interests revises our understanding of how the professions were built. Not yet ready to assume the role projected for them by Progressive theorists, experts in the early twentieth century were just beginning to reconstitute their professions on a scientific basis, to establish the institutions that would standardize that knowledge, to produce colleagues in sufficient numbers to influence policy, and to link more theoretical research to practical applications. For profession builders, power was the product of myriad choices and strategies. Far from being "hermetically sealed," professional behavior was constantly interacting and adapting to the environment in which it was nurtured. If they were to retain their authority in the twentieth century, the professions had to reconstitute the basis of that authority.

The early works of Hays, Wiebe, and Galambos concentrated on the broader social phenomena that dramatically reduced the classical professions' ability to explain the world in traditional terms. Increased interdependence, the component parts of which were industrialization, urbanization, immigration, and a shift from an extensive to an intensive economy, created massive new problems that resisted the kinds of solutions traditionally offered by the professions in the nineteenth century. Failure to resolve problems created by increased interdependence, in turn, challenged the traditional authority of lawyers, physicians, and the clergy.[51] Fortunately for forward-looking professionals, interdependence also offered a solution. Professionals—and many other groups—specialized in response to these upheavals caused by modernization. At the same time, they created new organizations to coordinate these specialized units on a national and eventually international scale.[52]

The first generation of organizational scholars was quick to point out the significance of the organizational impulse in the professions.[53] The American Medical Association (AMA) reorganized in 1901 and increased its membership from 8,400 in 1900 to over 70,000 by 1910.[54] The organizational equivalent of the AMA in the field of law was the American Bar Association. Founded in 1878 as the capstone of several local bar associations, it presided over 623 such organizations by 1916.[55] Even the clergy underwent an organizational revolution, becoming more hierarchically ordered and incorporating bureaucratic values into newly nationalized organizations.[56] Organizational specialization was the most visible indication of the revolution sweeping the professions.

While organizational adaptations were a necessary condition for survival in the new professional world, they were not a sufficient condition. To thrive, professions increasingly had to master a body of scientific knowledge. Expertise no longer rested on just experience and functional specialization. Increasingly it rested upon an esoteric body of knowledge, informed by scientific theory, tested empirically, and applied by the profession's practitioners. Again, this trend extended even to the clergy. As Andrew Walsh has recently pointed out, forward-looking clergy such as Graham Taylor at the Hartford Seminary made sociology a crucial component of the ministry's training. Taylor tutored his students in field work and argued that "if Christian society itself is to exist, or prevail, the ministry and membership of the Church must be instructed in the intelligent comprehension of the destructive and constructive social forces now at war. . . . They must moreover be trained in the practical use of the preventive, deterrent and reformatory measures by which death-dealing social evils are to be checked, restricted and eradicated."[57]

Recent scholarship has paid special attention to the dynamic relationship between a profession's cognitive base of knowledge and its organizational development. At a minimum, scholars have argued that professions have used the transition to a more scientifically oriented cognitive base of knowledge to justify claims to autonomy. More often, however, adopting specialized scientific knowledge as the new basis of authority was no less a matter of strategy and choice than the decisions driving the more explicitly political organizational developments.[58] At its extreme, the new scholarship insists that the professions have adopted a more scientific cognitive base for the sole purpose of enhancing claims to authority and political power. Thus Jerold S. Auerbach concluded that "law as science could not help but elevate the expertise, and therefore the power, of those who were trained to master its secrets. . . . The values of "objective science" were considerably less neutral than its proponents claimed; they were designed to provide conservative solutions by stressing stability, control, and order."[59]

The interaction between professional organization and cognitive base has been explored fully in recent accounts of professionalization in the social science and in medicine. In his study of the emergence of professional social science in the latter part of the nineteenth century, Thomas Haskell demonstrated how broader social forces promoted the adoption of new modes of thought on the one hand and new organizational forms on the other. The American Social Science Association (ASSA) was an organization built around a model of individualist causes and an approach to research that could not address the very questions that had stimulated its birth.[60] When the professional academic social sciences were founded separately in the 1880s and 1890s they began to build a body of knowledge that explained events in a world where causes—once seemingly identifiable by common sense and located in one's immediate environment—were increasingly perceived as the property of strange and remote factors.[61] Men like John Dewey, Richard Ely, and William James, who built the professional social sciences, looked for the causes of problems ranging from poverty to illness in a combination of environmental factors. This was a sharp break from the kinds of explanations offered by the generation that founded the ASSA, who were likely to attribute such problems to individual failure.[62] The social scientists of Dewey's generation built professional disciplines, ultimately housed in the nation's research universities, that provided full-time employment at the same time that they created a community of inquiry organized along the lines of specialized discipline.[63] The competition of ideas within this community, they argued, would insulate the new academic professions from public pressure; it would provide the autonomy that the new professionals so desired. Without such organizational articulation, little additional progress could be made in developing a scientific cognitive base of knowledge: Organizational base and cognitive base were integrally related.

In the hands of other scholars, the balance between intellectual and organizational motivation was decidedly tilted toward the latter. Academic newcomers such as William Graham Sumner used the mantle of science to bolster their position in the academy and to gain entrée to secular authority and political power, according to Dorothy Ross.[64] Thus it was not just autonomy that the social scientists sought; they hoped to forge monopoly control based on a claim to scientific knowledge that proved to be grossly inflated. From the outset, American social scientists "claimed to have established sciences before they were in possession of any firm body of scientific knowledge."[65] As results failed to live up to these claims after World War I, the social sciences articulated a narrower, harder, and more technical vision of this faith at the same time that they disengaged from some of the more unrealistic claims.[66]

Even in professions such as medicine that relied on a base of knowledge drawn from the physical sciences, and where concrete achievements came closer to matching professional claims, scholars argued that science was valued by practitioners for its ability to bolster a profession's autonomy, not for the benefits it might bring to that profession's clients. Broad scientific training put future professionals through a crucial first phase of unification and standardization.[67] That was particularly important in the case of medicine, a profession that did not succeed in establishing a standardized product around which it could unify until a mechanism for mass-producing this product was secured at the university. A scientific base was crucial to realizing the profession's demands for autonomy. Once established, doctors began to define the very standards by which medicine's success would be judged.[68]

Dismissing the major bacteriological breakthroughs of the 1880s and 1890s as leading only to a "slight increase in the effectiveness of the new medicine," E. Richard Brown attributed the rise of science-based medicine to factors having more to do with the economic and social needs satisfied by its new scientific base.[69] A new generation of managerial capitalists, Brown argued, embraced scientific medicine because it increasingly rejected a broader environmental explanation of illness rooted in living and working conditions. The germ theory of disease, which emphasized discrete, specific, and external causal agents of disease and which promoted research on specific therapies to cure certain diseases, was particularly appealing to the rising young capitalists, Brown argued. Disease was seen as an engineering problem that ultimately would succumb if sufficient resources were devoted to solving it.[70]

Even Paul Starr, who credited scientific breakthroughs in medicine with dramatic reductions in mortality rates, emphasized the independent value of medicine's new esoteric body of knowledge in a world where the average citizen had become dependent on specialists.[71] With the recession of causality, to use Haskell's term, not only had causes of problems become less apparent to the untrained eye, but the very identification of problems could no longer be trusted to the casual observer. As a Minnesota physician commented in 1923, "Ten years ago no parent brought a child to the physician for examination to make sure that nothing was wrong. Today, I venture to say that the greatest part of the work of a pediatrician is in preventive medicine."[72]

The recent literature on profession building is marked by a more fluid treatment of the construction and uses of knowledge in building organizational structure and in garnering authority. The professions were particularly attracted to a scientifically informed cognitive base not just because it enhanced their ability to explain and solve problems in an increasingly interdependent world, but because it also offered clear political advantages on the organizational front, enhancing professional authority and autonomy.

The recent professionalization literature has also explored more fully the implications of organizational structure for the construction of knowledge. The literature on the evolution of engineering provides the clearest example of this. Engineers followed many of the traditional steps toward professionalization in the nineteenth century. They formed professional organizations, starting with the American Society of Civil Engineers in 1852. They specialized, soon branching into mining and mechanical engineering by the end of the century and eventually electrical and chemical engineering in the twentieth century. Organizational beachheads were accompanied or soon followed by an intellectual reorientation that shifted the core of the engineer's expertise from experience to science-based knowledge. From 1870 on, the engineering curricula became increasingly science-based. In fact, in the newer subdisciplines of chemical and electrical engineering, chemistry and physics departments contributed as much to instruction as mechanical engineering departments had.[73]

Like other professions, engineers worked at the intersection of two powerful historical developments. The sciences were increasingly viewed as utilitarian, and the application of expert skill to problems increasingly drew on the development of science.[74] And like other professions, the place where the theoretical and applied came together was the university. That is where cognitive exclusiveness was refined and where professionals were reproduced.

Yet for all of these similarities, engineers never achieved the autonomy enjoyed by several other professions, medicine in particular. Organizational factors explain much of this difference. The failure lay not in the professional organizations established by engineers but in the nature of the clients ultimately served by engineers—large-scale industrial corporations.[75] With few entrepreneurial opportunities and with most of the dramatic advances coming from large corporate industrial firms such as General Electric and American Telephone and Telegraph, engineers molded their professional identity not just by the degree of scientific ability they achieved, but by mobility into corporate management as well.[76]

That engineers inculcated the values of their employers affected not only the conditions of their employment, according to David Noble, it affected the very base of knowledge that under other circumstances might have offered a path toward autonomy. Corporate engineers dominated curriculum development and shaped technological development.[77] The fullest expression of industry-education research cooperation occurred at the Massachusetts Institute of Technology (MIT). This cooperation not only produced research for corporate clients, but also groomed future managers for their climb up the corporate ladder. As Dugald Jackson, a prime mover in this effort, reported to the president of MIT in 1915, AT&T's contributions allowed the electrical engineering department to "put the more important problems . . . before graduate students and research assistants, who can prosecute their researches diligently and efficiently, under systematic and businesslike supervision, which not only enables these advanced students to be trained to higher effectiveness, but also enables their enthusiasm to be directed to definite ends."[78]

Robert Kohler's account of the emergence of biochemistry, though free of the strong social control argument that drives Noble's analysis, also chronicles how the organizational landscape shaped the way knowledge was defined. In this instance, however, would-be biochemists responded to opportunities created by a number of factors including existing relationships among several established academic disciplines (biology and chemistry among them), the demands of another profession (medical practitioners), and the evolving university in which this debate was set.[79] The catalyst was university reform. Reformers incorporated medical colleges into research universities and upgraded undergraduate curricula around the turn of the century. Thus it began to pay, in professional terms, to specialize. Because medical students now arrived with general chemistry and biology under their belts, specialists equipped to teach more advanced courses were suddenly in short supply. As Kohler notes, "What had been a marginal role for medical chemists became the basis for a new biomedical discipline." In the new spirit of incorporating scientific discovery into graduate training, research achievement was no longer icing on the cake when it came to establishing a school's reputation. It was now as important as teaching ability.[80]

That biochemistry remained in medical schools also contributed to the symbiotic relationship between biochemistry and clinical medicine. According to Kohler, "Each partner accommodated his professional role and ideology to the needs and expectations of the other." Professional biochemists, for instance, developed new diagnostic procedures that aided

clinicians, while hospital physicians were a never-ending source of experimental materials.[81]

This relationship ultimately influenced the intellectual basis of the discipline as biochemists adapted clinical imperatives to disciplinary objectives.
For the first generation of biochemists, it was the biological program that
provided much of the theoretical and methodological basis for creating a
new discipline, allowing them to escape from a more applications-based
construction of the field. But the institutional framework in which biochemists worked forced them increasingly to choose between clinical
applications and the evolving biological program. On the one hand, biochemistry had no edge over chemistry and biology in areas where a service
role in medicine was not required. These better-established fields did not
hesitate to expand into new nonservice areas. On the other hand, the topics
that biochemists pursued by the 1930s and 1940s were shaped by their
traditional service-oriented concerns. As a consequence biochemists missed
out on the revolution in molecular biology. Although Warren Weaver of
the Rockefeller Foundation saw biochemistry as the centerpiece of his program in molecular biology, grant recipients were almost all biologists and
chemists.[82]

Thus, the original organizational synthesis launched a concerted scholarly effort to expand the theoretical and empirical base upon which it had
been built. Its core remained intact and continued to guide the overall
direction of inquiry into the history of state-society relations. At least in
principle, that core emphasized process—whether in identifying causality
as suggested by Thomas Haskell's emphasis on interdependence or in constructing societal responses, as epitomized by Robert Wiebe's phrase "continuous management." The structures created to guide that process,
subsequent scholarship revealed, were far more malleable than the organizational scholars initially envisioned, particularly because professionalization proved to be a highly dynamic and politicized element. Thus, the
reorganized organizational synthesis demolishes assumptions that experts
reigned during the Progressive Era.

It replaces that rather stultifying foundation for twentieth-century
American development with an invitation to consider the implications of a
far more contingent set of relations that flowed from the quest to professionalize. Even in instances where professionalization was most advanced,
the revised synthesis pushes scholars to consider the process by which
would-be professionals compromised their ideals or acted on competing

ideals in order to garner the political support necessary to solve the problems created by interdependence. It also invites students to consider how the professionalization process affected the lives of millions of Americans who never fully embraced that particular response to industrialism. Most significantly, placing the struggle to professionalize in the Progressive Era strongly suggests that this crucial component of the organizational response was dynamic. Eventually it became an important catalyst for change in its own right and produced its own share of public reactions over the course of the century.

Building the State

The federal government's administrative capacity expanded significantly during the Progressive Era. The Interstate Commerce Act (1887) marked the beginning of a series of thrusts that extended regulatory authority upward from the states to the federal government.[83] In addition to the ICC and the Food and Drug Administration, the FTC and the Federal Reserve Board's regional banks and supervisory board were among the most visible institutions created by this burst of Progressive Era state building. The federal government also began to develop a cadre of professional civil servants and the capacity to oversee longer-term planning. The Pendleton Act (1883) created the statutory basis for a professional civil service. Throughout the Progressive Era, the service was gradually extended to increase its coverage. The Budgeting and Accounting Act of 1921, which established the Office of the Budget within the federal Department of the Treasury, laid the groundwork for the capacity to plan nationally. The Progressives also expanded the federal government's role in the application of science and technology. The Department of Agriculture (USDA) emerged as the nation's predominant scientific agency in the early decades of the twentieth century.[84]

Despite its expansion and a few exceptional agencies, such as the USDA, the American administrative state was compromised from the start by two powerful counterweights. The first was the legacy of the political system that the administrators sought to replace—what Skowronek has called a "state of courts and parties." The latter was a political culture distinctly antagonistic to centralized administrative authority.

In Skowronek's analysis, the early history of the ICC demonstrates just how strong the legacy of "courts and parties" could be. Although the ICC emerged by 1920 as perhaps the most powerful institution of continuous management at the federal level (with the possible exception of the Federal Reserve Bank) the path toward federal coordination of rail policy was strewn with obstacles. The political parties, adept at distributive politics but hamstrung when it came to distinguishing clearly between winners and losers, as regulatory actions often required, avoided the issue of national rail regulation for as long as possible. When the Supreme Court ruled in *Wabash v. Illinois* (1896) that the states could not regulate the railroads, Congress was forced to confront the issue. Congress, however, demonstrated that these difficult issues could be confronted without being resolved. By passing the problem along to a regulatory body, legislators denied the ICC a clear rate-setting mandate and saddled its new administrative surrogate with an inherently contradictory legislative mandate.[85]

ICC administrators stepped in to claim authority where none had explicitly been granted. The first chair of the ICC, Thomas Cooley, recognized that his agency would have to build a coherent policy in the interstices of the law. Rejecting a strict interpretation of the law, Cooley extended administrative discretion to his regulators. Had this been the end of the story, America might have emerged with a far more comprehensive approach to its transportation problems. Skowronek, however, skillfully demonstrates the power and range of well-established forces that centralized bureaucratic planners had to contend with in America, even once Congress was temporarily out of the picture.

The courts were not as accommodating as the parties on this issue. In 1897 the Supreme Court overturned this exercise in discretionary authority. The Court also challenged the ICC's tentative steps toward rate setting and its right to prescribe rates for the future. In essence, the Court blunted the commission's effort to rationalize a policy that a Congress bent on distributive politics had passed on to its administrative stepchild.[86] The economist Arthur Hadley summed up the ICC's predicament. There was a direct antagonism between rational economic planning and the practical workings of politics. Economists (rational planners, of course) were concerned with the collective good, according to Hadley. But "the practical workings of representative government, making each member primarily responsible to his district—or one might say the members of his own party in his district—means that the collective action of the whole is made to fulfill the separate wants of the parts—even though the satisfaction of those wants may antagonize the general interests of the nation."[87]

Even with strong presidential support, such state building would not be easy. Despite Theodore Roosevelt's mandate and a Republican Congress, it took all of the president's resources to make even small gains. Although the Hepburn and Mann-Elkins acts, which strengthened the ICC's rate-setting mandate, and a Supreme Court ruling in *Interstate Commerce Commission v. Illinois Central* granted the ICC greater freedom from judicial review, the ICC failed to act on its most pressing problem. It refused to raise railroad rates. Skowronek spelled out the reasons: "[It] was the commission's certain knowledge that action taken to relieve the railroads would raise the wrath of the agency's most ardent supporters in Congress." Legally more secure, the ICC remained politically fragile.[88]

State direction of corporate development outside the realm of public utilities clearly defined as natural monopolies was even more hesitant as Martin Sklar has demonstrated in *The Corporate Reconstruction of American Capitalism.*[89] The powerful Democratic chair of the Senate Committee on Interstate Commerce, Francis G. Newlands, summed up these divergent paths and attributed the difference to an administrative agency—the ICC— that gradually enhanced the state's presence in railroad planning and rate setting. In a letter to the powerful Democratic Speaker of the House, Champ Clark, Newlands noted that, because of the ICC, after "about 23 years of operation, through a gradual process of evolution, the regulation of railroads . . . has been practically accomplished." Administration of the Sherman Act, "on the contrary," Newlands continued, "has been lame and halting, changing with shifting incumbents . . . and according to the requirements of political exigencies."[90]

Sklar portrays in impressive detail why, despite the powerful thrust of corporate capital and its emergence over proprietary capital as the premier form of property relations in twentieth-century America, it was decades before a compromise could be hammered out that harmonized policy toward trusts in the three branches of the federal government.[91] Woodrow Wilson finally achieved the required political compromise in the legislation that established the FTC and the Clayton Act in 1914. According to Sklar, "Wilson's outlook articulated an awareness of the need to bring the system of authority and power lodged in capitalist property ownership . . . into phase with the system of authority and power lodged in the law, party politics and government."[92] Wilson's achievement, according to Sklar, was to extend the principle of flexible adjustment to corporate development that had been present in the Bureau of Corporations in the executive branch of government for some time to the legislative and judicial branches as well.[93] Juxtaposing Wilson's consensus position to that of both Roosevelt and Taft, Sklar sums up not only the reasons for the FTC's political success, but also the dilemma that Progressive state builders faced in general. "Wilson stood with Taft as an antistatist against Roosevelt," Sklar concludes. "He did not want the state to command society. Yet, he stood with Roosevelt against Taft, in wanting the state actively to serve society."[94]

In most policy areas, the legacy of "courts and parties" was built into the new administrative structure. The Budgeting and Accounting Act of 1921, for instance, created an outpost for expert advice on fiscal matters and an administrative apparatus for managing the budget within the executive branch. But for each executive structure established, there seemed to be a congressional counterweight as well. In the case of the new Bureau of the Budget, it was the General Accounting Office. In the case of the President's Civil Service Commission, it was the Congressional Bureau of Efficiency.[95] Courts and parties left a visible and lasting imprint on the shape of the emerging administrative state.

America's political culture played an equally significant though less visible role in that process. Explaining why welfare policy in America did not parallel developments in other industrialized nations, for instance, Ellis Hawley identified three sets of value structures that pervaded American political culture: free-market libertarianism, market-modifying republicanism, and managerial developmentalism. Each, on occasion, encouraged demands for a stronger state: to protect property rights in the case of the free-market advocates; to bring countervailing power to bear on those who would threaten the people's independence in the case of republicanism; and to promote and protect administrative mechanisms in the case of managerial developmentalism. Yet each, Hawley argued, contained a powerful antistatist strain, and each contributed to a cultural bias against the emergence of a powerful bureaucracy. The culture, Hawley contended, "was malleable enough to allow a bureaucracy geared to the performance of narrow, specific and pragmatically justified tasks but not one that had much of a capacity for overall social management or for developing and implementing a coherent national welfare scheme."[96] The cultural milieu was as resistant to the emergence of a strong administrative state as was the structure of politics.

The resistance of politicians wedded to a more decentralized and partisan system of politics combined with the pervasiveness of the antistatist strain in America's political culture severely restricted the development of federal administrative mechanisms. As Barry Karl has pointed out, even the reformers themselves, despite their commitment to greater government intervention, were ambivalent about using the federal government. It was at the state and local level that progressive reforms made their greatest impact.[97]

For instance, the public's role in aiding dependent children increased dramatically in the early twentieth century, but this was due to local, not federal, intervention. Between 1900 and 1904 the proportion of children in state and local institutions doubled. By 1919 thirty-nine states had authorized pensions for mothers with dependent children. At the turn of the century, cities and counties began to establish juvenile courts. By 1925 virtually all states had authorized such institutions.[98] Probation for adult and juvenile offenders and parole were two more criminal justice reforms instituted at the local level that required a new administrative apparatus and that claimed that the expertise of specialists would guide these institutions.[99] It was in the area of public health that states and localities made their most dramatic advances. The City of New York, for instance, administered almost seventy baby health stations by 1920.[100]

Andrew Polsky's analysis of the juvenile court movement and its institutionalization at the local level illustrates the distance between the Progressive ideal and Progressive Era reality when it came to harnessing expertise to a more powerful state.[101] The political catalyst for juvenile courts did not necessarily bode well for would-be state builders. The two thousand courts established in the first two decades of the twentieth century owed their existence as much to mundane fiscal considerations as to idealism. Probation, state legislatures believed, would reduce costs by shifting juveniles out of more costly institutions.[102] The juvenile courts, Polsky argues, turned out to be formidable institutions in their own right. Nevertheless, they continued to suffer from underfunding—a legacy linked to their early cost-saving rationale, and a product of the local base of their funding. Though the court owed its very existence to social scientists, who convinced reformers and philanthropists of their discipline's breakthroughs, in practice "every step in the process, from intake to disposition, fell far short of expectations," according to Polsky.[103] "Rather than provide a complete diagnostic tool, the preliminary investigation amounted to nothing more than a disjointed compilation of hearsay, gossip, and trivia," Polsky notes.[104] Clinics to support the court's therapeutic pretensions rarely existed. Although important advances in knowledge were made during the Progressive Era at a handful of institutes, the average judge rarely introduced science into the courtroom.[105] It is not surprising that the court movement was in "a precarious position," according to Polsky, by the late 1920s.[106]

In contrast to the direct services increasingly provided by localities—successful or not—action at the federal level was confined to limited grants-in-aid, the accumulation of statistics and symbolic acts. The Children's Bureau, established in 1912, was one such federal outpost. That it was able to exert such an influence on the child protection movement is a tribute to its leadership under Julia Lathrop, and certainly not the product of a great commitment to federal intervention. Its initial budget was $25,000.[107]

Federal grants-in-aid to the states were the most common form of federal expansion in the 1920s. Federal intergovernmental transfers grew from $7 million a year in 1902 to $123 million a year by 1927.[108] The major increases occurred in highway and education funding. The Sheppard-Towner Act, which provided grants-in-aid to state and locally administered maternal health programs, remained extremely small. In 1924 the Washington staff consisted of four physicians, a nurse, an accountant, a secretary, and a stenographer.[109] Even so, state and professional groups challenged the program, claiming that it reflected national, not state and locally determined, goals.[110] In 1913 the federal government spent nine cents per capita on civilian welfare; fifteen years later, it spent only twenty-five cents per capita.[111]

It was at the local level that major reforms in education, the delivery of basic city services such as sanitation and police, and planning for growth were implemented. There was a gradual shift upward in the locus of decision making. Decisions were concentrated in fewer, more expert hands. Local was defined more broadly—as county rather than ward, for instance.[112] To define such functions in national terms, however, still remained the exception, not the rule.

Only by compromising with the decentralized political structure reflected in the "state of courts and parties" and by accepting the restraints of America's antistatist culture could state builders achieve anything at all. Grants-in-aid from the federal government to the states were one form such compromises took.[113] Subjecting the administrative process to the veto power of influential interest groups, epitomized by the Army Corps of Engineers, was another. Powerful iron triangles developed that linked the fortunes of agencies not only to interest groups but to oversight committees in Congress as well.[114]

Operating within these constraints, however, there was ample room for aggressive administrators to enhance their policy-making leverage. Administrators could build support for their programs independent of established interest groups or congressional constituencies. In fact, federal bureaucrats soon learned how to create their own interest groups and constituencies. They could also seek the very kind of autonomy eventually granted to professionals, by claiming that the complexity of issues and the rapid pace of change required enhanced administrative discretion. Perhaps the best way that an agency could hope to control its own destiny was by claiming a monopoly on expertise. Forays into politics were not the exceptional product of power-hungry individuals. In a political environment as wary of centralized authority as America at the turn of the century, experts and administrators alike had to adapt politically if they were to carry out their professional and organizational missions. Their most significant adaptation—to embrace each other—still lay ahead. As was the case with virtually every other exercise in profession building and state building in America, this did not come about easily or naturally. The approach set in motion by the Progressives carried within it the seeds of a new political alliance between experts and federal administrators. This Progressive ideal, however, proved elusive until World War II, largely due to the underdeveloped condition of the professions and the legacy of "courts and parties" in the first decade of the twentieth century.

Part II

The Proministrative State

Building on the scholarship that has helped to revitalize the organizational synthesis, we can now extend the account of state and profession building into the late twentieth century, and track the emergent partnership between the two. While the Progressives envisioned the alliance of professionals and the central state, they did not realize it, nor did New Deal reformers. It took World War II and the ensuing Cold War to tie the knot. Once fused after World War II, professionals and federal organizations altered the trajectory of state-society relations significantly. The proministrative state—a label I have coined to signify the merger of professionals and federal administrative capacity—finally arrived in America three decades after Croly's vision and Lippmann's appeal.[115]

There were two critical differences between virtually all of the federal agencies' relationships to expertise before World War II and the kinds of relationships that emerged following the war. Before the war the federal government had little to do with the production of professional experts and as a result it exercised little influence over the cognitive base of the professions it employed or the number of professionals produced.[116] Second, and even more significantly, professionals were employed in Progressive and interwar federal bureaus primarily to apply skills already tested and routinized. The agendas dictated by the cutting edge of each profession's research—and, for that matter, basic research itself—remained outside the scope of the federal-professional relationship.

Why the delay? Despite telltale signs of one-night stands, the marriage vows between professional experts and the central government required that four conditions be met. Only two had been realized by 1940. The first condition that had just barely been realized by the time that World War II began was organizational and professional maturity. In organizational terms, this could be measured by the state's administrative reach, ability to plan, implement, and coordinate national policy, and also by the degree of sophistication that agencies had achieved in dealing with a variety of political actors, particularly elected officials and interest groups.[117] World War I and the economic crisis of the Great Depression finally pushed the federal government toward greater organizational capacity. In profession-building terms, maturity could be measured by professional autonomy and problem-solving capacity.[118] By the end of the Progressive Era, many of the professions were just establishing a scientific base of knowledge. The interwar years were crucial to the development of the professions. Most had not incorporated a scientific base of knowledge, learned to apply it, and disseminated it to practitioners until the eve of World War II.

The second condition met during the interwar years was integrally related to professional and organizational maturity. Both partners had to overcome what is best described as fear of commitment and learn how to work together to their mutual advantage. Administrators and professionals, while recognizing that each stood to gain valuable resources through a marriage of convenience, feared that their discretion and autonomy might be threatened by such a match. It was only when each felt more self-confident, and when living apart became financially impossible, that the wedding took place. Until the professions and federal managers could overcome their fear of commitment, the underdeveloped American administrative state was forced to work with "quasiprivatist" machinery, as Hawley called it.[119]

Broad, public legitimation was the third condition that had to be satisfied. America's political culture, even in the wake of the New Deal, remained strongly antagonistic toward centralized state control and insulated decision making by experts. It would take a series of dramatic events powerful enough to alter the cultural consciousness of millions of Americans in order to offset this antistatist bias. A series of dramatic displays in a highly visible arena—where the practical benefits of the union between experts and the central state could be demonstrated—was crucial to the success of this cultural task.

Organizing new sources of demand for the policies that the federal-professional alliance generated was the fourth precondition to establishing the prominist rative state. In the past, experts housed in the federal government had worked together most successfully when a narrowly drawn set of economic interests demanded services. Whether railroads and, eventually, truckers via the ICC, or the financial community through the Securities and Exchange Commission or Federal Reserve Bank, economic interest groups had pressed to institutionalize expertise in the federal government. The prominist rative state—whether offering electricity too cheap to meter or the eradication of poverty—promised services that outstripped the demand of organized economic interest groups for them. Samuel Beer was one of the first scholars to note that when it came to "technocratic politics," as he called the post–World War II period, the old pressure-group model did not apply. The merger of science and public policy, according to Beer, "shifts the initiative in government from the economic and social environment of government to government itself."[120]

A Long and Fruitful Courtship

Much of the organizational and professional development during the Progressive Era took place in the private, voluntary, or state and local sectors. Federal administrative capacity in the interwar years grew haltingly. Of course, administrative capacity varied across policy areas, as Theda Skocpol has pointed out.[121] Perhaps the best case study of such divergence in America is Ira Katznelson and Kenneth Prewitts review of U.S. policies toward Latin America. The United States, in comparison to other nations, had a strong capacity to intervene in Latin America, and the state autonomy to do so, but virtually no capacity to coordinate and plan domestic policies regarding Latin America.[122] Domestically, the only agency that came close to having a strong central capacity to plan policy nationally by the end of the New Deal was the USDA. Even before the Progressive Era, the USDA had spawned a specialized group of agricultural administrators.[123] The department, in the period after World War I, Skocpol and Finegold argue, was "an island of state strength in an ocean of weakness."[124] The factors that distinguished the USDA from other federal agencies were its long history; unified, flexible, and relatively autonomous management; strong research capacity; and an existing information-gathering ability crucial to the administration of complex programs such as the Agricultural Adjustment Act.[125]

The USDA was also distinguished by its political experience. For decades, it had dealt with the limits and possibilities of American politics. Skocpol and Finegold note that department experts were willing "to make policy *for*, rather than just *with* the farmers and their organizations."[126] They also noted that, "accustomed to the challenges of public office, their training and career experiences had given them a concrete sense of what could (and could not) be done with available government means."[127] Administrative and political experiences contributed to a USDA secure enough to spend money on basic research, confident enough to promote new policies engineered by its social scientists, and skilled enough to administer these new national policies.

The agricultural professions in America were as highly developed as the federal government's agricultural administration. A. Hunter Dupree dubbed the USDA a "predominant" agency of science in the early twentieth century. Dupree noted that the department was built around a system, not a personality; that the scope of its various branches ranged from land-grant colleges to state experimentation stations; and that the variety of functions it performed ran the gamut, coupling basic research to the application of science by individual farmers.[128] Expertise was merged with administration at the federal level so early in the case of the Department of Agriculture in part because the department's administrative capacity was so highly developed.

The USDA was one of the first federal agencies to engage in the production of expertise. It was able to do this through its integral links to state land-grant colleges created by the Morrill Act (1862), experimental stations funded by the Hatch Act (1887), and, later, the Extension Service created by the Smith-Lever Act (1914).[129] Almost all agricultural scientists were full-time government employees. Federal funding was no doubt a contributor to the "Golden Age" that this field experienced in the last two decades of the nineteenth century and the first two of the twentieth century.[130] The best proof that the USDA's managerial capacity promoted and used professions came not in the agricultural science but in the emergence of agricultural social sciences. By the 1920s, the department concentrated its developmental efforts on the social sciences. It formed the Bureau of Agricultural Economics in 1922. Like the natural sciences in agriculture, the agricultural social sciences were spawned by, and in turn embraced, their federal sponsor.[131] The Bureau of Agricultural Economics' chief was correct (although self-serving) when he gloated that in the seven decades since its inception, the USDA had developed from "essentially a collection of natural-scientific research workers with attachés for informational and publication services" into an agency that could formulate and implement economic and social policy.[132]

But for all this, agriculture was the clear exception to the rule. Much of the growth of science in the federal government during the Progressive Era was attributable to the government's enlarged regulatory role. Agency scientists concentrated on the routine tasks of inspection and testing.[133] The agendas dictated by the cutting edge of each profession's research—and, for that matter, basic research itself—remained outside the scope of the federal-professional relationship.[134] The professional's "expertness" was accepted, but the ever-changing cognitive base of knowledge and the professional's freedom to explore new research agendas—both of which were crucial to the maintenance of professional autonomy—fell outside of the federal government's reach.

Even in the "predominant" agency of science, it appears that the full extent of the professional expert's repertoire was rarely engaged. Most other agencies, and many bureaus within the USDA, survived only by ignoring basic research and carefully circumscribing the problems worked on by professionals. Although the federal government's Hygienic Laboratory began to develop an independent research laboratory during the first two decades of the twentieth century, a large part of the agency's political legitimacy rested on the routine task of enforcing the Biologics Control Act of 1902.[135] The same pattern occurred in the case of the USDA, which enforced the Pure Food and Drug Act of 1906.[136] Despite federal expenditures on research in 1900 that totaled $11 million—a staggering amount compared to other sources—federal spending did not dominate science because so much of it was devoted to practical day-to-day applications as opposed to basic research.[137] By the end of the Progressive Era, science had become distinctly specialized. Basic research was soundly grounded in the new research universities, while applied research remained the domain of government and was increasingly found in industry as well.[138]

Even when the federal government was willing to consider funding basic research, top experts balked. Well into the 1930s, leading physical scientists resisted federal funding. In 1934 the well-known astronomer and astrophysicist George Ellery Hale warned his colleagues that a National Research Administration might injure voluntary organizations such as the National Academy of Sciences and the National Research Council that housed science. "I do not believe," Hale warned, "that under a Government system the University of Chicago and other institutions of which I have personal knowledge would be what they are today."[139] His colleague Frank Jewett of the American Telephone and Telegraph Company was more blunt: "Outside of a restoration of scientific activities within the legitimate functions of the governmental departments, appropriation of Federal funds is a very grave question which goes to the root of the whole matter of state participation and control of functions which hitherto we have jealously guarded as the affairs of individual or nonpolitical cooperative effort." Sooner or later, Jewett continued, "There would be a large measure of bureaucratic control or attempts to control by the Federal government."[140] Basic science's elite researchers continued to resist federal funding throughout the 1930s.[141]

Outside of the USDA, leading social scientists also resisted proposals that might have brought federal funding at the expense of federal control. Economists, while relying heavily on the government's statistics-gathering ability, remained aloof from what they feared would be governmental control. They were housed in voluntary structures such as the National Bureau of Economic Research or the Brookings Institution. The vision they offered relied on voluntary cooperation in order to build a national countercyclical economic strategy or to improve economic and public administration's efficiency.[142] In explaining why so many professionals resisted the urge to seek federal funds, we must go beyond their concern for what federal funding might do to the professions and consider broader cultural reasons. These men and women were products of the same political culture described by Hawley and McGerr: They resisted expanding the federal government for the same reasons that millions of other Americans did.

Elected officials were also hesitant, particularly in regard to research and its application. That politicians were not eager to fund research where tangible results might be years off or nonexistent is not surprising. Nor did politicians leap at the opportunity to pass on the political discretion and resources that might accompany the application of expertise to problems. Such was the case in the social services. The increasing professionalization of welfare produced a fierce reaction among local welfare administrators—many of them elected. Their first line of defense was to question the accountability of the experts. As one county superintendent put it, the trend in charity was "towards vesting administrative details in the hands of distant Boards, who are only familiar with the clerical and academic aspects of the business and who are out of touch and sympathy with the individuals requiring relief."[143] Ultimately, by organizing nationally and emphasizing their own administrative skills, welfare directors fended off the challenge from social workers.

Because early twentieth-century American public administration was so underdeveloped—at least by European standards—the most enduring, and the most representative, relationship between experts and the public sector was licensing.[144] Through this relationship, states contributed to the authority of professionals and in many instances reduced competition from other occupations. Professionals, in turn, solved some of society's problems without disrupting the private or voluntary framework already in place. Rather than fuse expertise with a more centralized state, Americans viewed expertise as an alternative to an extended state. From the perspective of those steeped in America's antistatist culture, the hierarchy and self-governing mechanisms of the myriad professionalizing organizations were not unlike state and local governments: They dealt with problems without requiring the expansion of the centralized state.

By the 1920s there were four kinds of institutions that formed crucial bridges between professionals and the state. Each thrived precisely because of professional, public, and political reticence about the fusion of these two powerful forces. The first institutional bridge was the research university, which actually produced the new professionals. It was also where much of the nation's basic research was conducted. The second was the voluntary coordinating agency, such as the Social Science Research Council (SSRC) or National Research Council. The third bridge was the foundation, such as those established by Rockefeller and Carnegie or in memory of Laura Spelman. These foundations provided funding and sought to direct the development of both universities and coordinating agencies. Finally, there were the trade associations and professional societies that Hoover hoped would guide his associative state.

The voluntary sector's program to build the professions in the 1920s and 1930s demonstrates that, even by the close of the Progressive Era, the professions had a long way to go. When Beardsley Ruml moved to the Laura Spelman Rockefeller Memorial in 1921, he soon concluded that he could not attain the fund's objective of improving the nation's social welfare without a more solid foundation of knowledge. The fund he administered had in the past made large contributions to organizations like the Girl Scouts and the Young Women's Christian Association. But even these organizations, Ruml argued, recognized the need for greater knowledge of those factors influencing human behavior. Ruml claimed that the state of knowledge in the social sciences was embarrassingly low: "It is as though engineers were at work without an adequate development in the sciences of physics and chemistry or as though physicians were practising in the absence of the medical sciences."[145] Ruml used this argument to reorient the Memorial's funding, shifting it from practical social amelioration toward social science research. A large portion of the Memorial's funds was directed at the development of research centers within universities. The Memorial also supported coordinating mechanisms such as the SSRC. In all, during Ruml's six years as director, the Memorial disbursed more than $45 million to improve the social sciences.[146]

The unique combination of charity and faith in science that created foundations like the Laura Spelman Rockefeller Memorial filled a national void created by the tradition of federalism at the same time that it hastened the process of professionalization. Foundations existed, Barry Karl and Stanley Katz argued, because Americans were unwilling "to give their national government the authority to set national standards of social well-being, let alone to enforce them."[147]

Although the cognitive base for the physical sciences was far more developed than that of the social sciences, foundations played a crucial role in narrowing the gap between basic knowledge and its application—particularly in the field of medicine. It was at the nation's voluntary institutions that the business of producing professionals, funding their research, and applying that research was conducted on a national scale. The voluntary alternative to an enhanced, professionalized state carried the United States through the first third of the twentieth century.[148] It also foreshadowed the role that the federal government would assume after World War II.

Though Progressives initially branded it unthinkable, war, not reform, expanded administrative capacity and pushed professionals into these new positions on a national scale. Progressives like Dewey executed an abrupt about-face in their thinking about America's role in the war. Dewey felt that the crisis of war might lead to more extensive use of science for communal purposes, illuminate the public aspect of every social enterprise, create new mechanisms for "enforcing the public interest in all agencies of production and exchange," and temper America's excessive individualism.[149]

What the new wartime managers discovered, however, was that the science-based professions were nascent. The war made it the federal government's business to force-feed development. Karl summed up the problem in regard to the social sciences, writing that "in virtually every field the lesson was the same. From the economists who worked for the War Industries Board to the historians and political scientists who advised the president at Versailles, the issue boiled down to one basic problem: American specialization in such fields was essentially in its infancy."[150]

While the challenge for the social sciences was to demonstrate that the field's cognitive base was in fact scientific, the challenge for the physical sciences was to apply basic knowledge quickly enough to affect the war's outcome. That chemists and chemical engineers were able to produce in short order optical glass, nitrates, and poison gases justified the label "chemist's war" that was subsequently applied to the conflict.[151] Physicists, however, who before the war were viewed by the press as impractical scientists—good subjects for the staff humorists but not particularly newsworthy—had a hard time convincing the federal government that it needed their help.[152] Only through the persistent lobbying of the National Research Council—itself a product of the war—were physicists permitted to join the race to develop a submarine-detection device. Physicists were allowed to set up a small lab in New London, Connecticut, where, under the direction of Max Mason, they developed a detection device. Physicists also played an instrumental role in the work of the National Advisory Committee for Aeronautics and developed a range of signaling devices for the infantry.[153]

The wartime crisis convinced many Americans of the need for a far more centralized administrative apparatus. Woodrow Wilson dramatized the impulse when he nationalized the railroads in the waning days of 1917.

His actions came only after previous efforts at voluntary planning had failed.[154] Nationalizing the railroads, however, proved to be the exception. Responsibility for coordinating production and supply during the war fell first to the loosely organized Council of National Defense and ultimately to the War Industries Board (WIB). Even after it was reorganized to strengthen its authority, and after Bernard Baruch was named chairman in March 1918, the WIB lacked the power to command. Rather, it cajoled. The WIB was far more effective as a public symbol of rational control—largely due to Baruch's skills as a negotiator and promoter—than as a central planner.[155] Even the advisory apparatus set up to run the war was hastily dismantled the moment the fighting stopped. Congress was so quick in dismantling the nation's war machinery that it left some Washington office workers searching for funds to get home when their salaries were abruptly cut off.[156] For professionals who had served the federal government, there was also a quick return to the private or voluntary institutions in which they previously had been housed.

Yet the military crisis did have some long-term implications for what had previously been the parallel paths of state building and professionalization. If nothing else, successes were remembered. Stripped of the mobilization machinery, social scientists built a postwar equivalent around Herbert Hoover's vision of an associative state that used apolitical institutions like the National Bureau of Economic Research and the foundations as crucial sources of funding.[157] Even in instances where the institutional arrangements changed dramatically, as when federal control of the railroads was handed back to the private sector, the postwar arrangement reflected the wartime experience of central planning. The National Transportation Act (1920) completed the authority of the ICC. It granted the ICC far greater rate-making authority and for the first time allowed for a more cooperative approach, sanctioning pooling and allowing the ICC to plan rail consolidations.[158] Without the crisis of World War I it is not clear that even in this leading case, the administrative state would have broken the grip of "courts and parties."[159]

Eager to return to "normalcy," yet tempted by the mechanisms that allowed the nation to better plan and coordinate its economy during the war, a group of administrators led by Hoover embraced various techniques that promoted the union of national government and experts through voluntary mechanisms. The associative state proved most effective in those areas where the private sector was already organized.[160] Business and trade associations led the way in this regard, and they welcomed an arrangement that provided government-generated data and that encouraged more cooperative arrangements within each sector of the economy.[161] Hoover and the economist Wesley Mitchell also called on this network and the trade associations to support the president's boldest claim: the ability to control the business cycle. As a feat of institution building it was impressive; as for controlling the business cycle, Hoover is hardly remembered as its mastermind.[162]

Hoover's associative state represented the apotheosis of Progressive thinking about the relationships between the people, the experts, and the interests. State builders like Hoover turned the Progressive fear of the interests on its head, arguing for a society built on the smooth coordination of well-organized groups.[163] It was through this kind of interest-group politics that the people would be best represented. Experts, most often housed in the voluntary sector, would advise these groups how best to maximize their long-term success. The federal government had a distinct role to play, but it was one that respected the long-standing fear that direct federal employment of expertise would destroy the autonomy of that expertise. Rather than direct, the federal government would gather data—as it had begun to do during World War I—and coordinate. Besides data gathering and playing host to organized interests, the federal government would help promote the creation of interest groups and trade associations. Hoover's actions regarding professions hardly sure of their autonomy and a federal apparatus that was forced to bargain for even marginal grants of central authority recast Hoover as a practical Progressive, eager to extend the authority of the state through the cracks left behind by America's political structure and antistatist culture.

The Great Depression threatened to open gaping fissures in the American political system. Despite the acute economic crisis, surprisingly little professional and state convergence occurred. Given much of the credit for technological breakthroughs such as radios and other consumer goods that were mass marketed during the 1920s, scientists were often associated with some of the new technology's negative consequences—particularly "technological unemployment."[164] Rather than increasing inroads into the federal government during the Great Depression, the physical sciences came under increasing pressure to demonstrate their relevance. Franklin D. Roosevelt was persuaded to establish a Science Advisory Board, but the board received no funds and lasted only two years. The Roosevelt administration rejected its costly proposals. Meanwhile, budget director Lewis Douglas slashed scientists from the Bureau of Standards just as he cut jobs in other federal agencies in response to Roosevelt's campaign pledges of belt tightening.[165]

Where experts could demonstrate unequivocally that their skills were relevant, mergers at the federal level began to take place. Fusing expertise with direct federal administration began to extend the reach of the central government. For instance, the Bankhead-Jones Act in agricultural research and the National Cancer Institute in the field of biomedical research increased federal funding for basic research in areas that promised to lead to direct social applications.[166] Other experts were brought into the federal government as an expanded state sought to catch up with the technological breakthroughs of the twentieth century by regulating, or in some instances developing, new technologies in communications, transportation, and electrification.

While scientists demonstrated their relevance, administrators extended Hoover's concept of a society built around organized interests to far less-organized sectors of the polity. At the Tennessee Valley Authority, David Lilienthal brought the benefits of technical expertise to an entire region, mobilizing citizens through the mechanism of grass-roots democracy. What started out as an appeal to the grass roots, however, ended up looking like politics as usual through a series of compromises with firmly established interest groups like the American Farm Bureau Federation.[167] A more radical commitment to organizing at the grass roots, however, was carried out by administrators of the Farm Security Administration.[168] Whether appealing to established interest groups or beginning to create new constituencies, federal administrators recognized that access to expertise was an invaluable asset. Experts could produce concrete benefits for the agency's constituency. Experts also carried weight in Congress, where there was increasing competition for resources.

Professionals had their own money problems. By the 1930s the cost of research and training was threatening to outstrip private and voluntary sources of funding.[169] Even the social sciences were outgrowing their foundation support, forcing foundations to switch from funding entire programs to supporting narrower objectives.[170] The foundations had succeeded in stimulating a more research-oriented approach on the nation's leading campuses. Success, both in producing new scholars and scientists and in encouraging professional specialization, was a mixed blessing for America's voluntaristic/localized approach. By 1940 a number of professions had outstripped the resources of the voluntary sector.[171]

The federal government, however, was not yet prepared to fill that gap in a comprehensive way. Nor were professional experts entirely ready to accept the central government's embrace. Given the severe social upheaval that the Great Depression caused, it might have been expected that administrative capacity in areas that brought the expertise of social scientists to bear on these problems would be developed. There certainly were some early indications that this might happen. Again, the field of agriculture led the way. In the USDA, Richard Kirkendall has argued, proposals generated by economists and planners actually altered the behavior of key farm groups. Throughout the decade, social scientists were employed at top levels of the department, and they influenced policy. Ultimately their influence depended on political support. When a deteriorating relationship with the Secretary of Agriculture, exacerbated by Rexford Tugwell's confrontational style, eroded that support shortly before World War II, social scientists lost much of their influence.[172]

The National Resources Planning Board (NRPB) was another potentially powerful mechanism for combining the social sciences and federal administrative capacity. Besides the political opposition that ultimately hobbled the NRPB, social scientists continued to question a closer relationship with the federal government. The counterpart of the National Research Council—the SSRC—when requested by the NRPB to study the relationship of the federal government to social research "emphatically disapproved any government subsidization of research."[173] The SSRC committee was concerned that social research might deteriorate into "merely government propaganda" if federal dollars became the main source of support.[174]

Within the White House itself, of course, much was made of Franklin D. Roosevelt's "brains trust." Relying on academics interested in economic and industrial planning, such as A. A. Berle, Raymond Moley, and Rexford Tugwell, Roosevelt established new links between the presidency and the nation's campuses.[175] Yet for all of the attention these experts drew, it is not clear that their contributions had much of an impact on Roosevelt's program. Karl argues that working relationships between the president and his experts were "personal and basically political. [T]he edge was usually given to experience," Karl concluded, "and the newly established experts simply didn't have it. Roosevelt looked to academics for ideas, but his programs seem more traceable to the experienced political leaders and the community of managers he had always worked with."[176]

Roosevelt's sometime reliance on Keynesian economics was a case in point. Although he initially reduced government spending, he was soon willing to fund the New Deal's innovative programs by running up a budget deficit.[177] Yet when "prosperity" returned in early 1937, Roosevelt slashed government expenditures, touching off the "Roosevelt recession."[178] As the economy plunged downward, the president, in Leuchtenberg's words, "preferred to let the rival theorists war around him."[179] It was not until the following April that FDR announced that he was ready to spend big.[180] It was the massive deficit spending brought on by World War II, however, that ultimately demonstrated the impact that deficit spending could have on a sagging economy.[181]

Even when expert advice was housed in more formal structures such as the Temporary Economic Committee and the (equally temporary) NRPB, it seems to have had only a limited impact. Nevertheless, by employing social scientists and allowing them to apply their skills to high-priority problems, the New Deal experience expanded knowledge and technique in the disciplines themselves, even if these advances were not always applied.[182] Government service, as it had in World War I, also helped overcome some of the fears about the politicization that professionals and the broader public harbored. While prestigious organizations like the Brookings Institution voiced concern about the excessive independence of a reorganized executive branch and cautioned about the limits of expert-driven social policy, increasing numbers of prestigious social scientists were willing to take the plunge into government service.[183] As with Keynesian economics, however, it was service during World War II that institutionalized what up to that point was considered an exceptional situation.

Despite the crisis of the Great Depression, Roosevelt continued to struggle with the restrictions imposed by America's political culture. Wherever possible, FDR relied on existing administrative mechanisms to implement his new programs. Thus, all of the titles of the Social Security Act, with the exception of social insurance, were administered by state and local governments. Roosevelt was not happy about national administration of social insurance either, but he was persuaded that it simply was not technically feasible to administer this contributory retirement plan in any other fashion.[184] As a leading student of state-federal relations wrote about the New Deal approach to government expansion, "Whether gauged in dollar amounts, the variety of services aided, or the perfecting of the mechanism, the growth in federal grants during these years marked a major turning point in the history of American intergovernmental relations."[185] Federal aid to the states in 1939 was more than fifteen times higher than the 1933 level.[186] Voluntary coordination was also pushed to its limits. The National Industrial Recovery Act harkened back to Hoover's vision of an associative state, relying on voluntary cooperation between industry and labor, coordinated by the federal government.[187] While the New Deal changed the scope of government activity, its methods were familiar.[188] Given the conservative reaction that swept away some of the New Deal's more radical reforms—such as the Farm Security Administration, or the NRPB—it is not clear how much of the administrative capacity would have survived if America had not been plunged into yet another crisis.[189]

By the eve of World War II, many of America's professions had matured, had successfully integrated a scientific basis for their knowledge and skills, and, with the aid of the voluntary sector, had established mechanisms in the modern research university to transmit that knowledge to new generations. At the same time, the federal government enhanced its capacity, more by the exigencies of military and economic crises than by the perseverance of progressive reform. Yet administrative and professional development—though far more mature than it had been forty years earlier—continued to advance along parallel tracks. In the short space of a decade, that changed dramatically.

Demonstrating and Securing the Proministrative State

World War II pushed the maturing, increasingly committed partners together. The most dramatic example of the new marriage was the atomic bomb project. The Manhattan Project extended the federal government and its use of expertise far beyond the wildest dreams of Progressive, associative, or New Deal state builders. It drew on a well-developed profession, attracting some of the world's leading physicists. The crucial nature of their mission, the esoteric basis of their knowledge, and the secrecy of their quest brought them unparalleled resources. The federal government received in return the total commitment of respected experts. While some scientists bridled at wartime controls and secrecy, given the astounding rise in the cost of "big science," very few felt that voluntary techniques after the war would suffice.

Only the dramatic breakthroughs produced by expert-Federal cooperation during World War II satisfied a third condition for the proministrative state: a dramatic forum in which to demonstrate the practical benefits of this union. In a political culture wary of centralized government, such success had been demonstrated primarily by the USDA, which had accomplished this by serving two constituencies. It convinced the scientific community that it was at the cutting edge of research while persuading the public that its mission was crucial.[190] The Manhattan Project achieved the same end far more dramatically. The war proved that expertise—directed and funded by the federal government—could produce during a crisis. In other fields as well—military security and economic and social planning— experts put their theories into action, and events convinced many Americans that experts could solve large problems. Massive deficit spending during the war, for instance, accomplished what all of the New Deal programs had been unable to achieve: It lowered unemployment to politically acceptable levels, just as Keynesian economists had argued that it would. Americans might still bridle at explicit wage and price controls (though they would be used again during peacetime) but they embraced mechanisms such as the Council of Economic Advisers that institutionalized economic advice to the president (although Truman did not). By far the most decisive shift in the federal government's role following the war was its sponsorship of science and technology. Here, the war effort produced such highly publicized triumphs as the atomic bomb, radar, and penicillin.[191]

The mobilization model remained attractive long after the fighting in Europe and Japan stopped. Writing to Dwight D. Eisenhower shortly before the 1952 election, a longtime friend forwarded to the general a plan designed to head off the appeal of socialized medicine. Entitled "War on Untimely Death," the plan sought to eliminate the "Great Killer" diseases. Crafted to "smash the atoms" of disease, Edward Everett Hazlett wrote, the bomb project would serve as a model for this war on disease. "The attack on disease seems no more likely to fail than did that on the atom. It has, in addition, the spiritual advantage of being a campaign to save life and not to take it."[192]

Nevertheless, the fusion of central state and professional expert might well have dissolved once again following World War II had a fourth condition failed to materialize. As policies became more esoteric and planning more crucial, the ability to organize and concentrate demand for such programs was essential. In the absence of such well-articulated demand following World War II (or in the instance of military expenditures, even in the face of it), the powerful tendency in American politics toward decentralization and a weak central state triumphed when Truman slashed spending for the Army. Defense expenditures plummeted from $81.6 billion in fiscal 1945 to $13.1 billion in fiscal 1947 before beginning to rise again. Eisenhower hoped to return to where Truman had started. He conducted a rearguard battle, ultimately railing against the military-industrial complex in his frustration. Both presidents, however, failed in their quest to limit the scope of the prominstrative state.[193] They failed because a permanent crisis—the Cold War—cemented demand for the kinds of services provided by the prominstrative state.

Truman and Eisenhower, despite personal desires to return to a simpler, more traditional central government, took actions to ensure that America's professionals remained permanently mobilized by pronouncing the Truman Doctrine, implementing the recommendations of National Security Council Report 68 (NSC 68), and responding to Sputnik. Funding for federal research, which totaled approximately $97 million in 1940, jumped to $1.6 billion by 1945 and, after leveling off in 1948 at $865 million, climbed to $2.1 billion by 1953. Though frequently remembered now for his 1961 farewell address warning that the nation's public policy might become captive to a "scientific-technological elite," in 1946, Eisenhower was more concerned about "scientific and technological resources as military assets." Distilling these views in an April 30 memo with that title, Eisenhower argued that the nation's security required civilian resources that were crucial in an emergency "be associated closely with the activities of the Army in time of peace. . . . [The Army] must establish definite policies and administrative leadership which will make possible even greater contributions from science, technology, and management than during the last war."[194]

James Conant, the president of Harvard University and formerly the second ranking civilian overseeing the Manhattan Project, commented on the startling change in a secret address to military and government officials in 1952. Before the atomic bomb, Conant noted, technological conservatism was the military's chief stumbling block. Military officials had been "perhaps unduly slow in some cases to take up new ideas developed by civilian scientists." But in the wake of the bomb and the Cold War something akin to "the old religious phenomenon of conversion" had struck. "As I see it now," Conant continued, "the military, if anything, have become vastly too much impressed with the abilities of research and development." Underscoring the professional-federal union that the atomic bomb and Cold War had sealed, Conant noted wryly that some military professionals "have become infected with the virus that is so well known in academic circles, the virus of enthusiasm of the scientist and the inventor."[195]

The Cold War stimulated demand for centralized, expert responses to America's threatened national security. It was now the experts who often identified specific problems that required federal action. As the Cold War spread from military to economic and social fronts, experts in the social sciences and even the humanities linked national security to solutions offered by a broader range of disciplines. In the wake of Sputnik, policies as far afield from military security as civil rights and highway construction benefited from America's mass passion for national security. Even before Sputnik, however, educators claimed an increasing share of the national security budget by joining the drive for civil defense. Bert the Turtle warned schoolchildren that they not only had to learn to cross the street safely and know what to do in case of fire but also now had to know what to do in case of atomic attack. Americans turned directly to experts to soothe jittery nerves: Approximately one out of six white middle-class Americans consulted a professional for emotional or marriage problems by the mid-1950s. As one attitudinal survey put it, "Experts took over the role of psychic healer. . . . They would provide advice and counsel about raising and responding to children, how to behave in marriage, and what to see in that relationship. . . . Science moved in because people needed and wanted guidance."[196]

The Politics of the Proministrative State

The marriage between the professions and the federal government, announced as early as the Progressive Era, had finally been consummated. Drawing on a far more sophisticated cognitive base, confident, convinced that their very survival required federal assistance, respected for their dramatic accomplishments, and in demand everywhere, experts embraced federal support. Federal administrators, eager to capitalize on the prestige of experts and anxious to tap expert skills to solve a host of problems that, particularly in a crisis context and, given the government's wartime success, were seen as federal responsibilities, reciprocated. The newlyweds turned their attention to creating the proministrative state.

Their union, like millions of others after the war—and for some of the same reasons, including prosperity, wartime abstinence, and great faith in the future—soon produced heirs in larger quantities than ever before. The permanent crisis dwarfed the New Deal's contribution to state building. Federal expenditures more than doubled during the 1950s, increasing from $42 billion to $92 billion by 1960. Federal expenditures also consumed a larger share of the nation's gross national product (GNP). Federal expenditures accounted for 16.1 percent of GNP in 1950 and 18.5 percent of GNP by 1960. The explosion of federal administration and oversight was even more dramatic than the rise in expenditures. Agencies directly related to national security proliferated. The National Security Act of 1947 created a new Department of Defense as well as the National Security Council and Central Intelligence Agency. The federal government established competing bureaucracies ranging from the Agency for International Development to an Office for International Security Affairs within the Department of Defense. The proministrative state moved most forcefully to create an organizational infrastructure for science in postwar America. The Office of Naval Research, the Atomic Energy Commission, the National Science Foundation, and a greatly expanded National Institutes of Health soon housed and funded thousands of America's most sophisticated experts. Nor were the social sciences left behind. Established by the Employment Act of 1946, the Council of Economic Advisers, for instance, institutionalized economics within the White House.[197]

The professions grew at an equally extraordinary rate. Universities responded to the demand for highly skilled experts by minting record numbers of doctorates. The number of graduate degrees awarded between 1940 and 1959 doubled and quadrupled between 1950 and 1970, with degree programs in the most specialized fields leading the way. American universities conferred 3,277 doctorates in 1940, 3,940 in 1948, and 6,535 by 1950. Nearly ten thousand doctorates were awarded in 1960. With this burst of higher learning, the theoretical drove out the applied. Math and science began to dominate engineering curricula, for instance. Training for research replaced preparation for patient care at the most prestigious medical schools. As Frank Newman put it in his Ph.D. dissertation, "Increasingly, faculty saw their most important role as creating new researchers—a sort of institutionalized cloning." These new professionals led the drive toward federal support for graduate training. Within the proministrative state, these research interests also powered the drive for a host of new federal policies.[198]

At the heart of the new prominstrative state lay a symbiotic relationship between experts and the federal government. The federal government now actively produced and developed experts. Experts, on the other hand, just as was the case in the early days of foundation funding, actively defined what their benefactors' policy agendas should be. There was, however, by 1950 a significant difference between foundations in the interwar years and the federal government. While grants management was relatively centralized within the major foundations, the equivalent mechanisms in the federal government were scattered among hundreds of agencies and dozens of oversight committees and were at least potentially subject to pressure from thousands of interest groups. Under these circumstances, it was impossible to re-create the kind of direction that Weaver was able to achieve in the field of biomedicine at the Rockefeller Foundation. Nor was it so easy to distinguish between grantor and grantee: The federal administrators responsible for such decisions increasingly were professionals produced by this new relationship.

Having commented on our partners' adolescence, their courtship, and the wedding, it would be a mistake to abandon our analysis of this century-long relationship in the wake of that triumphant wedding.[199] The relationship was hardly static. Sketching its trajectory suggests one route by which a reorganized organizational synthesis might navigate the rapidly shifting post–World War II historiographic tides. As surely as Progressive reform and rhetoric altered the distributive style of politics that it, in part, supplanted, prominstrative politics revised interest-group politics in post–World War II America. This is not to argue that distributive or interest-group politics disappeared. Just as the distributive style of politics that pervaded the nineteenth-century "state of courts and parties" was built into the administrative state that emerged by the 1920s, elements of both distributive and interest-group politics were built into the very foundation of the prominstrative state that was constructed in the wake of World War II. Like their predecessors in the Progressive Era, post–World War II administrators and professionals had to build political support in order to acquire the autonomy necessary to pursue their distinct approach to problem solving. Federal administrators teamed up to create public demand for the increasingly esoteric services that they had to offer. Rather than simply responding to social and economic demands, postwar administrators, with the crucial aid of professionals, now had the resources to influence and sometimes even create demand autonomously. Precisely because the kinds of politics they engaged in excluded meaningful public participation in the details of complex policy decisions, general public support for, and belief in, expertise was crucial to the experts' success. Had such general support been lacking in the wake of World War II, the marriage of experts and large-scale federal organization would have been annulled before the honeymoon was over. Nor could massive public support—funded by steep increases in the income tax—be engineered by clever conspirators. Far from conspiratorial, the marriage of federal administrative capacity to professional expertise in America could only occur with the public's blessing. Support poured in because the professions and the central state had matured, and during World War II they demonstrated in dramatic fashion the powerful results that expert and federal fusion—which both partners were now ready to embrace—could deliver. When the crisis continued into the Cold War, the American public welcomed the proministrative state: The nation's very survival depended on it.

Beneath the veneer of expert consensus, however, another powerful dynamic—spurred by specialization—was at work. Massive infusions of federal dollars, expanded research universities, and the emergence of a knowledge-based economy accelerated professional specialization. Subdisciplines proliferated. Whether seeking or saddled with new responsibilities, the organizational infrastructure also specialized at a breathtaking pace. Nor was organizational articulation confined to the federal bureaucracy. Eventually Congress, state governments, and even local administrations specialized to keep pace. As each political actor acquired access to its own expertise, a tripartite matrix built on a specialized cognitive base, organizational perspective—now divided even within the same agency—and jurisdiction emerged. As experts, professional disciplines, and organizational subdivisions proliferated, the insulated debate crucial to expert decision making spilled over into increasingly public forums. The elaboration of expertise into specialized units, the inevitable differences in perspective that arose when a number of disciplines examined the same problem, and the political agendas engaged by various host institutions brought disputes between experts to the public's attention. When combined with the high visibility that experts courted in order to promote demand for their services, these disputes ultimately helped undermine both the authority and subsequently the autonomy of experts.[200]

The interplay of expertise and these structural factors created its own dynamic—a process that ultimately shattered public expert consensus and the nation's confidence in its experts. By the mid-1970s, expertise had been relegated to a necessary, but no longer decisive, condition for political success. With the federal government committed to the large-scale production of expertise, with research agendas incorporated wholesale into public policy, with each new subdiscipline looking at old problems from new perspectives, with today's knowledge—as it should be—under intense scrutiny by tomorrow's discipline builders, and, most significantly, with these once exclusively scholarly debates now reified in the halls of hundreds of agencies and subject to a thousand points of access, paradigmatic shifts have become a dime a dozen. They have undermined the once politically valuable authority of experts and left administrators and politicians alike in search not for order but for a new political resource with which to break the nation's painful policy stalemates. Far less significantly for the course of American politics, but of some interest to those seeking to understand twentieth-century America, charting the relationship between experts and the federal government might offer organizational scholars safe passage into the postwar era while sustaining the sense of discovery and exploration that the reorganized organizational synthesis has rediscovered.

Conclusion

The general thrust of my argument raises serious questions about the basic contours and direction of the organizational synthesis. More sophisticated, but also more cumbersome, the synthesis no longer glides through historical detail as it once did. Building conflict, end runs, and contingency into the organizational synthesis was essential to its survival. But with concepts like bureaucratization and professionalization that once offered safe harbor now buffeted by riptides themselves, is it fair to ask whether the revised organizational synthesis leaves us with any navigational advantages? I think that it does.

Its value can be illustrated by considering the promin; strative stage of federal-professional relations that an updated organizational synthesis reveals. Although the merger of federal and professional power envisioned by some Progressives finally arrived after World War II, and although it brought with it a disproportionate share of political clout for those with access to it, it ultimately proved to be no more stable than the historiography that had once placed that merger in the early twentieth century. Professionals and organizations continued to specialize, proliferate, and compete. This internal dynamic, as much as more explicit external events such as the Vietnam War and Watergate, ultimately undermined the authority of experts in the federal government and decimated their political clout.

What endures that is worth preserving in the organizational synthesis is the way it conceives of political conflict. Conflict was channeled into narrow, disaggregable demands, best pursued by tightly knit organizations capable of sustaining long-term political and legislative campaigns and, more significantly, of influencing the administrative implementation of these solutions. Discipline, occupation, organizational or associational allegiance, and access to expertise were far better bases from which to wage such a battle than class, party, or region, for instance. Even in the face of de jure segregation, the powerful bond of race did not manage to shift federal policy until the demands of the civil rights movement could be stated in the language of interest-group politics. Backed by organizational resources long after the broad social movement that helped generate them in the first place had subsided, civil rights interest groups carried their battle into the heart of legislative and administrative forums. There, more quietly than in Montgomery or Birmingham, they won some of their greatest battles in the struggle for equality.[201] The question in twentieth-century America was never to build or not build an "organizational society." Rather, the question was how organizational resources would be defined and distributed, what degree of political influence they would yield, what new political countercurrents they would create, and how losers in the early rounds would adapt in order to achieve greater success in later rounds. These are the central questions that a reorganized organizational synthesis can seek to answer. They flow from the assertion that remains as powerful today as it was when the predominant new phenomenon in state-society relations in twentieth-century America was the rapidly increasing pace of interdependence and when the most significant response was "continuous management" by bureaucrats and experts.

By the early 1960s, the federal government intervened regularly to resolve disputes about organizational resources, and it developed a powerful capacity to create those resources. Perhaps the greatest political advantage held by insiders in the heyday of the proministrative state was the discretion that they enjoyed to define and fund expertise and organizational support. Ironically, this advantage only hastened the evolutionary dynamic embedded in bureaucratic and professional development. Publicly funded experts proliferated, and so did conflicting organizational and disciplinary perspectives. The internal struggles they waged over shared turf ignited many of the political battles of the late 1960s and 1970s. This is a far different and, I would argue, far more illuminating way of framing the turmoil of the late 1960s than the more familiar (Progressive) perspective that pits the people against the experts.[202] By asking how groups organize, how they gain access to the resources necessary to organize, how this shapes their political demands and clout, and how they relate to the continuing evolution of the prominstrative apparatus, the reorganized organizational synthesis promises to reinvigorate interpretations of state-society relations. It may also finally free post–World War II political history from the mesmerizing spell cast by that first series of compromises hammered out by the Progressive Era's best-organized groups in their initial response to industrialism.

Chapter 5

Meeting the State Halfway:
Governing America, 1930–1950

The essays in this volume suggest an alternative way to narrate the evolution of politics and governance in the United States. They examine the interaction between state and society, paying particular attention to those institutions located within civil society and the private sector that mediated between citizen and state. I have mapped an "associational order" that was shaped, in part, by the state and that parceled out public authority to the voluntary and even the private sectors, relying on intermediary institutions to administer policies that achieved collective ends without trampling upon the rights of individual citizens. Federal administrators, like the nation's chief forester, Gifford Pinchot, and Secretary of Commerce Herbert Hoover, directed this associational order, effectively appealing to the logic of the market, even as they expanded the state's capacity to shape that market. Public administrators worked seamlessly with a broad range of nongovernmental professional organizations, interest groups, trade associations, and private corporations that coalesced around narrowly drawn public policies. At the ballot box, the elected officials who also guided this associational order began to take their cues from an array of interests that served as "mirrors of desires" for their constituents, sometimes offering a clearer portrait of voters' preferences than national political parties did. State builders repeatedly discovered that associating with the interests was more effective, and certainly more palatable to the public, than fighting the interests.

While cynics challenge this conception of victory, labeling it "capture" or "co-optation," a strong case can be made that a vast majority of Americans were willing to temper their individualism in order to achieve collective ends through a blend of state, voluntary, and private institutions. And when Americans believe that they are voluntarily embracing a collective agenda, they have done great things, even if the state's role in these triumphs is submerged.

Indeed, obscuring that public role is virtually a prerequisite for durable reform. Medicare remains a triumph of public health care provision even if Tea Party members insist that the government keep its hands off of it.[1] America's military strength remains second to none, in part because it has relied so heavily on the voluntary and private sectors to sustain it. Fierce debate has occasionally erupted about the ends toward which this exceptional form of public power should be directed. And more debate is needed about the degree of autonomy that any of the partners should enjoy in their tripartite relationship. Yet there is little doubt that some of the nation's most politically resilient collective achievements have been built upon foundations forged in public/private partnerships.

While scholars have incorporated many elements of this associational interpretation into their work, it has had little impact on the rhetoric used by public officials or popular accounts of political history narrated by leading public intellectuals. That popular narrative remains one that pits those who embrace a powerful state deployed on behalf of the people in the name of reform, against a narrow set of elites, overrepresented by the interests, who battle the cycles of reform that are said periodically to sweep across the political landscape. Today's version of this century-long division is usually stated, or in the case of cable news, shouted, as tax-and-spend liberals versus small-government conservatives.

This essay tackles the toughest case for those who seek to popularize an alternative narrative built around the evolution of an associational order. If the clash between the people and the interests, between advocates for big government versus elites who seek to stem the tide of reform explains any period of American history, it is certainly the decades that encompass the New Deal and World War II. That was a crucial era for forging a host of new, powerful federal institutions. Indeed, as the previous essay emphasizes, this era gave rise to a new kind of prominicrative state. The United States faced unprecedented challenges in this era. It was a period that witnessed the sharp delineation between classes—a division that helped forge the New Deal political coalition whose rise and decline continue to power a "cycles of reform" narrative, even today. Claims that associational networks endured and even thrived during the New Deal are further undermined by their chief proponent, Herbert Hoover's spectacular failure, and the fate of their seminal New Deal incarnation, the National Recovery Administration (NRA).

The purpose of my reexamination is not to dispute that there really was a man named Franklin D. Roosevelt or that he was informed by liberalism. It is not to deny, for that matter, the large number of conservatives who resisted many New Deal programs. Nor is it to downplay real differences between the ends sought by liberals and conservatives. That the federal government developed new administrative capacity, and, perhaps more important, enhanced its capacity to set professional agendas and influence key decisions in both voluntary and private sectors, is undeniable. Nevertheless, even during the heyday of class politics and newfound state autonomy at the national level, examining the ways in which a socially diverse set of advocates with sharply divergent agendas engaged the state's resources and explicating the ways in which the national government's powers to tax, coerce, guide, and coordinate were mediated through key institutions in civil society and the private sector, not to mention state and local government, are crucial to understanding these turbulent years. Doing so builds on the current trend among scholars to illuminate the symbiotic relationships among state, civil society, and the private sector and to identify how that associational order governed in a political culture that viewed distant, hierarchical state administrative structures as toxic.

As associational effectiveness displaces state autonomy as the measure of success, we need to revise the ways in which we assess the impact of government. The ability to realize ambitious goals such as managing the economy or improving quality of life, not the size of government as measured by percentage of gross national product (GNP) or the number of individuals that government employs, becomes the best measure of the state's effectiveness. Although it was hardly a straight path, bolstering a long-standing set of associations, such as organized labor, and offering it the same kinds of assistance that the state had long offered to business improved the lives of millions of Americans. Yet, measured by dollars appropriated or government personnel hired, the costs of implementing Section 7(a) of the National Industrial Recovery Act (NIRA), or the National Labor Relations Act that followed, were minuscule. Workers' lives were also improved by health care deductions that organized labor successfully bargained for after World War II. Those cost billions of dollars in taxes forgone, yet the health care that these tax deductions subsidize is considered to be a part of the "private" health care system.

This is not to argue that this kind of indirect approach was always effective. Too often broader objectives—precisely the kind that New Deal policy makers set out to achieve——fell by the wayside. Empowering organized labor or subsidizing larger commercial farmers through price supports clearly achieved the broader New Deal goal of providing economic security for important sectors of the middle class. As these interests, backed by the state's legal and fiscal power, exercised their political clout, however, another important New Deal goal—the inclusion of all Americans, especially the poorest, living in economically marginal regions—was sacrificed. In spite of the billions of federal dollars poured into the provision of middle-class benefits, those Americans who were excluded from such benefits, due to the lack of regular employment in the industrial core of the economy, or the quality or amount of land that they farmed, increasingly were viewed as the citizens who were living on "the dole," undeserving recipients of wasteful government largesse. Millions of African Americans and white women were denied individual access to a treasure trove of middle-class benefits, as a result of their race, gender, or both.

Even Ellis Hawley, who did more than any historian to identify and chronicle the nuanced interaction between state and society during the 1920s, acknowledged the limitations of the New Deal associational state. As Hawley put it, managing the political economy through voluntary mechanisms "lost credence and was rejected as being both unworkable and tyrannical." The dismal record of the NRA—which was Roosevelt's first (although I will argue, hardly his last) effort to shape the institutions of civil society toward state-directed ends—became a poster child for the failure of such voluntary techniques.[2]

These highly visible failures, however, did more to guide our *accounts* of how politics evolved from the 1930s through present times than to deter the actual articulation of associational mechanisms. Associational networks were activated by the state-assisted cultivation of underdeveloped assets arrayed on the shop floors of industries, for example. They also conceived of disparate populations through innovative policy frameworks based on river basins and regions. Besides state assistance to labor and the population served by the Tennessee Valley Authority, assistance intended to allow unions and citizens living in "underdeveloped" sectors of the economy to participate fully in the national political life, advocates of an associational approach to governance built up intermediary institutions—from the professions to research universities. And they increased the pace at which state authority and dollars were parceled out to thousands of private actors through the contractual relationships with the federal government. To force this long-standing pattern in American governance into an ideational framework that pitted liberals versus conservatives or to miss the ways in which policy makers governed through crucial intermediary institutions is to discard many of the essential ingredients of American political development.

Did millions of Americans demand, and ultimately realize a new set of rights, entitlements, and obligations during the New Deal and World War II? Absolutely. But they did so as the result of state-assisted efforts to organize various groups that in turn demanded more rights and benefits. And like those who had organized effectively before them—primarily businesses, trade groups, and the professions labeled "the interests"—these newly mobilized citizens appreciated the connection between political, economic, and social power, just as they endorsed state-assisted solutions to problems that were mediated through a host of voluntary and private institutions. It was access to the very associational mechanisms, mastered long ago by better-organized, often wealthier, Americans that ensured the good life from the individual's perspective. These same government-enhanced intermediaries, however, also held out the promise of addressing collective needs from a broader social perspective. Indeed, it is the battle over how these intermediary institutions would serve collective ends that deserves greater attention from scholars and that ultimately determined just how effective these associational networks would be.

Those looking to get into the associational game in the middle third of the twentieth century faced stiffer barriers than first movers. The legacies of slavery, racism, sexism, and class bias continued to impede progress for millions of Americans, not to mention resistance from entrenched opponents, especially well-established corporations that now disparaged as "big government" the very kinds of state activity that had secured their own place in the political economy. Remarkably, though many excluded citizens doubted the viability of both capitalism and the capacity of the voluntary sector during the darkest days of the Great Depression and war, few challenged the framework through which some of their fellow citizens had succeeded—a potent mix of politically responsive state assistance, more often than not doled out (a phrase that was *not* used in these cases) through an ever-growing army of intermediary institutions.

It is the degree to which these institutions were effectively stimulated, cajoled, guided, or simply mandated to serve progressive or conservative ends, and *not* whether New Deal Democrats were able to expand the state, or whether their conservative opponents succeeded in shrinking it, that should guide political history and enlighten contemporary political debate. It is only when history is employed to demystify the ways in which the false dichotomy between big government and small government has sidetracked a more substantive discussion of the ends of governance that a serious debate about ideological ends can ensue.

Associational Solutions to the Great Depression

In spite of the NIRA's spectacular failure, and even as the national government built powerful beachheads for bureaucratic autonomy during the New Deal and reinforced them during the crisis of World War II, the architects of America's political economy, social safety net, and muscular foreign policy returned to some of the associational approaches that had failed to stimulate the economic recovery promised by its proponents. The remainder of this essay argues that this associational approach structured a great number of New Deal policies and that the combined crises of World War II and the Cold War actually reinforced the associational state, forging a firm foundation for the remainder of the twentieth century. Many of the ways in which business and government had collaborated were "politicized" as a consequence of the economic and national security challenges faced by the nation. Nonetheless, key institutions in the private and voluntary sectors continued to serve as crucial intermediaries between citizens and states.[3]

The first step in employing that history is to make clear the degree to which public authority is infused through the institutions of civil society and how that process evolved. Most accounts of the middle third of twentieth-century America divide the New Deal—First, Second, and so on—thereby setting the stage for ensuing subdivisions of liberalism—Cold War, Great Society, and so forth. Proceeding from the premise that the most daunting challenge facing New Deal and World War II policy makers was integrating groups that were insufficiently organized to benefit from associational relationships with the state, I have created a different lens through which to consider public policy in the middle third of the twentieth century. In this regard, the role of the central state changed little from the nineteenth century. Its key challenge was to craft national rules and practices that would promote national development. The spectrum of issues that engaged it, however, and, more important, the array of intermediaries through which it worked expanded dramatically. The Great Depression exposed a pressing need to revise existing relationships and broadly expand the organizations available in the voluntary and private sector to ensure that past methods of parceling out national authority were adapted to current challenges.[4]

Rules that previously had applied to states and regions were nationalized. Segments of the population previously excluded from the political economy, or marginalized by it, were engaged. This pattern roughly followed the expansion of the franchise that exploded in the early nineteenth century, the 1920s, and again in the late 1960s. Just as was the case in the late eighteenth century and much of the nineteenth century, isolation was the greatest challenge to national development. Mid-twentieth-century public policy sought to break down political and economic isolation. Of course, the means differed. The problem was no longer ensuring political communications—something that the U.S. Postal Service addressed admirably in the early nineteenth century. Now the greatest challenge was crafting a new set of key intermediary institutions or adapting existing ones, as Americans were far more comfortable with this approach to governance than extending national authority directly by empowering federal bureaucrats.[5]

Both state and society were reorganized to integrate excluded or underrepresented citizens (and markets) and address the pressing problems (or satisfy the demands) of millions of Americans while avoiding the creation of an autonomous central state whenever possible. The national government intervened to shore up nascent associations of producers, especially farmers and industrialized labor. Federal policy makers also targeted regions that were isolated economically, primarily through agencies like the Tennessee Valley Authority (TVA) and the Works Progress Administration (WPA). Franklin D. Roosevelt's administration also sought to shore up segments of the private sector through a regulatory apparatus that relied on greater transparency. That transparency, in turn, stimulated the demand for a host of professionals. These professionals, far more than government bureaucrats, crafted, and (self-)policed the standards that they set within industries like the financial sector. While the role for accountants and economists grew, no profession was more instrumental than the law.

Universities were the training ground for most of these professions. But universities played a far more important role in mid-century America, emerging as perhaps the key intermediary institution that stood between citizen and state. From managing farm programs to administering complex contracts (primarily for the burgeoning defense sector of the economy) universities both benefited from federal aid and adapted the public authority that accompanied that aid in ways that were palatable to the vast majority of Americans. Indeed, universities had quite a bit to say about what it meant to be an American, as they proved to be schools of citizenship as well as science and the humanities. Universities also emerged as key testing grounds for many of the new goods and services that citizens would demand from both the public and spheres. Whether medical care or social work, these services were often developed and delivered by the private and voluntary sectors, even as they were increasingly funded by the government.

Finally, I will turn to a mechanism as old as American government itself—contracting. While much has been made about the acceptance of Keynesian pump-priming and its corollary stimulus of consumption, far less attention has been devoted to the channels through which the federal government distributed these funds. Besides allowing policy makers to calibrate politically the recipients of these tax dollars, contracting, more than any other mechanism, accommodated increased federal spending while ensuring that such spending was laundered through trusted intermediaries—from universities to charitable organizations to Northrop Grumman.

Recovering from the National Industrial Recovery Act

Even those receptive to the existence of such associational ties, however, have insisted that they died with the failed experiment of the NRA. Colin Gordon, for instance, characterized the NRA as beset by "dilemmas, inconsistencies, and contradictions." Elliot Rosen is blunter. "There was no corporate commonwealth in the nineteen-thirties, a nexus of business, investment banking, and government," he writes. "To the contrary, FDR regarded Wall Street bankers as crooks and sponsored legislation that discouraged business advance." Any notion that the NRA would serve as a back-door approach to planning was "stillborn." Criticism from the left was even more severe. As Mary Furner noted, statist liberals viewed the NRA codes as "little more than rent-seeking attempts to maintain prices by restricting production." Nor did Hawley disagree with all of these assessments of the NRA's fate. Indicting the NRA's formulators for "setting forth vague goals, giving industrial code-makers a virtually blank check," Hawley chastised the Act and its administration for failing to offer a definitive policy. Rather, it provided a "framework that different sets of administrators could use to build quite different versions of an industrial democracy."[6]

Yet Hawley's claim for continuity is unmistakable. Noting FDR's shift to "market restoration" in 1935, and a series of moves to regulate the economy through more explicit government intervention into the private sector, Hawley emphasized that by 1937 "the conflicting pressures shaping antitrust policy had produced a pattern resembling that of late 1934. The official goal . . . was 'market restoration.' Yet in large and crucial areas, the government was doing nothing to restore competition . . . and in others it was actively supporting anticompetitive arrangements." In the case of labor, as Colin Gordon has argued, ensuring minimum standards through the Wagner Act—an extension of Section 7A of the NIRA—became a crucial means of enforcing regulation, displacing the emphasis on trade associations or the explicit intervention of state regulatory bodies into the market. Despite the failure of many associational mechanisms after the crash (or even before in the case of lumber) Hawley also noted that some of them were incorporated into subsequent approaches to regulation.[7]

Although advocates of an associational approach struck out when it came to the NIRA, they built just such an approach into key farm legislation. The Agricultural Adjustment Act (AAA) was one of the first New Deal initiatives, and it is of particular interest to us as the U.S. Department of Agriculture (USDA) was also a model for the early American Political Development literature on "state autonomy" and the larger quest to "bring the state back in." The 1920s were characterized by federal efforts to reinforce and support cooperative marketing efforts organized along regional and commodity lines. The long-running farm depression prompted even more vigorous efforts on the part of the Hoover administration, culminating in the Agricultural Marketing Act of 1929, which provided government loans. It spawned hundreds of new cooperatives and supported national marketing initiatives for key commodities. Such "associationalism," Adam Sheingate noted, avoided the twin evils of "politicized policymaking and bureaucratic encroachments on personal freedom."[8]

With the passage of the AAA in 1933, the extension service emerged as a key mechanism for carrying out the nation's seminal agricultural policy, not to mention disseminating billions of dollars. By 1935 there were 3,300 county agents across the land. These were far from federal functionaries. Because federal and state funding was often matched with private funds, many of the county agents literally received a portion of their salaries from one of the era's most powerful interest groups—the American Farm Bureau Federation (AFBF). Under the AAA allotment plan, county agents decided how much acreage individual farmers had to take out of production, which, in turn, determined the federal payment these farmers received for enlisting in the fight against overproduction. Agents were also responsible for enforcing these production quotas. Secretary of Agriculture Henry Wallace shrewdly decided to carry out this controversial policy through the familiar faces of extension agents rather than creating a new federal bureaucracy. As the savvy Wallace put it in 1935, "Fortunately, we had the extension services with their corps of . . . county agricultural agents and a background of 20 years of experience with which to contact farmers."[9]

The AAA revived the Farm Bureau's sagging fortunes. "The organization of more than 3 million contract signers," the 1935 AFBF report noted, constituted "the greatest opportunity in the history of the Farm Bureau to strengthen its organization." Sheingate emphasizes that this cozy relationship fell far short of corporatism, as the Farm Bureau faced competition from other farm organizations—it never established dominance as a "peak organization." Meanwhile, the USDA splintered into warring factions by the late 1930s, with advocates for less prosperous (usually southern) farmers fighting the Farm Bureau.[10]

Through programs like the AAA, the New Deal state dramatically expanded its reach into the political economy, but it did so through a mechanism that blended state, local, and private associations. Small wonder that Wallace informed Congress in the late 1930s that "by decentralizing the responsibility . . . and using the full facilities of the Cooperative Agricultural Extension Service . . . it has been found practical to carry through operations involving from hundreds to millions of individual farmers." While many farmers used a language steeped in the populist tradition, it was government-induced production control and analogies to corporate organization that animated New Deal commodities programs.[11]

Bringing millions of farmers into a more secure and predictable relationship with the state and engaging them through the voluntary-sector intermediary of the AFBF was one of the signal accomplishments of the New Deal. Hardly a panacea, the AAA incorporated a sizeable segment of commercial farmers into the associational fold, tempering fears of heavy-handed, centralized bureaucratic control through the use of a now-familiar intermediary in the form of the county agent. Along the way it made "crop supports" as American as apple pie, sharply distinguishing them from "the dole."

If "business principles" could be applied to farmers, might they also encompass labor? That is precisely the way Ellis Hawley framed the issue in *The New Deal and the Problem of Monopoly*. "Here, too," Hawley concluded, "the effort to enlist governmental aid in the development of market power was making steady progress." Section 7(a) of the NIRA guaranteed collective bargaining rights for workers. Advocates argued that government oversight of this process would provide labor an equal playing field that had long been denied them in the courts, unleashing the inherent power of collective action to ensure adequate wage levels. This, in turn, advocates argued, would help maintain prices against a debilitating deflationary trend. Labor supported Section 7(a) because "strong union organization in each industry," as the American Federation of Labor put it, "can keep workers' income constantly moving upward as their producing power increases," ensuring that their "mass buying power" would fuel the economy.[12]

There was no substitute for the initiative, sacrifice, and courage of the workers themselves, which soon outstripped the poorly enforced provisions of Section 7(a) through a series of strikes that shook the nation in 1933. The Roosevelt administration responded by establishing the National Labor Board, succeeded by the National Labor Relations Board (NLRB). Both applied the principles of the "Reading Formula" that protected striking workers from retaliation and enshrined the principle of majority vote by the workers as the means for selecting proper labor representation. Labor agitation also pushed the NLRB to articulate and proscribe unfair labor practices. The passion and mobilization of millions of workers and effective leadership activated the explosion of union membership in the 1930s and the broad distribution of that membership, extending to core industrial sectors like auto manufacturing and steel. By 1940, 23 percent of the nonagricultural workforce was represented by unions, increasing to 25 percent by the end of World War II.[13]

Yet Section 7(a) of the NIRA set the overall framework through which labor's formal participation in the political economy would be channeled and that framework varied little over the course of the next fifteen years, although the degree to which the federal government insisted that the framework be accepted by both labor and management did. With each assertion of labor's demands, the national government responded by strengthening labor's hand in the battle to ensure that its collective clout could be brought to bear. Theda Skocpol summed up the sequence well, writing in *Diminished Democracy* that "labor unions needed the U.S. government's help fully to establish themselves—and in turn became the champions of New Deal economic and social programs." Those who charged excessive state intervention conveniently forgot the preceding fifty years of active state assistance to management under the "liberty of contract" regime and other favorable judicial interpretations that helped create a national market.[14]

When the Supreme Court threw out the NIRA in the *Schecter* decision, Senator Robert Wagner (D-NY), who had been instrumental in crafting Section 7(a), wasted no time in backing the NLRB's power with statutory authority. The National Labor Relations Act codified protections against discriminatory hiring and firing. It addressed one of the key impediments to organized labor's ability to assert its collective clout—the instrumental use by employers of "company unions." And it mandated that majority-elected unions would serve as the sole bargaining agent for the units they represented, undermining another management tactic that was used to dilute the power of organized labor—multiple bargaining units for workers performing similar tasks.[15]

From 1933 through the end of World War II the macroeconomic claims for this approach to labor relations varied. Advocates of the industry codes embodied in the NIRA insisted that comparable wages would provide a floor under prices, ensuring against overproduction and ruinous price cutting. Keynesian advocates of the power of mass consumption hailed the ability of organized labor to translate higher wages into purchasing power that would stimulate the economy. And wartime managers welcomed the opportunity to channel labor's demands during a period of scarce labor into wage and benefit concessions that kept defense plants humming. But underlying all three rationales was an idea shared by advocates for the state's associational relationship to business in the 1920s, the same conception of political economy that produced the ill-fated NIRA and the more successful AAA. That fundamental notion endorsed state authority to better organize, empower, and coordinate key sectors of the economy. Without such government assistance, those sectors would continue to suffer from the disproportionate power of economic adversaries—be they oligopolistic corporations, better-organized agricultural financiers and processors, or industrial managers in far-flung industries.

In the case of labor, this approach opened the door toward broader regulatory control of large sectors of the political economy without having to rely on more explicit forms of government intervention. As Colin Gordon has argued, long after the National Recovery Administration collapsed, many firms "sought stability as a byproduct of labor-management relations, hoping that the organization of workers and labor standards would act as a surrogate for the regulatory hand of the state." Business was divided over the efficacy of this approach. Some industry leaders worried that they would have to cede control over long-established management prerogatives. But in the face of the economic crisis and rising labor activism, the possibility of reining in competition by stabilizing labor costs and spreading them equally to competitors was a bargain that many business leaders accepted. Accommodating the spirit of Section 7(a) that was embodied in the Wagner Act and the NLRB that it empowered seemed like a good bet compared to many of the alternatives.[16]

If trade agreements could not be enforced explicitly in an environment that was just as suspicious of monopoly power as overt state corporatism, and explicit price fixing or wage requirements smacked of socialism, then empowering workers to demand a set of labor standards that could be enforced across firms and bargain for wages that would ensure a minimum standard of living seemed like a politically palatable way to increase consumption at the same time that it placed a floor under falling prices. Most importantly, it appeared to push the struggle for competitive advantage back into the private sector even though both industry and labor were now more subject to both administrative and judicial control than ever. Because unions failed to gain control over management on the shop floor or resource allocation within the industries that they bargained with, those businesses that bet on this approach won their gamble. They sacrificed few management prerogatives and, at least during the 1930s, avoided a major redistribution in income while laying the groundwork for more stable labor relations at the same time that they imposed standard costs on their domestic competitors. The "regulatory hand of the state" in this case, though far from invisible, operated indirectly through the collective bargaining process overseen by the NLRB.[17]

Shoring Up the Professions

For other sectors of the economy, bolstering the capacity to self-regulate through enhanced transparency was the key to the New Deal approach. As Louis Galambos argued in *The Creative Society*, the Securities and Exchange Commission (SEC), created in 1934, "brought a new level of reliable information to this important part of U.S. capitalism." The legislation that established the SEC was a prerequisite for this emerging associational network. It regulated the previously untamed practices of the New York Stock Exchange and other securities markets. Equally important was the commitment of the New Deal staff to ensure that the kinds of practices that contributed to the crash in 1929 would not be replicated. But these watchdogs carried out their mission through a uniquely American blend of public and private authority. The SEC's reporting requirements and rule making provided accountants with the authority required to stand up to corporate clients—a degree of autonomy that corporate engineers, for instance, never achieved. By empowering a crucial intermediary—the accounting profession—the SEC increased state capacity in a manner that many of the early students of state autonomy had not envisioned. State authority loomed large in this approach: A new regulatory body had been created in the SEC. Its power was enhanced, however, by the cooperative arrangement it worked out with firms marketing securities, employing a combination of transparency and accountability. This was ensured on a day-to-day basis by none other than newly empowered accountants. As Galambos summed up, by "extending power and status to professional experts, New Deal state crafting actually decentralized authority." The combination of statutory authority, the threat of more draconian state intervention, and the incentives for professionals to internalize the values of transparency that the state codified in both the Securities Act and its enforcement led to this hybrid regime.[18]

Christopher McKenna linked the emergence of the world's "newest profession" of management consulting to another seminal New Deal regulatory landmark—the Glass-Steagall Banking Act of 1933. Aimed at cutting off the flow of capital for the kind of speculation that led to the crash of 1929, this legislation severed the relationship between commercial and investment banking. It also prohibited the kind of supervision that commercial banks had provided to those accountants and engineers who conducted "investigations" of companies that sought to finance publicly their capital expansion. In this instance, accounting firms lost out after the SEC ruled that any consultation with clients as part of the "investigation" leading to financing would be considered a conflict of interest. Firms like Arthur Andersen subsequently focused on lucrative financial audits and steered clear of consulting. Men like James McKinsey, George Armstrong, and Edwin Booz stepped into this gap between two regulatory mandates, creating in its interstices the new profession of management consulting.[19]

This is the same profession that was grounded in the nascent cost accounting movement documented by Gerald Berk and that was integral to many of the associational relationships forged in the 1920s. It was ironic, McKenna noted, "that consultants should have benefited from the anti-monopolism of the nineteen-thirties, for as professional accountants and as engineers, like the managers to whom they reported, consultants had worked to consolidate the giant American oligopolies from the 1890s onward. Ultimately . . . the industrial engineers and cost accountants who benefited the most from the New Deal reforms of the nineteen-thirties were not trying to recast, but rather to promote, the growth of big business." Without the legislative mandate to separate commercial and investment banking embodied in the Glass-Steagall Act, and the SEC's determination to ensure transparency, this division of professional labor would not have occurred. As with their counterparts in accounting, the newly empowered management consultants, however, carried the state's agenda deep into the private sector itself. Maneuvering between those who feared too much competition and those who dreaded consolidation, housed in the private sector yet authorized by the state to serve as its agents in making information transparent and ensuring the objectivity of that information, professional intermediaries would have been invented if they did not already exist. In fact, in the case of management consultants, they were invented![20]

The legal profession served as an intermediary most frequently and was in turn enhanced by this role most dramatically. This was hardly the first time that attorneys served as the glue that affixed state and society. The Progressive reformer Herbert Croly insisted that "no other great people, either in classic, medieval, or modern times," had ever allowed "such a professional monopoly of governmental functions." Yet even by American standards, the number of lawyers grew dramatically during the New Deal. They were particularly visible in executive departments like State and the Treasury. They dominated the NLRB. And as Christopher Tomlins has shown, "professional legal practice" dictated both the organization and practices of that body. Nowhere were lawyers more pervasive than the SEC, where they flocked from top Wall Street firms or the top law schools that supplied such firms. Like the cost accountants who had benefited from corporate consolidation in the 1920s, many Wall Street lawyers had profited from serving corporations that operated in a relatively unregulated environment. Under the SEC, and in light of the financial calamity visited upon the nation, many were persuaded to take their public obligations as "gatekeepers to the capital markets" more seriously.[21]

Daniel Ernst has documented the distinctive qualities that these men brought with them and the enormous influence they exercised in crafting key New Deal programs. First and foremost was their experience in the private sector—they gained from a working knowledge of the Wall Street law firm. Such knowledge glorified the key practice that insulated law firms against investor lawsuits: "due diligence" investigations. Due diligence protected clients who unwittingly made material misstatements if their lawyers had conducted a "reasonable investigation." The law professor John C. Coffee Jr. dubbed due diligence a "Full Employment Act for law firms." Like the ongoing role that Glass-Steagall created for management consultants, financial incentives for professionals who were not employed directly by the state were crucial to the care and maintenance of effective intermediaries. Drawing on his review of New Deal legal practices to offer today's would-be reformers advice, Ernst urged that "policy makers should give gatekeeping professionals a financial and ideological stake in any new regulatory system. Well-designed schemes should empower private professionals to acquire information comprehensively and interpret rules and orders for their regulated clients."[22]

The ideology that Ernst alluded to was not one that fit neatly into liberal or conservative camps. Rather, it was a "theory of law as the adjustment of social interests." Felix Frankfurter epitomized this approach and trained a generation of lawyers, Ernst wrote, "to think of themselves as the master adjusters of social interests, experts at using other experts." Lawyers drew on firsthand knowledge of the industries that they sought to regulate but also operated within an ideational framework that viewed adjustment of social interests as the highest priority. They extended these values within the private and voluntary sectors, ensuring the success of such regulatory regimes. While many of these regimes ultimately failed, their long tenure suggested just how effective the state could be if it empowered professions like the law and dispersed its authority through its day-to-day practices. Those recent failures, in turn, from the Enron disaster to the collapse of the derivative market, are an important reminder that state oversight remains crucial to the successful maintenance of effective associational networks.[23]

Reproducing Intermediaries

No intermediary proved more versatile or ubiquitous in the middle third of the twentieth century than the research university. This development was hardly a foregone conclusion. Especially at elite universities, the kind of Ivy League enclaves that would compete for federal funding after World War II, accepting federal aid smacked of politics at best and socialism at worst. Even though the combination of rising laboratory costs and the economic crisis of the 1930s pushed universities to consider federal aid, leading scientists warned of the dangers to life as they knew it.[24]

Yet even as leading scientists warned of the dangers, universities forged various relationships with the national government. Their most important contribution to the associational order was to create and certify professionals. Universities helped professions like doctors and accountants establish control over an exclusive body of esoteric knowledge that allowed these professions to distinguish their members from competitors. Beyond this essential role, however, they began to provide the administrative mechanisms that allowed the very state that elite scientists feared to filter funds, and agendas, through less threatening hands, in a society still wary of visible trappings of central government.[25]

Universities became key sites for reproducing and coordinating intermediaries. Those county agents, for instance, were the product of long-standing federal support for the extension service—created by the Smith-Lever Act of 1914. To farmers, at least the right kind of farmer, the county agent was a neighbor. To the extent he represented state authority, that authority had been leavened by his association with the American Farm Bureau Federation, the land-grant college that the extension service was connected to, and local Bureau representatives. The New Deal state dramatically expanded its reach into the political economy but did so through a mechanism that blended state, local, and private associations under the umbrella of higher education. By the end of the 1930s a broad array of federal agencies operated through the extension service, from the TVA to the Rural Electrification Administration.[26]

Universities, of course, were an important intermediary in their own right. Even though Harvard's James Conant declined (along with 139 other college presidents) when the federal government extended its Federal Emergency Relief Administration grants to students at private schools in 1934, other private universities accepted the much-needed grants that paid for part-time student jobs. At Stanford, where President Ray Lyman Wilbur just a few years earlier had warned of federal aid pushing universities into the "arms of the government," economic need trumped fears of big government. By the 1934–35 academic year, 12 percent of Stanford's students received federal work relief funds. Stanford was part of a much broader national trend. Over the next decade, federal work-study funds flowed to more than 600,000 students, 13 percent of all students.[27]

As Christopher Loss has noted, federal work-study fit a larger pattern for the New Deal and the federal-university partnership more generally. "State-level emergency relief administrators, educational bureaucrats, and university leaders handled the day-to-day managerial duties of the work-study program." Loss documents how the back and forth between students and college officials personalized the federal presence in what a few years earlier had been regarded as a sacred private or state-level endeavor. This decentralized approach also assured southern Democrats the discretion required to maintain segregation.[28]

"Higher education played a crucial part in helping the New Deal achieve administrative capacity in a political culture uncomfortable with a sprawling national bureaucracy," Loss notes. "The university's placement between citizens and the state made it an ideal para-state for the federal government to connect with citizens and, in turn, for citizens to connect with their government." New Dealers used universities and their surrogates, like the extension service, to naturalize the federal presence. Tapping key institutions in civil society to deliver federal programs and services "naturalized the New Deal's expanded natural reach and made it politically palatable to average Americans and to conservative, especially southern, politicians." The university's service to the state would only grow with the looming national security crisis of World War II and the subsequent Cold War. Both increased demand for federal funding and direction, at the same time that they underscored America's distinctive antistatist tradition, whether contrasted with fascist Germany or the communist Soviet Union and People's Republic of China.[29]

That is because universities proved to be crucial intermediaries between citizens and their increasingly bureaucratic state. Universities served this role by pioneering and adapting a social technology that mediated between individual desires and collective needs in modern American democracy—personal adjustment. Loss argues persuasively that psychological techniques were disseminated broadly through the medium of education. Thus, education became a process that both imparted knowledge and created skills and provided a means through which individuals learned how to adapt to hierarchical organizations. Universities discovered this inadvertently during the 1920s when they faced high dropout rates and tried a variety of remedies. The military was indoctrinated during World War II as psychologists demonstrated the links between education and effective soldiering. Education served as a means of adjusting soldiers into and out of military life. Americans eager to shore up the commitment of citizens in the twilight struggle against communism after World War II soon adjusted education toward patriotic ends. As these hardened into efforts to sway public opinion, the implications of education for a democratic republic emerged as a central question on college campuses. Buffeted by youth-driven social movements ranging from the quest for social justice to efforts to end the Vietnam War, educators gave up on their half-century quest toward adjustment and embraced difference—the root of contemporary diversity programs.[30]

In the meantime, universities cashed in on a form of aid that states, localities, and the private sector had long benefited from: government investment in infrastructure. The Public Works Administration (PWA) provided $200 million to universities to modernize their physical plant. They funded a range of projects from classrooms to libraries. By the time it expired, the PWA had funded construction at the vast majority of state and land-grant universities, subsidizing more than six hundred projects.[31]

Building a New Deal

This was a tiny portion of the construction funding authorized by the PWA, which was created as part of the original NIRA in 1933. Jason Scott Smith has demonstrated the continuity between the PWA, the WPA (created in 1935) and the Federal Works Agency (FWA, created in 1939) to consolidate public projects and which extended these crucial New Deal programs into the wartime era. Historians of the New Deal have treated these public works projects as jobs programs. Most have noted their failure to create enough jobs to stem the downward economic spiral, correctly crediting the wartime buildup with the eventual return of prosperity. As Smith notes, the rationale for public investment in infrastructure alternated between economic development under the PWA and again with the FWA, and social welfare under the WPA. Running through all three programs, however, was a commitment to "wide ranging investments in national infrastructure" that transformed not only the political scene but also reshaped the physical landscape of the United States. The objective was to modernize that infrastructure. Nor was this commitment perfunctory. Approximately two-thirds of New Deal emergency expenditures between 1933 and 1939 were disbursed through public works projects.[32]

Smith's contribution was not simply to remind us of the importance of rebuilding the national infrastructure for the purposes of long-term economic development. He also painstakingly traced the way that this investment reshaped attitudes toward the federal government and, conversely, how these construction programs adapted to prevailing preferences. Probing the objects of and conduits for this massive spending, Smith chronicled the way that public works "helped justify the new role of the state in American life, legitimizing—intellectually and physically—what has come to be known as Keynesian management of the economy." In doing so, he shifted our focus from the more abstract debate over the structural reform versus Keynesian consumption-oriented strain of liberalism that dominates the scholarship today to an older literature, recently refurbished by scholars like Richard John, Bill Novak, and John Laurentz Larson. They have recovered the long-standing tradition of government funding for economic infrastructure.[33]

While Smith framed his study as an opportunity to better understand liberalism, his account transcends that framework. Although Smith dutifully engaged with the preponderance of New Deal literature that is informed by Progressive historiography, his own approach appears to be influenced far more by scholars like Hawley, Hurst, and the Handlins, scholars who examined carefully the ways in which the state penetrated civil society, crafting the legal mechanisms that shaped the market and interpretations of "private property." "I have relied on an older literature that clarifies the historical relationship between government and the economy," Smith wrote. "This interpretive focus restores the New Deal public works programs to the broader narrative of American economic development, a narrative that acknowledges the importance of World War II government contracts to American business and highlights the central role played by government spending in the subsequent growth of the postwar period, but has comparatively neglected the events of the New Deal years."[34]

That "older literature" is primarily grounded in the nineteenth century and the 1920s, connecting Smith's story of active government assistance to economic development. It is a story that defies a simple alliance between Progressives and government activism, or precludes conservative support for dramatic legal intervention on the part of the national government. In short, it is a framework that challenges the central tension that inheres in Progressive historiography. As Smith points out, many New Dealers themselves recognized this. Senator Lewis Schwellenbach (D-WA) enumerated the government advantages advocated by conservatives during the nineteenth century: bounties for railroads, vast tracts of timberland, a protective tariff, and so on. "There were bounties galore," Schwellenbach noted. "But the people who worked, and who bought and consumed our products never got in on them." Now that groups previously left out of these cooperative arrangements with government were empowered, they too should enjoy the benefits of government-directed economic development. One could portray this as the people using government on behalf of the people, as Charles Beard might have framed it, or as Hawley or Galambos might put it, the possibility for sectors of the population who had not been sufficiently organized in the past to access the assistance of government to do so now.[35]

The details of Smith's account made clear the associational framework that pervaded the federal construction programs, regardless of the acronym. The PWA, under the guidance of Harold Ickes, relied heavily on private contractors. It awarded almost 55,000 contracts to more than 20,000 private contractors. Funneling funds through the existing private mechanism for construction was a valuable way to ease public acceptance. The PWA was quick to seize on this fact, broadcasting in 1937 a series of discussions about the PWA that highlighted this feature. As one interview with an architect noted, "The PWA saved the contractors and the whole construction business." Perhaps the best proof of the degree to which PWA projects relied upon private oversight was the outcry when Harry Hopkins, whom contractors dubbed "the High Prophet of No Profits," cut contractors out of construction projects under the WPA. Eager to speed the flow of money and the provision of jobs, the WPA employed relief workers directly, circumventing long-established intermediaries.[36]

However, the PWA relied on more than private contractors to combat charges of central bureaucratic control. For instance, it distributed funds through local governments. Big city mayors, in particular, were thrilled at the potential for controlling these funds, going so far to create an association of their own, the U.S. Conference of Mayors, in 1933. The PWA adopted this practice and also relied heavily on a federal agency that had a century of experience dealing with delicate intergovernmental and partisan political issues, the Army Corps of Engineers.[37]

The New Deal extended an approach to economic development that the federal government had carefully constructed over the past 150 years to segments of the population that had been passed by or recently cut out of this largesse. Jerome Frank, a legal adviser to Harold Ickes at the PWA, summed up the trajectory, placing it in the longer sweep of American history. According to Frank, nineteenth-century America was "an era of the most stupendous pump-priming in the history of the modern world. Our continent was developed by individual private initiative—but that private initiative was stimulated and aided, and its exploits were made possible, by billions and billions of gifts from the government of these United States." Frank could not believe that a country that rose to greatness through "gigantic government aid to private enterprise" would "arrest its present development, and stifle its amazing potential future growth, merely because governmental aid to private enterprise must now take on a new form." If pump-priming was "essentially sound and conservative then," Frank concluded, surely it must be so during the present crisis.[38]

The PWA and its successor programs were popular with the public precisely because many of the techniques they used fit neatly with both private-sector and intergovernmental relations as configured at the time. Even measured by one of the most stringent tests, local elections about bonds that would fund matching shares of PWA projects, the federal construction program was popular. As Smith reported, 83 percent of the time, in more than 2,600 elections, localities voted to match federal funds for public works. For a small town like Chula Vista, California, Smith wrote, "The spirit of the New Deal meant the improvement of local streets by private contractors employing a combination of skilled labor and workers taken from the relief rolls, funded by a mixture of federal grants, loans, and locally issued bonds." It meant that the same federal government that was instrumental in developing the transportation, irrigation, and market structure that made the very idea of California possible, was now going to home in on some of the acute problems that had crippled the economy and would do so in a way that used familiar intermediaries to deliver these benefits.[39]

Organizing the Nation's "Internal Frontier"

Federal development of the infrastructure had long been directed toward the nation's frontier, and that meant the West. While New Deal construction programs continued that pattern, they were also informed by new regional priorities in the quest to integrate economically underdeveloped areas. The pump-priming that Jerome Frank believed would yield "lasting physical improvements of the highest economic and social value . . . unquestionably supplying us with that needed stimulus to private initiative which spells national prosperity" was now directed at the nation's "internal frontier." That internal frontier was colonized by massive federal undertakings like the TVA but encompassed other parts of the South as well.[40]

In April 1933 Roosevelt asked Congress to create the TVA, which his special message to Congress called "a corporation clothed with the power of government, but possessed of the flexibility and initiative of a private enterprise." Five weeks later Congress complied, beginning an experiment that, on its face, constituted a bold departure for the federal government. The legislation empowered this new agency, which transcended state and local jurisdictions and that did not fit neatly into any federal chain of command, to undertake regional development, pursuing conservation, flood control, power production, and agriculture among other tasks. It was the shared river basin that formed the Tennessee Valley, not traditional intergovernmental relationships or functionally defined missions. While the TVA's mandate was as vague as it was encompassing, Commonwealth and Southern (C&S), the holding company that owned private utilities in the region, viewed the TVA as an immediate threat. C&S urged the TVA to sell its power to existing utilities that would continue to distribute government-generated power through the C&S network.[41]

The youngest TVA commissioner, David Lilienthal, fresh from the Wisconsin Public Utilities Commission, had different ideas. He refused to play ball with the large utilities, insisting on competing with them. Competition, Lilienthal argued, would establish a "yardstick" that could be used to compare the full cost of providing power, including distribution and transmission, along with production. That yardstick, Lilienthal hoped, would keep trusts like C&S honest and force them to provide reliable service at fair prices. The TVA bandied about other ideas that threatened to disrupt folk ways and challenge the existing system of private enterprise. Especially ominous to many was all the talk about government planning. To make matters worse politically, Lilienthal was a northern Jew, with liberal leanings, and the chair of the TVA, A. E. Morgan, another Yankee, was considered to be an "idealistic dreamer."[42]

Lilienthal countered the opposition by appealing to the populist impulses of electricity consumers. The yardstick was one way to keep costs low. But the best way to ensure lower rates for electricity, Lilienthal believed, was to increase its use. Lilienthal conceived of the Electric Home and Farm Authority, which would lower the cost of electrically powered appliances. He worked with large appliance manufacturers like General Electric to reduce the costs of these appliances to farmers, in order to create customers for TVA power. Building on his experience, Lilienthal insisted that the blessings of nature, even when harnessed by engineers and other experts, meant nothing if the people did not participate in that development. This was a principle that he spelled out later in a popular tract titled *TVA: Democracy on the March*.[43]

The TVA was able to provide electricity at low rates, although private utilities insisted that this was attributable to generous PWA construction loans, not to greater efficiency. Lilienthal also initiated a distribution system that, with the assistance of other government agencies, operated through cooperative, publicly owned utilities in a number of towns and rural areas. After a key Supreme Court ruling against Tennessee Electric Power Company, C&S, its parent company, finally agreed to sell a large portion of its holdings to the TVA and local distributors. C&S agreed to defer to the TVA and local distributors in the Tennessee River basin. This was a huge victory for public power, sealed by a congressional appropriation of $61.5 million to finance the purchase of C&S properties in that territory.[44]

Yet Lilienthal's conception of democracy on the march, or what he sometimes called grass-roots democracy, was not one that community organizers of the 1960s would recognize. In fact, Lilienthal worked through many of the very local and private institutions that latter-day activists excoriated: local government, the extension service, and voluntary associations. Lilienthal's approach to grass-roots democracy was another way of ensuring that the TVA made peace with the local establishment. Ironically, grass-roots democracy became a defense against incursions by competitors, like

Harold Ickes, who were within the federal government itself. Looking down, Lilienthal argued that the people were on his side; looking up, the grass-roots mantra became a justification for greater TVA autonomy from Congress and the executive branch.[45]

In a brilliant analysis of the functions that the grass-roots ideology served at the TVA, the sociologist Philip Selznick summed up the TVA's dilemma in *TVA and the Grass Roots*. "It was felt that an imposed federal program would be alien and unwanted, and ultimately accomplish little, unless it brought together at the grass roots all the agencies concerned with and essential to the development of a region's resources." This included "the local communities, voluntary private organizations, state agencies, and cooperating federal agencies." This was the definition of the grass roots that the TVA pursued.[46]

Lilienthal's diaries reflected his innate impatience with this approach. Outlining his thoughts for a speech in 1940, Lilienthal appeared to carica-ture this indirect and cumbersome path toward achieving a public objec-tive. "The farm program with its circuitous educational process through university, extension service, county agent, assistant county agent, etc., etc., is an example," he fumed, "since the easy, direct, simple way of helping these farmers would be to avoid all this business and make a direct educa-tional job of it." The other Lilienthal, however, the experienced administra-tor and astute student of bureaucratic politics, prevailed. "By going the circuitous route," the patient Lilienthal continued, "you are developing a whole framework of living, in which independence and participation become not only a part of the individual farmer's thinking and way of living but imbue the institutions that are all around him with that same point of view."[47]

It was the latter approach that ultimately informed the TVA's behavior, one that even Selznick agreed was probably a political necessity. Precisely because the TVA did not emerge out of a political debate that engaged key interests, and because it was imposed on a number of powerful constituen-cies, it had to curry favor with these forces if it was to succeed. As Selznick said, "It had to feel its way." It did so by forging cooperative relationships with many of the preexisting intermediaries that stood between it and the real grass roots, emerging as the guardian of local prerogative with all of the implications that this entailed for existing social and racial relations.[48]

When it came to the rest of the South, investments were vetted by local elites from the start. But they were bankrolled by the federal government.

In July 1938 Roosevelt stated publicly what most Americans already suspected: The South was "the Nation's No. 1 economic problem—the Nation's problem, not merely the South's." Eight years later, a novelist who made a career fictionalizing some of those problems confirmed that Roosevelt's administration had responded to the president's call. "Our economy is no longer agricultural," William Faulkner noted. "Our economy is the Federal Government."[49]

As Ira Katznelson has written, "[t]he South permitted American liberal democracy the space within which to proceed, but it restricted American policymaking to . . . a 'southern cage,' from which there was no escape." As other scholars from Linda Gordon to Jill Quadagno have illustrated, federal social policy was subjected to the southern veto power. Social benefits, whether the job categories covered by social insurance or the grant levels paid to welfare recipients, were held hostage to southern racial hierarchies and preferences. Although social insurance was the exception, the mechanism that protected these regional predilections was federalism. It offered local administration and discretion while pumping federal dollars into the region.[50]

The ways in which the federal government armed America to fight World War II and the impact of these policies on the South ultimately did more to transform the South than Roosevelt's letter or even the *Report on Economic Conditions of the South* that prompted it. Like the New Deal's social and agricultural programs, the nation's war efforts were diffused through an elaborate set of local, state, voluntary, and private-sector filters that limited federal autonomy even as they reshaped the relationship between the South and the federal government. The contractual state that emerged after World War II, its military justification, and the investment in infrastructure required to support both military preparedness and a more fully integrated economy were initially justified in compensatory terms when applied to the South. But it soon defined the nation's fastest growing region—the "Sunbelt"—and its leading economic sectors in aerospace and electronics.[51]

Even before Roosevelt's regional call to arms, liberal legislation like the Fair Labor Standards Act and rigorous enforcement had targeted the South. But as Bruce Schulman has documented, "War mobilization soon made the Fair Labor Standards Act obsolete." Manufacturing employment expanded by 50 percent in the South over the course of the war and annual wages increased 40 percent from 1939 to 1942.[52]

Yet wartime investment in the South got off to a slow start. Even though FDR wanted to marshal state resources to jump-start southern industry, the military asserted its independence, favoring the kind of large, reliable contractors it had used in the past. Few of these existed in the South as the military sought to speed up production. The military was quick to expand bases in the South, however, and forged a "military-payroll complex." More than one-third of the military facilities built in the continental United States were constructed in that region. The TVA's autonomy also served the South well after that agency jumped on the mobilization bandwagon, ramping up its power production, churning out strategic materials like magnesium, and training local workers for work in defense plants. In the wake of Pearl Harbor, this outpost of technical and engineering know-how enlisted its skills to combat the enemy, perfecting new processes for manufacturing aluminum. "The Authority assembled a team of research scientists for this and other projects," Schulman concluded, "and its success dramatized the economic benefits of industrial research." This "home-grown" technological community, aided by the revelation of the Atomic Energy Commission's secret complex at Oak Ridge, Tennessee after the war, stimulated the love affair with science that would soon spawn endeavors like Research Triangle Park in North Carolina.[53]

Although wartime production in the South got off to a slow start, government policy, the labor shortage, and the overwhelming demand combined to give southern startups a chance. The South accounted for 23 percent of the new plant facilities built over the course of the war. Entrepreneurs like Andrew Jackson Higgins benefited from these opportunities. Out of the small boat producer he presided over in Louisiana, he created a transportation equipment giant with 20,000 employees and annual sales of more than $100 million. He couldn't have done it without the government's support for the high-wage, mechanized approach to manufacturing. When Higgins's contract for liberty ships was canceled due to a shortage of steel, Roosevelt reminded the War Production Board czar Donald Nelson that even though Higgins, who called Washington the "District of Confusion," could be difficult to work with, "the fact remains that he has production facilities and can do a good job." "I have no idea what he should make," the president continued, "airplanes or corvettes or something else, but I do want his plant utilized." Higgins was soon offered a contract to produce 1,200 cargo planes. While the South manufactured a disproportionate amount of explosives, creating plants that presumably would be of little value after conversion, it also acquired important footholds in sectors that would endure, from synthetic rubber to steel.[54]

The attitudes of local elites mattered. North Carolina lagged behind the rest of the South and far behind the Southwest when it came to attracting wartime industry. That is because it was already the most industrialized state in the South. Those industries were heavily invested in low-wage traditional manufacturing, such as textiles and tobacco. The men who ran these companies were influential in North Carolina politics and were not eager to attract defense contracts that would threaten their access to cheap labor.[55]

But federal policy mattered too. One of the reasons that men like Donald Nelson were drawn to public service was the opportunity it offered to address the South's problems. The War Production Board affirmed that the sites chosen for production should not only be secure and efficient, but also should be considered for "important and permanent consequences for the economic development of different parts of the nation." Nor did many of these benefits dissipate after the war. During hot or cold wars, the military contracted with universities, spawned prime contracts and subcontracts in the private sector, funded research, and reshaped the regional wage structure. Massive investments in infrastructure, from the Interstate Highway Act, which increased federal funding to 90 percent of the costs in 1956, to airport construction were justified by proponents because they contributed to the nation's defense. "The South's relations with the national government—at first so peculiar," Schulman concluded, "more and more came to define national attitudes and experiences."[56]

The Emergence of the Contract State

The West Coast's Higgins was Henry Kaiser. Kaiser dominated the nation's headlines in the summer of 1942. Introduced at the National Press Club in July as "the modern Paul Bunyan" for his remarkable success in churning out ships, Kaiser was surprisingly candid for a man who thrived on a do-it-yourself image and perception that his entrepreneurial can-do attitude had built his empires in ship building, magnesium, and aluminum. "Every time I take anybody to a shipyard, they want to see the ways and they think that is the shipyard. Well, that isn't the shipyard at all," Kaiser chided. "I will tell you where the . . . shipyard is," Kaiser continued: "it starts in

Washington." Kaiser was indeed an entrepreneur, but his greatest innovations turned on parlaying his skills as a California construction contractor into a national policy maker—a "government entrepreneur"—based in the private sector. He linked business and government through a web of contractual relationships.[57]

While the American public celebrated Kaiser's wartime contributions, Washington insiders had long been familiar with Kaiser's large-scale projects that ranged from dam building to aluminum plants. As Stephen B. Adams concluded in his penetrating study of Kaiser, he "did not take the road to Washington only during World War II. As the federal government grew during the thirties and forties he was a regular visitor to the nation's capital." Kaiser's path epitomized the shared endeavors that narrowed the distinction between the national government and the private sector in the middle decades of the twentieth century and, indeed, continued a long-standing tradition of joint ventures initiated by the developmental state.[58]

While Americans streamed west, Kaiser commuted east to cement (sometimes literally) his relationship with Washington, DC. He had grown up in the East, a few blocks from the greatest public undertaking of the nineteenth century—the Erie Canal. Perhaps it was no accident that the man who would one day build the Hoover Dam regularly watched barges labor through a canal that was built with massive government investment. Kaiser got his start as a road builder in Canada, but in 1921 he successfully bid on his first job in California. He set up shop in Oakland and never looked back. As tens of thousands of private contractors had confirmed over the course of the nineteenth century, state and local governments were an enduring source of business. What's more, their emphasis on building an infrastructure for economic development led to even more opportunities if those bets paid off. Most of Kaiser's bets did. He perfected contracting at the very time that many of the endeavors that he was engaged with were beginning to draw increased federal attention and funding. Kaiser was one of a cohort of "private" industrialists who ensured that the political infrastructure, in this case defined as the network of private, voluntary, and public partners, was hospitable to extending local and regional development to a national scale of unprecedented dimensions.[59]

Kaiser honed two sets of skills that had nothing to do with engineering per se but that proved crucial to his development as a government entrepreneur. Early on he learned how to work effectively with lawyers. It was virtually impossible to build a road in California without being sued, and Kaiser quickly learned how to maneuver through these legal roadblocks. Because the contract itself was so crucial to his success, lawyers who could negotiate, interpret, and litigate contract disputes were essential. And the right kind of lawyer provided entrée into the world of politics. Kaiser had an eye for legal expertise and political access. Over the course of his career, he worked with some of the best at both skill sets, including Thomas Corcoran and Lloyd Cutler.[60]

Kaiser also quickly discerned the crucial role played by trade associations in a business that was enmeshed in the public sector. Kaiser the contractor was also a trade association man. As president of the Northern California Contractors, he waged war against the use of day labor supervised by the Army Corps of Engineers. He also led a campaign to increase the gasoline tax in order to build more roads.[61]

Although Kaiser would apply his skills to bigger projects and tap federal, rather than state, financing, negotiating private means for realizing public ends through contractual agreements was the consistent theme that ran through his entire career. California proved to be the ideal training ground in which to refine these skills. As the editor of the *Engineering News-Record* noted, "In the Far West political considerations govern engineering." Whether building roads or dams, Adams concluded that Kaiser "had learned that government contracting was an organic process rather than a predictable series of discrete events. . . . Just about everything was negotiable, especially after the acceptance of the bid." And Kaiser learned one more thing. He learned how to portray himself as self-made individual entrepreneur, fitting into a long line of individuals from David Sarnoff to Howard Hughes, who in fact had gotten their big break from a change in government regulation or a government subsidy.[62]

Like the radar system that MIT scientists developed (under contract) to guide Allied aircraft, contracting undergirded wartime mobilization and postwar demobilization: It was quiet, invisible to the broader public, yet remapped landscapes regardless of topography or cloud cover. It provided a flexible, politically popular way to mesh ambitious government programs with the private incentive structure, allowing the associational state to fly in any kind of political weather. And like radar systems employed by the air traffic control system after the war, it soon expanded to a host of civilian enterprises.

In theory, military contracting was overseen by the National Defense Advisory Commission and the Office of Production Management—

agencies run by civilians like Nelson. In practice, as Paul Koistinen has argued, fierce divisions within these civilian oversight mechanisms allowed the military to call the shots for key aspects of both mobilization and demobilization. Like World War I, many of the civilian agencies were staffed with dollar-a-year men. In the case of World War II, a liberal, New Deal–oriented faction, headed by Nelson, warred with one that was more oriented toward meeting industry's needs, headed by Charles E. Wilson.[63]

The military offered industry several important advantages in the vacuum created by these power struggles. In a polity without an effective upper-level civil service system, the military provided professional continuity. Despite interbranch rivalries, the military was also able to come together if necessary and speak with one voice, the product of its command structure. Koistinen suggested a third factor that appealed to national corporations: The military was relatively free from the complications of dealing with the confusing array of state and local interests, although it could hardly ignore congressional representation of those interests. While the military borrowed financial and legal expertise from the private sector, industry capitalized on the military's statutory procurement powers and its ability to follow through on its priorities. Generous cost-plus contracting and reconversion agreements built and sustained this alliance into the postwar era. The military also financed $16 billion of the $25 billion in new war manufacturing capacity built during World War II. Along with the support of business federations like the "US Chamber of Commerce, National Association of Manufacturers, and Business Advisory Council (and spinoff Committee for Economic Development)," Koistinen argued, an alliance of military and industrial interests was able to "head off or temper efforts by New Dealers and other planners to dominate reconversion." Once again, the legal profession played a crucial role as brokers and mediators. As Bat Sparrow has noted, the Navy's Procurement Legal Division changed contract negotiation into a flexible, discretionary tool over the course of World War II, a practice that continued long after the fighting stopped.[64]

Just as categorical grants would come to dominate the relationship between the national government and the states after World War II, changing the nature of federalism, contractual relationships came to dominate the relationship between the federal government and civil society. Contractual relations were essential to heading off the "garrison state" that Harold Lasswell feared, even as federally subsidized agendas increasingly guided key portions of the private sector. Aaron Friedberg has documented the way in which a combination of liberal ideology and structural factors etched into the Constitution shaped the nation's reaction to the crises of World War II and the Cold War. The United States turned to the private sector, not government arsenals, for its defense needs during World War II. In peacetime, "and even during war," Friedberg argued, "the federal government has typically sought first to shape the behavior of individuals and groups *indirectly*, through the use of exhortation, tax incentives, procurement contracts, and transfer payments, rather than resort to the direct application of coercive power." Friedberg illustrated how this approach shaped strategic policy—with its emphasis on "flexible response" that relied on a strong nuclear deterrent, eventually supplemented with other conventional options during the Kennedy administration. It also shaped defense expenditures, channeling them into contracts with private corporations, which were viewed by many as simply another form of market exchange.[65]

Universities were the primary beneficiaries of this alternative to the garrison state, constructed by military planners and civilians alike. A new alliance between science and the state was forged after World War II but, like the vast network of procurement for military purposes, that research was housed largely outside the state. Just as procurement contracts were viewed as market exchange, federal research grants became part of the voluntary sector that universities anchored. For some, like Stanford and MIT, federal research funding was instrumental to their rise to the top of this hierarchy. For hundreds of others, contracts for research in the health sciences, education, and even social policy became a marker of success. If universities were indeed shaping citizenship by the 1950s, as Loss argues, they had every reason to share many of the incentives and goals that those citizens saluted.[66]

Conclusion

The state mattered in all of these associational relationships. In some instances, such as the AAA, legislation was the crucial catalyst for the creation of an effective intermediary in the private sector. In other cases, administrative discretion was just as important, stimulating the emergence of the contractual state, for instance. Professionals, especially lawyers, played key roles in staffing many of these associational networks and in merging statutory mandates with customary practices in the voluntary and private sectors.

In virtually every instance, the creation of associational mechanisms was merely a means to an end that could serve conservative *or* progressive objectives. Indeed, the history of many of the intermediaries described in this essay, and the networks they forged with the state, suggests that each has served a broad range of ideological ends at different points in their histories. Which ends prevailed often *did* depend on the ideological DNA of those who occupied key positions in the state. For that reason, even if most citizens, the fourth estate, public officials themselves, and especially partisan elected officials, continue to conflate conservatives with limited government and insist that only liberals advocated for a more powerful state, historians should resist the urge to follow. Disaggregating this alluring but misleading synthesis of ends and means remains one of our profession's most important challenges.

Chapter 6

Making Pluralism "Great": Beyond a Recycled History of the Great Society

Explicit in the title of this essay is a seemingly innocuous term: "pluralism." For many leading scholars, the Great Society killed pluralism. Nelson Lichtenstein, for instance, has castigated pluralism as a Trojan horse (designed by liberal intellectuals, no less!) that co-opted social democracy only to succumb to self-absorbed rights consciousness. Hugh Heclo, on the other hand, has underscored the schizophrenic pressures that pluralism faced in the 1960s when citizens asked government to do more at the very time they trusted it less. This overwhelmed a system built upon compromise. "Combining ferocious opposites and keeping each ferocious," not the compromise and bargaining essential to pluralism, animated 1960s civics, as Heclo sees it.[1] Whether celebrating its demise or bemoaning a cultural shift that crippled the capacity to compromise, so essential to pluralism's effectiveness, most scholars agree that the old "iron triangles" that had mediated between the mass public, and effective governance from the New Deal through the mid-1960s, failed catastrophically or were subsumed by the passions and social movements of the last third of the twentieth century.

This essay weighs the historical evolution of pluralism and concludes that it survived the Great Society. No doubt, the social tumult, radical demands for democratic access, and a dramatic increase in the venues for policy making stimulated by the 1960s have altered pluralism significantly. Nevertheless, the Great Society democratized politics without destroying the basic pluralist fabric that bound Americans to the public sphere in the twentieth century and that endures today. While associational relationships between state, voluntary and private institutions connected citizens who shared discrete sets of interests to governing structures that governed those interests, it was the pluralist give and take between these associational orders—not ideology or partisan marching orders—that resolved the never-ending conflicts that roiled the polity as a whole."

The "Challenge Constantly Renewed"

The relationship between politics, public policy, and society shifted during the "long" 1960s. "What was new about sixties civics," Hugh Heclo insists, "was not policy but *policy mindedness*" which was "an outlook that elevates and cleaves to one essential insight—when governing is happening or when partisan politics is churning, when all the affairs of public affairs are coming and going, the one thing that is *really* happening are choices about policy."[2] That liberal Democrats might envision the world in these terms should come as no surprise. That the New Right ultimately embraced this perspective suggests a more fundamental shift in social and intellectual perspective.

The breadth and complexity of the "Great Society" as a concept found no better expression than Lyndon Johnson's words at the University of Michigan commencement in May 1964. "Most of all," Johnson cautioned, "the Great Society is not a safe harbor, a resting place, a final objective, a finished work." Rather, it is a "challenge constantly renewed."[3] That its ambitions were boundless, its commitment sincere, and elements of its initial agenda long overdue meant that Great Society programs sometimes identified new problems and shifted their angle of attack as initial challenges proved to be more intractable than anticipated. The Great Society was a work in progress. Its progress elicited demands for more work.

Johnson's words triggered an ambitious agenda. LBJ challenged the Michigan students to "enrich and elevate our national life, and to advance the quality of our American civilization." With imagination, initiative, and indignation, they could move "not only toward the rich society and the powerful society, but upward to the Great Society." Such a society would fulfill man's desire for beauty and his "hunger for community." It would be a place where he could "renew contact with nature." The Great Society would even address loneliness, boredom, and indifference. Schools would prepare students to "enjoy their hours of leisure as well as their hours of labor."[4]

The means to these sweeping ends, however, were unclear. Employing more experts was one solution that Johnson offered to a nation locked into a space race and supposedly on the verge of producing electrical power "too cheap to meter."[5] Expertise was tapped in the social and human sciences, not just in physics and engineering. Johnson told the Michigan students, "We are going to assemble the best thought and the broadest knowledge from all over the world to find . . . answers for America." But the president also cautioned against the very kind of statist intervention that many Progressives sought. As LBJ told the Michigan audience, "The solution to these problems does not rest on a massive program in Washington, nor can it rely solely on the strained resources of local authority." Rather than specifying the means, Johnson instead retreated to the far more politically cautious mechanism of "creative federalism." Of all of the idealistic assumptions built into early conception of a Great Society, the belief that bold ends could be achieved without redistributing income and power nationally was certainly the most optimistic.[6]

Within months of the Michigan speech, Johnson created the first of what ultimately swelled to more than one hundred task forces that would bring the power of expert problem solving to bear on the nation's social problems. LBJ understood the importance of timing. Departing from the inaugural ball that crowned his landslide election over Barry Goldwater, the president put his aides on notice: "Don't stay up late. There's work to be done. We're on our way to the Great Society."[7]

If legislation could make society great, the Johnson team was the one to beat. In the first half of 1965, the president sent sixty-five messages to Congress. James Patterson has labeled the most significant achievements in this unprecedented legislative onslaught the "Big Four": aid to elementary and secondary education, Medicare and Medicaid, immigration reform, and the Voting Rights Act. Even before the "Big Four," Johnson had declared war on poverty, adopting a set of community-based experiments funded by the Ford Foundation as the centerpiece of his Office of Economic Opportunity.[8] By 1966, Johnson delivered on his promise to address Americans' quality of life. He passed legislation addressing clean air and wilderness areas. Congress also created the National Endowment for the Arts and the National Endowment for the Humanities, and it expanded aid to college students.[9]

At its outset, the Great Society was a dynamic, though scattershot, effort to bring the good life to all Americans. But to do so meant addressing the problem of inequality. Those Americans who had been left behind due to poverty or racism had to be brought into the middle class. The Great

Society sought to extend to all Americans the kinds of New Deal programs that had helped to broaden the middle class in the 1940s and 1950s. It started by completing the missing link: federally subsidized health care for elderly Americans with steady work histories. It was compulsory, and it was financed by payroll taxes.[10]

Although social security benefits came to be viewed as an entitlement for those who had steady employment in the core sectors of the economy, the program was built originally on the cultural bedrock of "equal opportunity." By providing for the security of hardworking Americans after retirement, during times of high unemployment, the Social Security Act and its extensions rewarded the work ethic. Over the years the types of work covered slowly expanded outward from the industrial core to include agricultural and other workers who initially had been excluded from benefits. Social security administrators celebrated the date (1951) that the work-related social insurance coverage finally outstripped the hated means-tested old-age assistance.[11]

Yet for millions of Americans, opportunity remained "blocked." The Great Society addressed this neglected constituency, seeking to remove barriers to political and economic opportunity. The most straightforward, and perhaps most successful, legislation was the Voting Rights Act, which brought unprecedented federal enforcement to bear on what traditionally had been localized responsibilities: registration, redistricting, and municipal expansion. Under the banner of community action, the federal government helped to organize poor and dispossessed citizens, urging them to challenge local and state bureaucracies like welfare departments and school boards. Johnson framed his claims for aid to the poor in the rhetoric of self-sufficiency. This was not welfare. Rather, LBJ sought to increase opportunity through training for jobs and through education.[12]

Historically, education had been the great avenue of opportunity in America. But it had failed to achieve this end, particularly in urban areas. Loath to redistribute income directly or to guarantee jobs for poor people, Great Society planners viewed the Elementary and Secondary Education Act (ESEA) as the most promising engine for equalizing opportunity. A powerful equity rationale—the removal of barriers to equal opportunity— lay behind the ESEA. It was the federal government's responsibility to promote social and economic opportunity through education.

Equal access to a good education also raised the federal government's stake in desegregation. With the emergence of Black Power, frustration with the pace of progress, and a wave of riots that swept the nation's cities, programmatic liberals shifted from emphasizing opportunity to insisting upon results. But the initial ESEA legislation provided little federal control as it funneled additional resources to disadvantaged students through state and local school systems. As funding directed toward traditional ends and middle-class constituents increased, the federal government intervened. As a result, the political debate shifted from whether the federal government had an obligation to promote educational opportunity to the effectiveness and unintended consequences of these efforts.[13]

During the 1960s, the federal courts and the Office of Education leap-frogged each other in a race toward southern compliance with school desegregation. Faced with losing what, by the end of the decade, was a major source of revenue, southern systems complied with federal mandates and in many instances achieved levels of integration that far exceeded the North.[14]

While the Great Society was built on an important historical foundation of programs dedicated to the ideal of equal opportunity, the Johnson administration's vision was results-oriented from the start when it came to serving those who already enjoyed "equal opportunity." For middle-class Americans who had long benefited from hefty government subsidies rang-ing from social security to veterans' benefits to the home mortgage deduc-tion, the Great Society promised results where it most mattered: quality of life. In February 1965, the president urged Congress to adopt environmen-tal policies that considered "not just man's welfare, but the dignity of man's spirit."[15] Some of the most assertive new extensions of federal authority occurred in policy areas such as the arts or the environment, in programs that historically had been run by state and local authorities if they existed at all, and in policies that disproportionately advantaged middle-class and wealthy patrons.

By the end of the Johnson years, nine separate task forces had explored a range of policy issues that resulted in hundreds of conservation and beau-tification measures costing $12 billion.[16] Congress weighed in, passing legis-lation like the 1965 Water Quality Act, even though public opinion polls at the time showed that only 17 percent of the American people considered air and water pollution a problem worthy of government attention.[17]

For the poorest quarter of Americans, the Great Society authorized the War on Poverty in order to remove barriers that denied equal opportunity whether the problem was racial discrimination, access to the political system, or unequal education. When these barriers proved to be more intractable than anticipated, those who had already embraced federal public policy as the solution to social and economic problems demanded results, not just "opportunity." Understood as a challenge constantly renewed, the Great Society did not insist on equalizing Americans' incomes or quality of life, but instead sought to improve every American's quality of life.

Cyclical, Linear, and Proximate Historical Influences

Cycles of Reform

New Deal reforms were supported politically by a coalition that retained the Democratic Party's base of support in the "solid South" but captured millions of new adherents among northern African Americans, working-class ethnics, and union members. Frayed from the start at the local level, this coalition proved to be a powerful force at the national level during the Great Society. It even drew millions of newly suburbanized voters into its ranks. The New Deal coalition was able to maintain this balancing act by deferring regularly to local administrative preferences. From welfare to public housing policy, from road building to public power, national enabling legislation was implemented through various brokers who adapted New Deal programs to local preferences.

But as the Great Society nationalized public policy, some of these local arrangements fractured. As African American constituents embraced Black Power, long-standing fissures between this key northern constituency and the Democratic Party's southern base tore the party apart.[18] Nor were the cleavages purely regional. Programs like the Equal Opportunity Act of 1964 were designed to take political advantage of millions of African Americans who had moved north, but these programs also fueled fires already smoldering at the local level. Figurative fires were soon replaced by real ones, as race riots swept through virtually every major American city by the end of the 1960s, illuminating even more starkly the firewall that now stood between segments of the New Deal coalition.

Cycles of social reform in twentieth-century America were also limited by war. The Great Society's ambitious program ended in the Vietnam War, just as World Wars I and II brought the Progressive and New Deal reform eras to a close. Carey McWilliams summed up this insight, observing that "foreign policy is to a Great Society like a third party on a romantic date, a disruption of the mood, prose muddling poetry."[19] While a number of scholars have demonstrated that war has often contributed to significant social reform—the emergence of the modern civil rights movement and the capacious package of veterans' benefits after World War II being just two examples—there is little doubt that some of the principals, especially Lyndon Johnson himself, worried that war would kill the Great Society.[20]

Enduring Legacies

Most of the connections between the Great Society and the past, however, simply defy the "cycles of reform" framework. Indeed, there was a powerful strain within the Great Society that resonated deeply with some of America's longest-standing legacies. The quest for growth and mastery was one. While America's intervention in Vietnam came to symbolize the apotheosis of military, technological, and ideological optimism (if not hubris), it was just one of many examples, such as the space program, that sought to conquer the boundaries of time, place, and material restraints. Johnson was a nationalist and, like all the American presidents who came before him, was committed to the goal of "mastery, abundance and command over nature."[21] Like most Americans in the mid-1960s, Johnson believed that America could not fail—in Vietnam, or in its quest to build a Great Society. While it is easy to criticize this arrogance of power in the wake of the Vietnam disaster, the noble dream embodied in the Great Society would not have been possible without that kind of chutzpah.[22] Nor was it uncharacteristic for Americans to believe that the remaining barriers to social and economic obstacles could be overcome, given the exceptional advantages in the political system, resources, and technical ingenuity that America enjoyed.

Regrettably, the history of exclusion and bias toward women and minorities is another legacy that stretches back just as far in American history and is inextricably linked to the quest for growth and mastery. Moreover, the role of the state in enforcing these racist and sexist norms has been even more prominent than its support for expansion and technical mastery.[23] A committed handful of racial activists and a far larger number of anonymous citizens battled racial discrimination throughout the century. It was courageous work among "local people" that set the stage for the legal breakthroughs of the 1960s. Liberal leaders, however, had not been as willing to take political risks as their supporters at the grass roots. Stepping out of the shadows of the New Deal, the Great Society explicitly acknowledged America's racist history, addressing the problem directly in the Civil Rights Act of 1964, the Voting Rights Act of 1965, and the aggressive interpretation and enforcement of both.[24]

When "equal opportunity" alone failed to erase hundreds of years of racial discrimination, Great Society programs did not shy away from emphasizing results in their administrative interpretation of legislative mandates, despite the long-standing history of liberal emphasis on equal individual rights. Doing so required that certain groups be designated as "official minorities." But, as Hugh Graham noted, "A major barrier to designating official minorities in post–World War II America was the liberal political tradition itself, which emphasized equal individual rights, not group rights, and protected them through the negative action of antidiscrimination."[25] Thus, advocates of results-based Great Society programs had to reconstruct liberalism before they could mobilize it effectively to end racial discrimination.[26]

The Great Society had less to say about the long-standing tradition of sexism. Sex distinctions remained acceptable among liberals in the mid-1960s. Nevertheless, Great Society programs did begin to incorporate a subtle shift in attitude toward women and work that was reflected in training programs as early as the mid-1950s. These programs stressed the role that training and education might play in preparing women on welfare for the workforce. By 1962, federal welfare directed toward women began to build work-related income incentives into the program, and in 1967, the Work Incentive Program was initiated, allowing states to end assistance to parents (of older children) if the adults refused to work or accept training. This transition paved the way for treating women and men alike—at least when it came to the relationship between work and welfare.[27] Given the system's expectation that women would continue to care for children while they worked, the biting criticism of the welfare rights activist Johnnie Tillmon hit home. She compared welfare to a "supersexist marriage. You trade in *a* man for *the* man."[28]

The Great Society was part of another linear trend in the twentieth century—the growth of the administrative presidency.[29] This trend, which dates back to the Progressive Era and gained momentum during the New Deal, divorced the presidency more and more from party and congressional control. Like many of his predecessors, Johnson sought alternative bases of support. Johnson established one such beachhead in the Community Action Program, which enabled the president to reach grass-roots constituents by going around ossified local institutions and more traditional levers of power.[30] Indeed, the Great Society pushed the administrative presidency to the breaking point. When push came to shove—whether in the form of urban riots, increasingly radical demands from newly empowered constituents, or opposition to the Vietnam War—Johnson's extension of the administrative presidency left him insulated, if not isolated, from his party and large segments of Congress.[31] For the previous thirty-five years, strengthening the presidency had reinforced its stature. For the first time since Roosevelt's ill-advised court-packing scheme, a majority of Americans began to question the legitimacy of the administrative presidency.[32]

The Cold War Influence on the Great Society

Both the ubiquitous, cyclical interpretations of reform and those grounded in persistent patterns like the quest for mastery or racism have crowded out a more proximate, and the most significant, historical influence upon the Great Society: the Cold War. The post–World War II growth of the administrative presidency, for instance, had been nurtured and in large part underwritten by the Cold War, which encouraged Americans to defer to insulated, distant institutions, especially the federal government. Experts had been glamorized by their crucial role in developing the atomic bomb, radar, and other scientific triumphs that helped win World War II, and they enjoyed unprecedented authority and status by the early 1960s. Some of the luster of the physical sciences had even rubbed off on the social sciences. Many of the programs that emerged as part of the Great Society were the product of ideas supplied by well-meaning professionals, not responses to popular demand.

This merger of professional and administrative capacity, which I have labeled the prominent administrative state, reached the height of its influence during the early years of the Great Society. Ironically, at the very time that Americans were looking more and more to government and to experts to solve an ever-growing list of problems, they also began to question the ability of those experts to deliver public policy that worked. By the end of the decade, and in part as a result of failed policies in Vietnam, the American faith in even science and technology had been shaken.[33]

Yet for fifteen years, from roughly 1950 through 1965, Americans granted experts unprecedented discretion, especially in the area of national security. Few questioned the safety or economic viability of the government's role in subsidizing a nuclear power industry that promised cheap electricity at the same time it strengthened the nation's defense. Environmental considerations, civilian health and safety, and local zoning traditions were trampled in order to accommodate the needs of the nation's university-military-industrial complex.[34]

The prominiistrative state, responding to the pressures of the Cold War, led the national government in the 1950s to undertake major new initiatives, such as the interstate highway system and the St. Lawrence Seaway. The Cold War, as Mary Dudziak has argued, added a new rationale for improving race relations, as racial oppression in the United States was a heavy burden in the nation's competition with the Soviet Union for the hearts and minds of the so-called third world. It also provided a new rationale for deficit spending, as the National Security Council called for permanent mobilization to counter the Soviet threat even though it would create a deficit situation. It was the National Defense Education Act of 1958, passed in the wake of Sputnik to provide federal assistance to states to improve science, math, and language instruction, that laid the groundwork for the explosion of categorical grant programs for domestic social programs that made up so much of the Great Society and ushered in a new era of federalism. This path of social reform was far from cyclical, nor did it owe its legacy to the New Deal, as the Johnson White House relied on critical resources and precedents created during the height of the Cold War—most significantly deficit spending—oftentimes simply taking them for granted.[35]

The Cold War also had a dramatic impact on liberalism. For all of Johnson's self-reflective comparisons to Franklin Roosevelt's administration, it was Cold War liberalism that informed his thinking as he sought to sustain both guns and butter. The gritty insider politics of the Truman and Eisenhower presidencies and Johnson's tenure as Majority Leader were more proximate influences on Johnson's career as president. It was Cold War liberalism that dominated ideological debate on both sides of the partisan aisle in the early 1960s.[36]

The liberalism that built the New Deal, Heclo has argued, was constructed upon a foundation of disinterestedness. Embodied in Walter Lippmann's 1929 call for an educated public that could employ a mature and self-controlled outlook to process objective information, disinterestedness lay at the heart of public-spirited Progressivism.[37] Heclo contrasts this ideal to the new realism embedded in the outlook of Cold War liberals like Arthur Schlesinger Jr. "Coolness," the characteristic most associated with John F. Kennedy's attitude toward public policy, was now the norm. This "realistic and hard-edged cast" continued to offer a positive view of the federal government's ability to carry out reform.[38] But in the wake of Nazi Germany, World War II, and the use of atomic weapons, mankind had to be regarded as flawed and corruptible. The positive attitude toward government was thus combined in Cold War liberalism with a negative view of humanity's behavior. This incubator for "big policy" grew out of Cold War, not New Deal liberalism, and provided the impetus for a "New Liberalism" that emerged during the Great Society.

What Was Distinctive About the Great Society?

Sensitivity to the historical context from which the Great Society grew should not obscure the social and political transformation that occurred between 1964 and the end of the decade. We cannot understand this transformation, however, if our analysis is confined to the White House or even to the formal political and policy-making arenas. Instead, we need to consider profound changes in American political culture and social relations in the mid-1960s. Politicians and policy makers adapted to and, in some instances, guided this rapidly changing environment.

Social Movements

Social movements transformed liberal ideology and the Cold War pluralist system. The civil rights movement fashioned a template for mobilizing hundreds of thousands of committed citizens around a concrete set of programmatic objectives and publicizing this agenda to millions of sympathetic supporters. This model was soon adopted by students protesting restrictions on free speech and, eventually, by millions more who challenged the administration's policies in Vietnam. Public interest groups, epitomized by Ralph Nader's crusade on behalf of consumers, proliferated during the second half of the decade, carrying finely tuned policy pronouncements deep into the inner sanctums of all three branches of government.

Social movements, as well as the networks of issue-related public interest groups they spawned, cared not only about the substance of policy problems, but also, and sometimes more intensely, about the process by which citizens engaged public policy in a modern democratic republic. Although the solution crafted by New Left theoreticians—participatory democracy—failed in practice, the overwhelming demand for transparency left its mark on the process of governance.[39] An acute sense of "rights consciousness" powered many of the demands advanced by social movements, issue networks, and plaintiffs who filed class action suits. From initial demands targeted at destroying the Jim Crow regime in the South to the right to a minimum income, clean air and water, or special education, the language of entitlement expanded as the decade progressed.

The civil rights movement led the way in this regard. It demonstrated the transformative power of organized protest and also exposed the relatively fragile condition of political institutions that had for so long upheld the prerogatives of Jim Crow segregation.[40] The New Left, another seminal social movement that animated student protest against the war during the 1960s, was deeply influenced by the triumphs of the civil rights movement. A sense of hope and possibility—even a utopian spirit at times—pervaded the New Left in its early years.[41] The civil rights movement also provided the "how-to" guide for would-be organizers, as activists from civil rights moved on to the New Left, feminist, and even the environmental movements. The lessons went well beyond personal experience. In a society that increasingly turned to the electronic media for its news—first television, then the World Wide Web—the power of the video image was a lesson that activists soon mastered. Nonviolent resistance, marches on Washington, confrontations with reactionary opponents—all of these were tactics adopted from the civil rights movement and used again and again by other groups demanding a hearing for their issues.[42]

Linking virtually all of these movements was a radical reconceptualization of the boundary between public and private. Again, the civil rights movement led the way. It trained its tactical guns on activities previously considered "private": lunch counters, transportation, employment, recreation, and even religious observance. It exposed the public power behind the seemingly private sets of decisions that excluded citizens based on race in all of these areas. The landmark civil rights legislation of 1964 and 1965 was "radical," to use Hugh Graham's adjective, because it embraced "the permanently expanded federal authority with effective enforcement power over vast areas of behaviour previously free of national coercion, including private as well as public employment; customer choice in stores, hotels, restaurants, and places of amusement; and voting procedures."[43] It mobilized a political, rather than a personal, response to these affronts to African American rights and dignity, and it demanded public solutions. Armed with the mantra that "the personal is the political," students at elite college campuses began to see connections between the courses they were required to take and the federally subsidized military-industrial-university complex; women noticed the discrepancy between male and female wages; and environmentalists glimpsed the relationship between personal health and protective regulation. Once engaged, issues previously considered inappropriate for public action emerged as a crucial source of new policy agendas.

Social pressure from the grass roots was instrumental in breaking the legislative logjam. The 1964 Civil Rights Act and the 1965 Voting Rights Act created templates that ultimately served the needs of many other groups. Famously, Title VII of the Civil Rights Act, originally drafted with racial discrimination in mind, was redirected toward sexual discrimination in the workplace.[44] The Voting Rights Act was expanded to a broad range of minorities.[45]

Indeed, the relationship between the Great Society and the emergence of feminism illustrates the enduring relationship between social movements and the policy legacy of the civil rights movement. Women's issues were ignored by most Great Society planners. Despite the valuable work of the network of professional women who eventually formed the National Organization of Women, the organization they created focused on relatively narrow issues of employment discrimination and electing women to office. As late as the mid-1960s, the lives of most women were circumscribed both within the family and in the workplace. It took grass-roots activism and mass mobilization of women to bring changes in society that led to greater equality for women.[46] Only after the emergence of feminism, with the broad-based pressure it was able to exert on the political system and in the private sector, were women able to use legislation and administrative procedures initially crafted to secure the rights of African Americans to protect the rights of their sisters. The breakthrough for women required redrawing the boundary between public and private to place issues previously considered personal or private on the state's agenda and to pursue "liberation" in places previously considered "private." "The vast majority of the newly minted feminists across the country," Linda Gordon has observed, "did not belong to any organization. Participation in the move-ment was as much private and domestic as public, it was a new way of challenging the boss, a new way of understanding daily interactions. You were in the women's movement if you thought you were."[47] Women, just as millions of African Americans had when they embraced Black Power, addressed the political culture. The movement radically reoriented wom-en's views about power. By embracing identities as African Americans, women, or both, activists exposed sources of repression, whether private or public, and sought to redress the balance of power in all of their relation-ships. They demonstrated that so-called private matters, whether in the home or at work, were in fact public concerns and that public conscious-ness could reshape "private" relationships.

Big Policy, Little Trust

Cumulatively, these powerful thrusts from the grass roots upward democra-tized the political culture of the mid-1960s. As Heclo put it, the "overbelief," virtually a theology, of the 1960s was "a vision of the people redeeming a flawed society, if you will, democracy in a modern passion play."[48] Distrust of government and faith in public policy were not sequential. Rather, there was a "singularity" to this symbiotic relationship as Heclo describes it, and public trust in government plummeted between 1965 and 1975.[49] Clearly, Vietnam and Watergate were contributing factors, but mistrust of govern-ment went well beyond these seminal events. It became embedded in the very relations between students and teachers, doctors and patients, elected officials and constituents. Significantly, trust in government declined at a faster pace among liberals than conservatives. By the 1970s, nothing seemed to alarm liberal consumer advocate Ralph Nader more than the prospect of actually sharing power with the "establishment."[50]

At the same time, liberals embraced "big policy" and turned to the federal government for it. The explosion of new policy demands from dem-ocratically inspired social movements called for more government, not less. Liberation—whether black, Hispanic, gay, or female—invariably required an active state. Even Lyndon Johnson was caught up in the rhetoric of liberation that permeated the political culture. It resonated with his popu-list roots. Johnson's Great Society speech at the University of Michigan echoed language of the Port Huron Statement drafted not far from there in 1962.[51] As late as 1966, Johnson's State of the Union address called for "liberation," which would use the nation's economic success for the "fulfillment" of our lives.[52] Still, liberals retained a suspicion of government authority. Even the new administrative structures created by social pressure—the Equal Employment Opportunities Commission (EEOC), the Office of Economic Opportunity (OEO), the Environmental Protection Agency (EPA)—were themselves objects of suspicion and constant vigilance by the grass roots.

Ambivalent activists quickly embraced a discourse that had become more pervasive in post–World War II liberalism—the language of individual rights.[53] While the roots of nineteenth-century liberalism lay in protecting the integrity and rights of the individual, the "Rights Revolution" or "Rights Talk" that had exploded by the end of the 1960s differed from classical liberalism in its demand that the public sector, especially the national government, actively enforce a broad range of rights and fund a generous array of direct government services in order to uphold these rights.[54] The New Deal laid the groundwork for this, but the range of rights pursued before the Great Society was limited.

Advocates of the vastly expanded rights agenda also stressed procedural rights, which reflected their ambivalent attitude toward a government that was asked to do more yet was not fully trusted by the very interests demanding its expansion. Policy got "bigger," while the bureaucratic discretion required to implement expanded policy was circumscribed, in order to ensure the right of equal access to all. Robert Kagan has labeled as "adversarial legalism" the juxtaposition of demands that an activist government protect individuals from serious harm, injustice, and environmental dangers on the one hand, and the heightened fear of concentrated power and demands for access on the other hand.[55]

Rights-based liberalism ultimately overwhelmed and constrained the administrative structure, especially the capacious conception of the presidency, founded during the New Deal. It opened the New Deal's entrenched administrative structures to attack from both the left and the right.[56] In education, for instance, the theme of "equal opportunity" was superseded in the 1970s by a rationale that emphasized entitlements and protecting rights.[57] Along the fractious boundary between work and welfare, the National Welfare Rights Organization broke with the Great Society's early emphasis on equal opportunity, demanding a guaranteed income as one of the rights of citizenship.[58] It was Richard Nixon, not Lyndon Johnson, who translated these demands into public policy, proposing legislation that would have ensured just such an entitlement. The quest for civil rights evolved from an equal opportunity rationale to one that featured "hard" affirmative action and equal results. Once again, it was Richard Nixon, through the Philadelphia Plan, who enshrined this rights-driven program.[59]

Lowering the Legitimacy Barrier

A conception developed by the political scientist James Q. Wilson, the legitimacy barrier, operated to constrain the scope of public policy, identifying certain options—such as state-owned businesses, for instance—as illegitimate, except, perhaps, during times of crisis. In many instances, the legitimacy barrier was breached when the national government moved into policy areas traditionally handled at the state and local levels—such as civil rights enforcement and voter registration. Once lowered, Wilson argues, "no program is any longer 'new'—it is seen, rather, as an extension, a modification, or an enlargement of something the government is already doing."[60] The new wave of social regulation introduced in the 1970s is another important example of the legitimacy barrier being breached. "In the past going back ten or fifteen years," Bernard Falk of the National Electrical Manufacturers Association complained, "you didn't have a consumer movement. The manufacturer controlled the make-up of his own product, and Washington could be ignored. Now we all have a new partner, the federal government."[61]

Starting with Johnson's expansive goals, which ranged from combating boredom to the search for beauty, Great Society policies propelled the national government into a variety of new policy areas.[62] Each new breach in the legitimacy barrier was significant in its own right. But the most important consequence, one that Shep Melnick has called the "most profound legacy of the Great Society," was cumulative.[63] During the 1970s, the federal government's expansion was routinized. It no longer took a presidential assassination or powerful social movements to recalibrate the legitimacy barrier.

The Great Society gave birth to a new set of institutional patterns that privileged big policy and garnered support from conservatives as well as liberals. The implications of this shift are evident today. As President George W. Bush sought to fulfill traditional conservative pledges to rein in "big government" by reducing domestic spending and federal regulation, he faced opposition from some of his supporters, concerned that programs that their states have come to rely on would be targeted. As the *Washington Post* reported on January 26, 2003, "Two of the Senate's most conservative Republicans, Sens. John E. Sununu and Judd Gregg of New Hampshire, supported an amendment aimed at having the federal government play a more active role in protecting New England from Midwest air pollution."[64] Conservatives could play the "big policy" game too.

The Therapeutic Ethos

Where did such demands come from in the first place? Perhaps the most distinctive source of new demands during the Great Society grew out of a phenomenon broadly referred to as the "therapeutic ethos." At the core of this worldview lay the notion that virtually any problem could be solved, even problems previously defined as "personal" or "emotional." If the personal really was the political, then public policy might well hold the key to satisfaction and fulfillment. The ever-expanding list of problems, concerns, and rights to be protected by government was easier to sustain during a time of economic prosperity and rising federal revenues, which made it appear that the government could afford to meet these demands without redistributing income or power. The range of remedies for society's problems offered in the name of therapeutic progress—and the broad public acceptance of this legitimacy—helps explain why public obligations ballooned during the Great Society, ranging from the expansion of mental health and education programs to "identity-based" programs such as affirmative action.[65]

Society was seen as a sick patient in need of therapy that public policy experts can supply. Contrasting therapeutic and socialist perspectives, Heclo wrote that "socialists had thought the great change in political society would come from collectivizing the means of production. What actually turned out to be the leverage point was collectivizing fault. The source of disorders troubling the people was not any class, section, or individual ethical failings, but society itself. Policy became modern democracy's answer to socialism, communism and every other ism claiming a master plan for society's future."[66]

In "The Triumph of Group Therapeutics," Peter Sheehy elucidated the key to understanding why the New Left embraced the therapeutic ethos, breaking with the Old Left's disdain for such considerations. The origins of the therapeutic ethos were individualistic and hierarchical, drawn directly from Freud's conception of the doctor-patient relationship. Sheehy, however, historicizes the rise of the therapeutic, documenting the growing emphasis among social scientists on environmental influences on the individual and the power of the group to incorporate individuals into society. This portrait of the therapeutic ethos that permeated society by the 1960s is one that supported and in some instances even served as a catalyst for collective action. Self-realization, in a collective setting, proved to be a fruitful catalyst for exploring the possibility that the personal and the political were integrally connected.[67]

The therapeutic ethos influenced the way that Americans conceived of politics. The "environmental turn" in the therapeutic ethos shifted the emphasis in therapy away from its exclusive focus on the individual and focused it instead on the relationship of the individual to his or her environment. It also relied on group relations—not just the hierarchical analyst-patient relationship—to empower individuals. The changing nature of therapeutic theory and practice explains why techniques like "consciousness raising" proved to be effective politically. The women's liberation movement placed private life at the center of its concerns, recognizing that subordination in the private realm could not be separated from subordination in the public realm.[68] A hybrid of some of the organizing techniques that grew out of the civil rights movement and group therapy, consciousness raising was particularly effective at excavating discontents that previously had been submerged and at framing these discontents in a broader political context. Just as the evolution of therapeutic practice had broken down the older Freudian hierarchy between analyst and patient, consciousness raising abolished the distinction between political organizer and organized, reinforcing the democratic nature of this movement and connecting it to the New Left through its embrace of participatory democracy.[69] Linking the personal and the political corroded the legitimacy barrier, generating many of the demands that fueled "big policy" in the last third of the twentieth century. Public policy was now the key to protecting not only individual life and property, but also an individual's well-being.

New Venues

Policy advocates turned to new venues in order to press their claims. As with so many features of the Great Society policy-making system, the quest for civil rights led the way. Graham summed up the explosive potential of

the Civil Rights Act of 1964 and the Voting Rights Act of 1965: "The radi-
calism of these measures lay not in their command against harmful discrimination. . . . Such nondiscrimination policy had characterized liberal
reform proposals and measures since the Reconstruction era." Rather, new
laws were radical because they extended federal authority into venues previously untouched by the national government.[70] Local and state prerogatives were the most significant among these.

Facing restraints and the outright opposition of Richard Nixon in his
second term, liberal policy advocates replaced the New Deal–inspired tax-
and-spend formula with a more intricate, but equally effective "mandate-
and-sue" strategy. Building on a power base that now lay in congressional
subcommittees, the lower federal courts, and a cadre of permanent federal
civil servants, liberal reformers expanded policy from bases that lay outside
the White House. There were fewer "big bang" legislative initiatives, but
far more incremental growth through new interpretations of existing laws.
There were fewer novel constitutional arguments in the Supreme Court
and more "creative" statutory interpretations at the district court level.[71]
Advocates of big policy worked across all three branches of government. A
federal district court judge, for instance, ordered the EPA to implement a
rural air-quality program. The court's decision rested on a few fragments of
legislative history, but this was sufficient to trigger an elaborate regulatory
program. Once ordered by the Court, Congress expanded the program still
further.

As Gary Orfield's classic study of southern school desegregation
recounts, this administrative-judicial pattern of leapfrogging was established even while a liberal Democrat was president. Here, a landmark legislative act—the ESEA—got the ball rolling. But progress on desegregation
only followed after civil rights advocates in the Justice Department used a
combination of district court decisions and threats to cut off funding under
Title VII of the Civil Rights Act to pressure both the federal Office of Education and local school districts to desegregate.[72]

By the late 1960s, the strategy of mandate-and-sue featured three venues
that emerged as crucial forums for crafting public policy: intergovernmental relations, congressional oversight, and the federal judiciary. Martha Derthick has chronicled the radical shift in the nature of federalism during the
1960s.[73] The scale and scope of federal grants-in-aid increased significantly.
Initially, many of these grants were administered in the age-old tradition of
local discretion. But as federal funding increased, and the demand for

results intensified, federal administrative agencies grew more assertive. The federal Office of Education had a long history of supporting states through statistics and advisory notices. As funding grew through the ESEA's categorical grants, the Office of Education moved from a supporting role to far more active supervision and oversight.[74] But at least these mandates *were* funded. This was not the case in another program overseen by the Office of Education: special education. Established by an amendment to the ESEA in 1966, special education grew by leaps and bounds. So too did the number of children served under it. Although total public school enrollment had declined between 1968 and 1986, the number of children served by special education almost doubled.[75]

Improving environmental quality proved to be another classic case of unfunded federal mandates. Established in 1970, the EPA was originally envisioned as an agency that would work in concert with the states. Indeed, pollution control had been a traditional responsibility of state and local government. But seven days after taking office, William Ruckelshaus, EPA's administrator, announced that Atlanta, Cleveland, and Detroit would have just 180 days to comply with water-pollution laws. Matters only grew more heated in the early 1970s when the EPA sought to enforce the Clean Air and Clean Water Acts. "This oversight," Ruckelshaus later reflected, "created a very, very difficult period between the EPA and the states. The states thought we dictated too much, were too intrusive."[76]

Eager to press ahead with big policy, yet wary of granting the administrative discretion required to fulfill demanding policy promises, Congress micromanaged programs through detailed statutory provisions and intensive oversight. In an era of divided government, if such detailed provisions could not compel executive compliance they at least could be used to pillory executive incompetence should administrative agencies fall short of these demanding mandates. Congressional hearings became an important venue for articulating still-new demands and exposing executive or local foot-dragging. Increasingly shut out of the executive branch, liberal policy advocates often sought to expand public policy by exposing government failures.[77]

Perhaps the most distinctive new arena for making public policy was the federal judiciary. The Warren Court produced a series of landmark cases that invited or mandated assertive new public policies. Some, like *Reynolds v. Syms*, which proclaimed the "one person, one vote" principle, or *Harper v. Virginia Board of Education*, which eliminated the poll tax,

imposed federal standards on long-standing local prerogatives. Others, like
Green v. New Kent County, which ordered busing to desegregate schools,
and *Goldberg v. Kelly*, which ensured the right of welfare clients to a "fair
hearing," propelled the Court into arenas that would soon require elaborate
policy decisions on the part of the Court. Decisions that required complex
policy solutions were often made with the assistance of court-appointed
masters.[78]

While federalism, fine-grained congressional management, and an
activist judiciary served as beachheads for expanding the range of public
policy, they would not have been effective without the dense networks of
activists that circulated through them and that connected bureaucrats to
social movements, judges to grass-roots citizens' groups. The judiciary
loomed as a formidable policy player in part due to the revolution in standing for plaintiffs that swept the courts by the 1970s. As Melnick notes, the
Great Society created new centers of policy advocacy both inside and outside of the government.[79] Thus civil rights agencies, from the EEOC to the
civil rights division of the Justice Department, worked hand in hand with
advocacy groups like the Legal Defense Fund of the National Association
for the Advancement of Colored People or the National Organization of
Women. It was through these more staid, button-down iterations of the
civil rights movement that the courage and energy that inspired a mass
movement continued to shape public policy.

As already noted, advocates of big policy during this era were wary
of empowering the instruments needed to carry out big policy. The most
important mechanism for ensuring democratic accountability was the "citizen suit," which one environmentalist described as "a means of access for
ordinary citizens to the process of governmental decisionmaking" and "a
repudiation of our traditional reliance upon professional bureaucrats."[80]
While these suits sometimes allowed individuals to enter the policy-making
arena, the increased use of citizens' suits more often provided entrée to
organized advocacy groups, such as the Natural Resources Defense League
in the case of the environment.

As the number of venues available for making public policy multiplied
during the 1960s, the opportunity for state-created advocacy groups multiplied as well. Hybrid creations of the new era in intergovernmental relations, like the Community Action Program or the Model Cities program,
actively recruited advocates for the poor and helped organize pressure
groups to represent them. The voluntary sector also played a crucial role in

shaping advocacy groups. The Ford Foundation sponsored initiatives that led to the creation of Mobilization for Youth, the Mexican American Legal Defense and Education Fund, and the National Resources Defense Council.[81]

With the explosion of policy demands, techniques long used by the federal government in defense policy, arguably the training grounds for "big policy" during the Cold War, were applied to new fields. After plans to have the Department of Defense run job-training centers fell through, the OEO turned to a practice that was actually more familiar to those in the Pentagon: contracted services. The provider, in this instance was RCA, which had vast experience in the defense field and was hired for its expertise in systems management. Programs that addressed environmental quality also adopted systems analysis, a technique originally engineered by the military. Under the guidance of political scientist Arthur "Muddy Waters" Maass, the Harvard Water Program developed "multi-objective planning." As Paul Milazzo revealed, such techniques reoriented the practices of even such inveterate dam builders as the Army Corps of Engineers. By the mid-1960s, the Corps had begun to develop alternative water-use policies that factored in water quality—not because this bureaucracy had turned "green" but because water quality was essential to water supply for economic development in the drought-stricken East.[82]

Thus, the Great Society reforms extended public policy into venues previously considered "private" or voluntary, linking interests to policy making in new ways and expanding the methods of administration. Areas previously free of federal authority succumbed to federal "coercion" during the Great Society, but that was only part of the story. The list included private as well as public agencies and encompassed stores, hotels, restaurants, and places of amusement.[83] In education, the key to passing the ESEA was a compromise device that targeted federal aid at students rather than schools, thus broaching the divide between public, parochial, and private schools.[84]

Making Pluralism "Great"

Business and professional groups forged the parameters of twentieth-century interest-group pluralism.[85] When the economic crisis of the 1930s offered the possibility of social democratic alternatives to the prevailing political structure, labor also came to embrace pluralism. With its acceptance of the Wagner Act's collective bargaining provisions in 1935, labor pushed pluralism toward a far more capacious framework than the one dominated primarily by well-organized businesses, trade associations, and the professions. While many working people were shut out of trade union pluralism, interest-group bargaining during the New Deal and the following decades secured a broad range of benefits for those workers who *were* represented by powerful unions. No wonder economists and political scientists by the 1950s treated organized labor as an interest group: Labor was a powerful interest deeply invested in maintaining the pluralist system, and its inclusion in pluralism was the definitive development in the policy-making system since the mid-1930s.[86]

Cold War Pluralism

The Cold War constrained pluralism as it hardened the boundaries between those insiders safely welded to iron triangles and constituencies excluded from these policy-making communities. It is no accident that terms such as "iron triangles" gained popularity in describing the reinforced, insulated subsystems that parceled out power and guarded access to crucial public policy decisions. Established interest groups coveted their access to congressional subcommittees and administrative bureaus. Public officials returned the favor, carefully nurturing well-organized interests. The resulting policy-making structure was indeed insular; it was best suited to deal with limited issues. It was designed to preserve stability.[87] Once inside, bargaining and negotiation were the qualities that participants valued most. New recruits, like labor, had to be reminded of this sometimes, but as long as the economy and tax revenues grew, negotiation yielded outcomes acceptable to everybody included in the game. During the Cold War era, pluralism hunkered down, seeking to win the twilight struggle with formidable foes, emerging as a "fighting faith," in order to vanquish totalitarian alternatives.[88]

By parceling decision making out to dozens of iron triangles, the national policy-making structure was geared to contain conflict over issues as divergent as race relations and tax reform. "Protected by their pressure group, served by their governmental agency, assuaged by their friendly congressmen," Louis Galambos writes, "they were satisfied with triocracy. They were not going to be foot soldiers in a battle to eliminate privilege for others—and certainly not for themselves."[89]

"Big Policy's" roots were firmly grounded in the Cold War system of pluralism, "with its shrewd, utilitarian acceptance of selfish interests." It was a focus of the new realism, Heclo writes. "With policy came programs that could be designed to use those competing interests for public ends. Thus the philosophy of liberal realism shaded into programmatic liberalism and the burst of government initiatives in the Great Society era."[90] If the New Deal cast a shadow on Johnson's Great Society, Cold War liberalism illuminated many of the paths that the Great Society would forge.

Key policy makers during the Great Society era, from Lyndon Johnson to Earl Warren, rose to power, of course, by mastering the Cold War pluralist system. No wonder LBJ was appalled by the unwieldy politics of "the street" despite his intense desire to make society great for all Americans. Johnson, who was persuasive in small groups and one-to-one encounters, never mastered mass politics.[91] The cloakroom, the subcommittee, and, when pressed, the Senate floor were the forums in which Johnson rose to power. In his preference for insulated politics, Johnson was very much a product of his political culture, a practitioner of the "suprapartisan politics," as Byron Hulsey has called it, that was practiced by the Washington establishment during the Cold War in a fashion that "celebrated pragmatic compromise and ridiculed ideological obstinacy."[92]

Democratic Pluralism: Lift Every Voice

Yet this Cold War system proved vulnerable on the very front that its advocates claimed to revere: democratic participation. As E. E. Schattschneider noted half a century ago, "The flaw in the pluralist heaven is that the heavenly chorus sings with a strong upper-class accent."[93] For influential scholars of the mid-1960s like Theodore Lowi, interest groups were, at best, necessary evils and the notion that the problems pluralism might encounter were self-correcting, a joke. Among political scientists, pluralism bashing became a growth industry.[94]

The treatment of African Americans was the most visible reminder of pluralism's elitist repertoire. Beginning with their efforts to convert the courage and energy of grass-roots activists into social reform, Great Society programs revolutionized access to the policy-making system.[95] The Great Society reached out to some of pluralism's severest critics: African Americans abused by what for them was only the latest system of oppression as well as a broad range of Americans who insisted that "beauty and health" were legitimate objects of national public policy.[96] These Americans took matters into their own hands, massing in unruly and sometimes fractious movements that ebbed and flowed with the latest insult to their members' status as full participants in the exclusive pluralist chorus. The Great Society took these demands seriously, converted some into effective policies, and raised the hopes of millions that other objectives might soon be realized—that they might encompass the hopes of *all* Americans, not just a privileged few.

Lyndon Johnson embraced reforms that democratized Cold War pluralism and made the public policy process accessible to millions of citizens for the first time. Whether the Supreme Court's willingness to grant class action status, the Community Action Program's "maximum feasible participation," or the Medicaid program that opened a world of federally funded benefits to those without steady work records, public policies that shaped the Great Society expanded the scope of debate.[97]

Momentarily lost in the shuffle, however, was the bitterness expressed by more conservative business and even some Cold War liberal interest groups, forced to share the pluralist stage with insurgents and activists who would have been considered intruders just a few years ago. At the same time, critics on the left scorned the now-enlarged pluralist system for its tendency to retreat from or, more often, to fail to identify the moral high ground. No sooner had some interests, excluded for centuries, stepped through the conference room door than they were charged with selling, or "copping," out.[98]

Even as pluralism expanded access to groups previously excluded from the political system, prominstrators retained a partial grasp on their privileged perch. They played a particularly crucial role in narrowing broad-gauged demands for reform into policy packages that might fit the pluralist mold. While high profile advisory bodies like President Truman's Committee on Civil Rights put the issue of racial discrimination on the policy making agenda, it was the actions of obscure government officials who first asked employers to report the number of "negro" and "other minority" employees who mattered most.[99]

This development was noted by other racial and ethnic groups, who lobbied members of Congress to pressure responsible administrators for them to be included by name. Responding to the League of United Latin American Citizens and the Mexican-American Political Action Committee,

Henry Gonzales (D-TX) succeeded in 1962 in having "Spanish-Americans" included as a specific category on Standard Form 40. In turn, the Japanese American Citizens League, with the support of Senator Hiram L. Fong and Representative Daniel K. Inouye of Hawaii, won the addition of "Orientals" as a required category on Form 40. It was through the system of iron triangles that epitomized the way Cold War pluralism worked that agreements were hammered out behind the scenes with little public debate and even less publicity.[100]

The number of "insiders" and the style that they brought to pluralism were changing as was intended in landmark legislation vesting new groups with a stake in the system. The Civil Rights Act of 1964 was one of the pillars of Johnson's Great Society Program. It established the EEOC, which, among other responsibilities, was charged with contract compliance. This was a high-profile, and highly publicized, body that by 1965 operated at the epicenter of one of the most highly contested issues in post–World War II history. Martin Luther King, Malcolm X, and the Student Nonviolent Coordinating Committee (SNCC), representing three strains of a powerful social movement, were at the height of their influence. Yet the decision about which groups to include on the EEO-1 form that replaced Standard Form 40 for contract compliance purposes suffered from bureaucratic inertia: The groups that employers now had to count were Negroes, Spanish-Americans, Orientals, American Indians, and Whites.

When the Philadelphia Plan propelled the government into "hard" affirmative action a few years later, it had at its disposal a list of four official minorities. Yet, as Graham notes, "there is no record of civil rights leaders addressing the issue of which groups to include on the EEO-1 form, no hearings or record of discussion by the presidents' contract compliance committees or by the EEOC." Instead, the initiative "came from appointed federal officials and served their immediate political needs."[101] Even at the height of the Great Society's quest for participatory politics, in a highly contested policy area thrust on the nation's agenda by the century's most powerful social movement, crucial decisions were still hammered out in a manner that military contractors, dam builders, or the United Auto Workers and their congressional and prominative partners would be quite comfortable with.

The Great Society was an era of big policy: It both identified new problems and insisted that there were policy solutions to these problems. Before society could be "great," however, it had to be more egalitarian. Racial inequality was the most glaring discrepancy, and in the eyes of most Great Society advocates, little could be accomplished until this problem was addressed. As the highly visible racial divide was narrowed, it revealed another gaping discrepancy—income.

Expanding equality, or at least access to public resources in the pursuit of equality, changed the very nature of the "society" slated for greatness.[102] It was now far more diverse, but there was little consensus. The diversity and range of perspectives that penetrated America's policy-making system was the direct result of hard-won victories by the civil rights movement and, to a lesser extent, the New Left. By the end of the decade, feminism accounted for additional victories in the quest to democratize mainstream politics. The Great Society imbibed the rhetoric of "community" and the commitment to participation expressed by these social movements. The Great Society even subsidized, within limits, challenges to older, less representative, and far less participatory state and local bureaucracies.

There was a price, however. New entrants into the policy sweepstakes had to play by pluralist rules. In racial politics this produced what Peter Skerry has called a "hybrid" organization: the Mexican American Legal Defense and Education Fund (MALDEF). "The organization's lawyers have played the inside game of clientelist politics," Skerry writes, excelling at the "back-room maneuvering and inside politicking needed to negotiate the maze of today's administrative state. But MALDEF has also played an aggressive outside game of high-visibility, media-oriented entrepreneurial politics."[103]

As one effervescent movement after another stepped into the policy-making arena, the shape of pluralism itself changed.[104] The size of the chorus expanded, the backgrounds of its singers diversified, and rehearsals grew more raucous. Democratizing pluralism opened the door to a host of new participants. For the first time since pluralism adapted to the demands of working-class Americans during the New Deal, the pluralist chorus really did sing with different accents and sway to a variety of beats.

Nor was the chorus intimidated by its director. Pluralism grew unwieldy. It expanded the venues in which the chorus performed. It invited audience participation in its highly publicized performances, some of which seemed like they would never end as court-composed codas and regulatory encores kept the music going long into the night. Although liberals and conservatives both complained bitterly about the outcomes, African Americans, women, the disabled, those who sought to infuse public policy with moral and religious values, and a host of other Americans had far greater access to the system than they did in 1963. Access, inclusion, and the claims upon full citizenship that went with them made pluralism—despite all its problems—"great" in the 1960s. The decade democratized pluralism.

Some have discovered in this raucous cacophony the death of pluralism.[105] Of the current condition of labor, Lichtenstein concludes that "individualistic, rights-based assumptions replaced group pluralist ones and turned solidarity into a quaint and antique notion."[106] For Heclo, the demise of pluralism is also an important turning point. That collapse was engineered by the demise of trust, goodwill, and the belief in disinterestedness, qualities Heclo believes to be essential to any pluralist system.

I disagree. Pluralism not only survived the Great Society, it remains the central feature of the American policy-making system today. It was democratic pluralism that neoconservatives and the New Right mastered as they sought to turn public policy to their own ends, and it is democratic pluralism, that for better or for worse, characterizes the way public policy is made today. What ultimately distinguished the Great Society from more radical approaches or, for that matter, conservative critiques that saw little role for the federal government at all was the determination to break down broad social demands—the kinds of objectives that would have been considered unrealistic just a decade or two earlier—into digestible bites. These could then be converted into public policies. The central mechanism used to achieve this—just as it was during the New Deal—was interest-group pluralism, albeit a more vocal and energetic form of pluralism.

Pluralism remained a powerful framework, although it now reached out to a vast array of groups, many of which claimed to speak for the "public interest." Whether working in the governmental nodes of the issue networks that pushed this pluralist infrastructure to the breaking point, or on the public advocacy end of the spectrum, policy promoters embraced far more ambitious and demanding ends.

To some, the results were cacophonous; for others, polyphonic. As conservatives soon discovered, however, the restructured pluralism that emerged from the Great Society could serve the purposes of more than one ideological program. Far steadier than "cycles of reform," pluralism, toughened by the Cold War and democratized by the Great Society, offered a mechanism for expanding the size and diversity of the chorus while ensuring that its music was still acceptable to the congregation and church elders alike.

Conclusion

How We Got Here

The year 2013 was not good for the Obama administration. Despite his earlier accomplishments—navigating landmark health care reform through a hyper-partisan Congress and spearheading the successful assault on Osama Bin Laden—implementation proved to be a challenge for the former community organizer, law professor, and U.S. senator. The rollout of "Obamacare" was a self-acknowledged disaster. And on the homeland security front, the aggressive pursuit of the very goals that most Americans supported raised concerns about privacy from both Democrats and Republicans in the wake of revelations by Edward Snowden, the former National Security Agency (NSA) contractor turned whistle blower. While each of these headline-grabbing setbacks for the Obama administration may well prove inconsequential over the long arc of American history, Obama's response to each underscores a pattern that has defined the very shape of that history.

In both instances, President Obama turned to the private sector to enhance political support for assertive federal programs. On the health care front, Obama got help from unanticipated quarters: Republicans. While some Republican governors eschewed Medicaid expansion, others, like Republican Rick Snyder of Michigan, simply could not afford to walk away from 100 percent federal funding for 400,000 uncovered constituents. The key to obtaining the necessary support from Republican lawmakers, however, was Michigan's track record of privatizing Medicaid delivery in that state. State Representative Al Pscholka, a Republican leader in the House, was no fan of Obamacare. As he put it to a National Public Radio (NPR) reporter, "When people say Medicaid expansion, I think to a lot of us that meant bigger government. And it meant expanding a program that doesn't work very well."[1] But when Pscholka looked into the actual administration of Medicaid in Michigan, he changed his position. "When I understood how it worked, and what we had done in Michigan in the late '90s that was actually pretty smart—we've privatized a lot of that already, which I think a lot of folks didn't understand." Pscholka's support for the expansion of Medicaid in Michigan—which was crucial to the success of Obamacare— was contingent on the continued use of private health maintenance organizations (HMOs) to administer Medicaid to the hundreds of thousands of newly eligible residents.

While Pscholka's position quickly drew a primary challenge, the Republican legislator counted on the support of hospitals, doctors, and the statewide small-business associations to win reelection in his heavily Republican district. And President Obama counted on the appeal of such public-private solutions to reassure millions of voters that their health care was in trusted hands. Defending the Affordable Care Act, Obama doubled down. Having already eschewed a unitary payer system in favor of health care exchanges that relied on private health care insurers to deliver services, the Obama administration turned to the private sector once again to expand Medicaid coverage in the state of Michigan.

When it came to defending the homeland, the NSA worked closely with the nation's largest telecommunications companies to peruse metadata for millions of phone calls. In the wake of the Obama administration's review of this controversial intrusion into Americans' privacy, the president stated that the NSA would no longer maintain a database that retained such information on government servers.[2] He proposed instead that the data either be retained by the private telecommunications companies that collected it originally or by a third party that would store the data.[3] Obama was clear about the reason for this decision: "Given the unique power of the state, it is not enough for leaders to say: Trust us. We won't abuse the data we collect. For history has too many examples when that trust has been breached."[4] A nation that trusted its most intimate conversations to Google and Facebook presumably breathed a sigh of relief to know that Verizon or some unnamed third party, not the NSA, would now stand guard over these data, even though the NSA continued to access it, just as it did in the past.

Remarkably, neither the popular discourse of American politics or common understandings of American political history can capture the braided nature of public authority that both these examples highlight and that has characterized American political development. Even though scholars have long since moved past the stark binary that still informs "liberal" rhetoric about state action, and "conservative" talking points about "big government," the findings from this scholarship have had little impact on the ways in which most public officials and informed citizens conceive of the political challenges Americans face today. Never mind that the actions of these very same citizens and public officials, whether liberal Democrats or Tea Party Republicans, embrace federal authority and private and civil sector deployment of that authority in most instances. For all the pathbreaking scholarship that has charted the evolution of "salus populi suprema lex est," the ways in which the mail was actually delivered, the cultural adaptations to the "warfare state," the operations of the "submerged state," and "infrastructural power," the nation's understanding of its history remains one that is too easily encapsulated by Fox News and MSNBC.[5]

The chapters in this volume have drawn on a deep reservoir of scholarship that leveled the boundaries between state and society to craft the outlines of an associational synthesis. This framework can provide an alternative perspective for elected officials and cable news networks in the future. To reach that audience I will shift to a more user-friendly genre to sum up the contours of the associational synthesis: a pitch to the mythical "Associational News Channel." "How We Got Here" highlights six scenes that shift our understanding of American governance over the past century. Stay tuned.

Scene 1: Gifford Pinchot on Horseback, 1905

Set against newsreel footage of Teddy Roosevelt and still photographs of Gifford Pinchot in the woods, the documentary opens with some of the landmarks of national conservation—one of the pillars of the Progressive agenda in the first decade of the twentieth century. Unlike many of the Progressives' reforms that took place in state or local government, Pinchot's Forest Service placed millions of acres of national forest under the direct management of the national government. And it did so while purportedly battling greedy corporations and parochial Western settlers. Professionally trained foresters, primarily from Yale—civil servants with an irrepressible "espirit de corps"—triumphed over America's long-standing commitment to laissez-faire and local control. Or so the story goes.

That story is incomplete. It features the naked expansion of the national government and the rise of planning with little or no reference to the key moves that made these possible or the key associations that made national intervention politically palatable. Three of the legs of the early administrative state are reexamined in this segment. Expertise is the first. Pinchot's own expertise was questionable at best, obtained on the fly in Germany as his mentor, the world-renowned forester Sir Dietrich Brandis, never ceased to remind his student. As for the Yale School of Forestry, the Pinchot family founded it with a major gift and quite literally nurtured it in the backyard of their Milford estate over the summers. To call the expertise that emerged from these origins "independent" took a leap of faith. The second foundation of the modern administrative state—the civil service—was built on rather shaky ground as well. Many of the would-be civil servants who went from Yale directly to the Forest Service were financially beholden to their boss. While spirits may have run high out of a genuine commitment to forestry and the mission to extend its reach across the land, it was Gifford Pinchot's personal largesse, not a government paycheck or organizational incentives, that ensured loyalty in this far-flung bureaucracy.

The reason that the conservation story has anchored the foundation of the modern administrative state is that the Forest Service intervened directly in the market by placing millions of acres of national forest under active forest management. Yet it is highly unlikely that this milestone in progressive governance would have ever come about during the Roosevelt administration if Pinchot had not appealed directly to the logic of the market. This appeal to the market is the third intervention that revises the traditional understanding of the origins of the modern states. As was the case with Pinchot's so-called expertise, self-promotion was essential. Pinchot's brief for managing George Vanderbilt's Biltmore Forest was the same as the chief forester's appeal to Congress years later: Scientific forestry paid. Effective management of forests would yield long-term revenues that would profit both Vanderbilt and, subsequently, the nation. That these calculations were based on faulty assumptions seemed to matter little (except to Vanderbilt!). Perhaps that is because Pinchot's plan was ultimately supported by some of the very corporate lumber interests that Progressive rhetoric pilloried. Frederick E. Weyerhaeuser and the National Lumber Manufacturers Association backed Pinchot's plan for transferring the nation's forest reserves to the Department of Agriculture's Forest Bureau, effectively consolidating Pinchot's ability to manage those forests, by creating the Forest Service.[6] Just as large sheep and cattle grazers soon learned that it was not such a bad deal to empower the national government to bring order to common grazing lands, large lumber interests understood that it was in their best interest to use taxpayer dollars to fight forest fires, which, after all, did not respect boundaries between public and private land. Besides, how bad could it be for business to take large swaths of forest *off* the market, thus pushing up the value of the lumbermen's privately held acres?

To revise our historical understanding of the key components of the Progressive Era story is not to challenge the significance of Pinchot's utilitarian philosophy of the greatest good for the greatest number in the long run. Achieving these ends, however, in a polity that continued to value the market and distrusted autonomous administrators and experts was another matter. Pinchot's contribution, and that of the men like him who pioneered extensions of highly visible national authority, was to work with the language of markets, and some of the interest groups that were organized most effectively to create the political space necessary to allow the national government to serve as a more effective coordinator for these associations. While the key legislative moment for this arrangement in the case of forestry came in 1905 with the creation of the Forest Service, Pinchot had built the infrastructure for this network since the 1890s, and indeed he could not have succeeded without the increasing national reach of important partners in the private sector and civil society. Pinchot's successors strengthened these connections—at Yale, in the forestry industry, and with the public more generally.

Scene 2: Personnel in Military Uniforms Hand Out Aid to Italian Civilians, 1918

This segment opens with these men handing out American flags and pictures of Woodrow Wilson to Italian civilians along with humanitarian aid. But these were not members of the American Expeditionary Forces. Rather, they were foot soldiers in the American Red Cross (ARC). In order to ensure that the relief being dispensed along with the flags possessed "an American character pronounced enough to constantly remind everyone connected with it that this help comes from America," the War Department authorized the ARC to don military uniforms and even assign ranks to these volunteers. Smarting from criticism that the United States was slow to send American troops into combat, authorizing Red Cross volunteers to wear uniforms made it easier for the volunteers to operate in a war zone and it underscored American military commitment to the war effort. As Julia Irwin has documented in *Making the World Safe*, the ARC played a crucial role in carrying out American diplomacy and a commitment to international engagement through voluntary means.[7]

While authorizing the use of military uniforms was an exceptional policy for special wartime circumstances, exercising public authority through this powerful voluntary organization was the norm. Indeed, the ARC derived its virtual monopoly over domestic and international relief efforts from the federal charter that it procured in 1900. The charter designated the ARC as the nation's official voluntary relief organization, providing a legal foundation for this public-private relationship.[8] The ARC was authorized by Congress to represent the government in treating wounded soldiers and in mitigating the impact of disasters on civilians domestically and beyond the borders of the United States.[9] Congress renewed this charter in 1905 by tying the ARC even more tightly to the federal government.[10] Under the new provisions, the president of the United States appointed six of the ARC's eighteen-member Central Committee.[11] As important as the national government's formal hand in the governance of the ARC was the active participation of the sitting president, Teddy Roosevelt, when the San Francisco earthquake struck in 1906. Until that point, TR had withheld his personal endorsement of the ARC. In the wake of the San Francisco disaster, Roosevelt appealed to the American public to support relief efforts through the ARC, initiating a long-running commitment by America's chief executives to this voluntary mechanism for relief.[12]

A congressional charter and the executive branch's endorsement secured the long-running relationship between the ARC and the federal government. This framework, in turn, provided an organizational structure for another important set of intermediaries—the professions. Social workers were instrumental to the approach that the ARC took to delivering aid—an approach informed by "scientific charity."[13] The social work profession was soon joined by the medical profession, both nurses and physicians, in the ARC's international work.[14] They tackled health issues from typhoid to yellow fever.

The real value of this informal diplomacy built around humanitarian aid became apparent as Woodrow Wilson's plans for the League of Nations encountered fierce opposition after the armistice that ended World War I. The ARC pursued postwar relief efforts in Eastern Europe and Siberia even as Americans repudiated Wilson's more formal diplomatic proposals. As one American Red Cross official working in the Balkans after the war put it, even as Wilson's plans for America's entry into the League collapsed, "There is no more practical or effective agency to demonstrate friendship than the American Red Cross."[15] Against a backdrop of flagging interest in international affairs by many Americans during the 1920s, the international humanitarian impulse remained alive and was asserted repeatedly through the ARC.[16] As Irwin concludes, "At a moment when U.S. citizens and government officials grappled with their nation's growing power and influence in the world, the ARC became a principal means for them to engage with world health and welfare issues. Through relief and reform activities— many of them quite comprehensive—the ARC served state diplomatic agendas while offering private citizens a way to fulfill their aspirations to alleviate suffering in the world."[17]

Using the ARC for "soft diplomacy" fit into a long-standing pattern of executing foreign policy through nonstate actors, such as financial advisers counseling foreign administrations or encouraging loans and investments by private American banks. Third Party relations with Latin America and management of World War I reparations with European countries through such mechanisms allowed the White House to avoid direct intervention, bypass congressional approval, and avoid strategic entanglements from the Progressive Era through the 1930s. As was the case with the associational approach to domestic policy, the ideals of direct control and greater efficiency were sacrificed in return for an approach that was politically palatable. And as was also the case with domestic policy, the challenge was to ensure the proper balance of public control over private and voluntary intermediaries.[18]

The United States also asserted its foreign interests by shaping the legal systems and jurisprudence of nations like the Philippines long after American troops withdrew. As Clara Altman has argued, "Through the reform of the islands' system of jurisprudence, the U.S. state gained the tools, honed the techniques, and developed the discourses, for a twentieth century empire premised on the capacity to intervene abroad to create the central features of 'modern' rational systems of laws: efficiency, the free flow of capital, predictability, and 'stability.'"[19] The hybrid of American, Spanish, and indigenous Philippine jurisprudence that emerged accommodated American interests without committing more tangible American resources. American efforts to reform Philippine law sought to change the legal culture both by funneling American legal expertise to the islands and by training Filipino lawyers at American law schools.[20] As Altman argues, state building (or re-building) in the Philippines was conducted largely through the legal system, eschewing the imperialist rhetoric embraced by America's national competitors in the first half of the twentieth century and embracing instead the language of modernization and efficiency.

Placed alongside the traditional pillars of the history of foreign relations in this period—America's entry into World War I, Wilson's failure to secure approval for the League of Nations, the isolationism of the 1930s, and the growing power of the presidency—an associational perspective provides an important corrective. National authority was parceled through a set of intermediaries that engaged the world continuously and, quite often, informally. Those intermediaries consisted of organizations like the ARC and the professions that ranged from social workers to nurses, lawyers to accountants. And they operated through institutions, like the court system, embedded deeply in foreign societies. Although the thrust of this associational approach redounded to the benefit of the expanding liberal democracy that was America, this approach to foreign relations insisted that the nation's foreign relations were not a zero-sum game. The international system, as well as those countries that embraced this vision, advocates argued, would benefit by modernizing and rationalizing their affairs as well.

Scene 3: Newsreel Footage of a Hooverville in Seattle, 1933

Herbert Hoover's name will forever be associated with the crash of 1929 and the ensuing Great Depression. That Americans quickly named the collection of shacks that sprang up in most American cities "Hoovervilles" indelibly linked the "Master of Emergencies" with America's longest-running emergency. Hoover failed to solve it, and indeed he may well have exacerbated it. Clinging steadfastly to his policy of volunteerism, a central component of Hoover's "associative state," Hoover refused to tap the full resources of the national government or provide aid directly to the American public. The failure of the National Recovery Administration in the early Roosevelt administration, which was built on Hoover's idea of voluntary cooperation on wages, hours, and prices within key industrial sectors, ostensibly buried associational techniques for the remainder of the century according to scholars. FDR did not hesitate to tap federal resources in order to aid an ailing nation. The president served up a steady diet of alphabet soup to cure the nation. Each letter described a new or repurposed federal agency, from the AAA to the WPA.

Yet powerful alliances between federal, state and local, voluntary, and private organizations animated many of the New Deal programs. In this regard, the national government continued to serve as lead developer for the nation's political economy. Given the scope of the problem, however, it now sought to shore up sectors of society that were insufficiently organized to serve as effective partners on the associational team. Mid-twentieth-century public policy sought to break down political and economic isolation. The national government intervened to bolster nascent associations of producers, especially farmers and industrialized labor. The Agricultural Adjustment Act (AAA) paid farmers to take land out of production in order to establish a floor for prices. The flip side of federal efforts to encourage cooperative marketing arrangements in the 1920s, the feds relied on a powerful partner to cultivate this lagging sector of the economy—the county agent. County agents were the product of earlier efforts to apply scientific knowledge developed at state-subsidized agricultural schools to commercial farming and organizing efforts in the 1920s of the American Farm Bureau Federation. The county agent, who often worked for both of these masters, was empowered by the national government to determine which land should be taken out of production, triggering federal support payments. The AAA revived farm prices by relying on agents of this key interest group to regulate production.

As with agriculture, if the national government did not have an effective partner to represent producers in the industrial sector, it would have invented one or, at least, empowered one. The mechanism used in this instance was Section 7(a) of the ill-fated National Industrial Recovery Act (NIRA). It protected the right of workers to bargain collectively through their union with their employer. When the NIRA was overturned by the Supreme Court in 1935, Congress quickly restored and strengthened these rights in the National Labor Relations Act (the Wagner Act). Section 7(a) and the Wagner Act were the product of hard-fought political battles, waged on the shop floor and in the halls of Congress. But they also benefited from an approach that capitalized on state authority to better organize, empower, and coordinate key sectors of the economy. Without such government assistance those sectors would continue to suffer from the disproportionate clout and logistical advantages of economic adversaries—be they oligopolistic corporations, better-organized agricultural financiers and processors, or industrial managers.

The ongoing crisis of the Great Depression, followed by another national emergency—World War II—changed the balance within the associational alliance of state, civil society, and private sector. Increasingly, the national government took the lead in addressing problems, especially when sectors of the economy or regions of the nation threatened to drag down the entire economy. A pragmatic strain of progressive thought embodied in New Deal liberalism garnered strong support in the electorate, a home in the Democratic Party, and no shortage of adherents in the opposition party by the end of World War II. At the heart of New Deal liberalism lay the commitment to ensuring economic security for all Americans, even if this required greater intervention into the market by the federal government. Yet, given the prolonged nature of the crisis, it is quite remarkable the lengths that Americans went to in order to meet these obligations without redistributing income or empowering a central government to plan, fix wages and prices, or mandate from a distance. Massive spending for the war effort demonstrated the power of fiscal pump-priming. But beyond that new and increasingly accepted role for the federal government, Americans preferred to pursue collective goals through a refurbished associational team, perhaps led by Washington, but anchored by intermediaries in state and local government, the professions, universities, and the civil and private sectors.

Scene 4: A Reenactment of Hostesses for Hoover Listening to Hoover on the Radio, 1928

There is no newsreel footage of this event, which occurred in hundreds of households across America because it harnessed personal relationships to create a more intimate connection between a presidential candidate and a newly enfranchised group of voters who were viewed as more likely than many men to vote independently, crossing party lines. The actresses, dressed in middle-class garb of the late 1920s and huddled around a radio in the living room of the kind of house featured in Hoover's "Better Homes for America" campaign, are listening to the end of a Hoover campaign speech. Once the radio is turned off, they launch into a discussion of "good government" and the kinds of threats to it posed by "wet" urban politicians like Al Smith.

This scene opens a segment that runs from the 1920s to the present day. It explains the *electoral* evolution from enduring partisan ties, literally passed from father to son, to connections that are grounded in occupational, business-based, and eventually issue-oriented ties. It considers the ways in which elected officials reconceptualized constituencies, from simply Democrats or Republicans, northerners or southerners, Italians or African Americans, to car dealers and "hostesses." Because the farmers or union members discussed in the previous segment provided better, and more specialized, cues about their preferences than older networks of partisan intelligence, elected officials sought new ways to tap into these sentiments and were better able to craft specific public policies that appealed to disaggregable sectors of the electorate, regardless of their partisan leanings. These policies, from the Sheppard-Towner Act to the AAA or the Wagner Act discussed above, or subsequent antipoverty programs in the Great Society such as Medicare, banked on intense support from well-organized groups who stood to benefit from such policies or who were empowered and more effectively organized in the wake of these policies. While much of the literature focuses on poorly organized groups, from the poor to the elderly (who were also the poor before Social Security and Medicare), the sector of the economy that best represents this phenomenon is defense contracting. Embraced by Republicans, who before the onset of the Cold War had been wary of military entanglements and commitments, America's "Arsenal of Defense" was now a permanent fixture among the interest group–driven politics of the second half of the twentieth century.

To be sure, the ability of such interests to funnel campaign contributions to candidates was important. More valuable, however, was the capacity to provide intelligence about voters' preferences and to capture votes by explaining the advantages of favored public policies, thus linking electoral support, elected officials, and appealing public policies. Even civilian administrators who relied on defense contractors—men like James Webb who ran NASA under John F. Kennedy—were acutely aware of the contracts and subcontracts that spanned most congressional districts. Webb carried around a raft of notecards with the names of every NASA subcontractor in every congressional district. He could count on the subcontractors themselves to let voters know the economic impact that putting a man on the moon had on any given district.

The irrepressible Mrs. Silas Strawn, who directed Hostesses for Hoover, envisioned limitless possibilities for the model she crafted. In revealing her plans for the future, Strawn embraced the associational spirit spawned by the Hoover campaign. "With more time and sufficient funds in subsequent campaigns," Mrs. Strawn concluded in her final report, "the plan could be enlarged upon by emphasizing the organization of industrial workers, welfare groups, churches, hospitals, business women's and social clubs, farmers' organizations and fraternal bodies. This would be in addition to the radio parties in private homes. An organization embracing *every activity in life*, both men and women, can be developed."[21] Her vision was soon realized as elected officials augmented their partisan intelligence with that of an ever-increasing number of interest groups. Although it is not likely that any of these politicians had read Harwood Childs, increasingly it was the AFL-CIOs, the American Farm Bureau Federations, and the Grummans and Raytheons that were "at the same time reservoirs of ideas, mirrors of desires, sifters of major from minor policies, agencies for leading and directing the legislative activities of the government."[22]

As I argued in "Mirrors of Desires," conceptualizing the electorate as a congeries of group preferences best discerned through the platforms and policy agendas of interest groups constituted a distinct period in American political development. Just as elected officials adapted an era of partisan allegiance in the late nineteenth century to a world of interests in the middle third of the twentieth century, their successors adapted that partisan/interest-group world to two important developments in the media that might be more fruitfully labeled "mediation." The first mediating technology was broadcast television, which dominated mass media between the late 1950s and the early 1980s. The second mediating technology was regularized, relatively inexpensive, public opinion polling, along with the subsequent data mining that provided far more fine-grained portraits of segments of the electorate than even interest-group intelligence was able to.

These developments pulled candidates in opposite directions. While the homogenizing impact of broadcast television encouraged messages aimed at the broad middle—encouraging politicians to offer up "corn" that could easily be digested by the masses—the ability to discern more fine-grained voter preferences and the ability to target such preferences through more specialized media (starting with direct mail, but soon expanded through multiple cable and satellite television outlets, and, ultimately, the Internet) kindled dreams of turning out voters with strongly held views at either end of the ideological spectrum. In a political system where partisan ties, ideological preferences, and interest-group bonds were more perfectly aligned, identifying, motivating, and turning out those voters on the fringes through targeted messages might prove to be the key to success in a close election.

From the 1950s through the 1970s, candidate-centered campaigns in both parties beamed their messages back to voters through three television networks. By the late 1950s, television displaced radio as the mass media of choice for the vast majority of Americans.[23] The three broadcast networks were, in effect, an oligopoly that reached roughly 90 percent of all viewers for much of this period. Whether they liked politics or not, most Americans were exposed to it through television, especially when all three networks carried a debate or press conference. Roughly 60 percent of American households tuned in to watch John F. Kennedy debate Richard M. Nixon in 1960. It was not uncommon for presidential speeches to attract 80 percent of those watching in the early days of television. Limited to three networks with roughly equal shares of viewership in the 1960s and 1970s, the savvy candidate aimed for the broad middle. When presidential aspirants diverged from that steady diet of corn, as Barry Goldwater and George McGovern did, they paid a hefty price.[24]

Accounts of the activities of early political consultants, the experts who replaced party functionaries in election campaigns by the late 1950s and early 1960s offer a valuable portrait of campaign strategy in the early days of broadcast television and public opinion polling. The firm credited with creating the profession of campaign consulting, Whitaker and Baxter, noted that a campaign's theme "must be simple and have a strong human interest appeal." "It must have more 'corn than caviar.'" Whitaker and Baxter's advice was illustrative of the early days of candidate-centered campaigns that broadcast their messages through radio, television, and other mass-market media.[25]

While television was a godsend for shoring up a presidential candidate's broad base, the inexorable march of special interests continued unabated, and its pace quickened dramatically during the 1960s and 1970s, pressuring candidates to attend to minority interests while remaining "presidential." Presidents, presidential candidates, and their parties might have been stuck with corn when it came to televised communications. But that did not mean they could not experiment with a sophisticated array of variations on that staple, from cornbread to high fructose corn syrup. The rise of public opinion polling by the 1970s offered candidates the chance to enjoy the best of both worlds.

As presidents grew comfortable with polling, they sought more from the torrent of data that flooded in. Capturing a snapshot of broad public opinion that could also be broken down by cross-sectional analysis to home in on specific segments of the population without having to rely on intermediaries, be they political parties or interest groups, was simply too tempting to ignore. In this era, no politician viewed polling as a panacea. With broadcast television the only game in town, whatever a candidate might learn about the nuances of a sliver of the electorate would still have to be reconciled with a message that met the average viewer at his own level. But polling might serve as a panopticon that could survey both majority perspectives as well as dissenting perspectives. Polling data might reveal the secret formula for balancing corn and caviar—discovering ways to serve both. By the end of the twentieth century, polling expanded the candidate's capacity to discern the voters' preferences as much as possible, while candidates crafted various techniques for circumventing broadcast television, or making the best of it, through adjustments in the image projected and lavishing attention on commercial placement.

Even as such efforts flourished, rapidly digitizing databases and the plummeting costs of computers made the analysis of information that every voter inadvertently provided through day-to-day activities the next frontier for identifying preferences. Such data included a voter's hobbies, gleaned from magazine subscriptions and patterns of consumption reported by credit card companies. When these data were combined with digitized census, voter registration, and polling data, they produced profiles that were snapped up by candidates. These profiles offered candidates even greater assurance that it might be worth considering taking a position that was a bit out of the mainstream but that resonated forcefully with an identifiable minority. Rather than signaling preferences to party and interest-group elites—Washington insiders who used privileged knowledge of their constituents' preferences as crucial bargaining chips in a pluralist negotiation—voters signaled their proclivities through a variety of outlets. The proxies that intermediaries between the voter and the candidate once held were now replaced by direct communications between voter and candidate. Like travel agents, video stores, and insurance agents, political middle men were being replaced by consumers who could now order directly from the service provider. Governing, however, required far more room for negotiation between competing interests and perspectives than streaming a video or booking a flight.

Once convinced of the advantages, candidates gambled on tactical flights to the margins for two reasons. The first, made famous by Karl Rove, was to "stir up the base." The other, however, could not have been more different. It entailed salvaging voters from the political waste land of *inat*tention (in contrast to that highly motivated base) or, even more boldly, poaching voters from the opposing party. Such sorties could be costly—both financially, and politically—if the gambit alienated too many other voters in the candidate's coalition. But growing confidence in the kinds of data that could identify fruitful targets combined with the growing range of mass media alternatives to broadcast television encouraged candidates on both sides of the aisle to roll the dice.

Polling remained an essential ingredient in the candidate's repertoire, just as cues from parties had, despite the rise of interest groups, and intelligence from interest groups had, despite the rise of public opinion polling.[26] Nevertheless, by the last decade of the twentieth century, the marginal advantage in what had become a highly competitive contest between the two parties appeared to go to the candidates who could leverage massive databases in order to "microtarget" selective audiences for narrowly tailored messages.[27]

Today's parties and interest groups are crippled when it comes to the actual business of governing, as the job of reassembling the odd-shaped coalitions that elect a president for the far less dramatic business of passing legislation has proven near impossible. In the absence of key brokers who can both claim access to a unique perspective on their constituents' preferences and the authority to reach a deal on their behalf, presidents are often left with the option of tailoring bite-sized policies that will poll well without activating too much opposition, or exhorting Congress to take bold actions even though such calls are used primarily to enflame segments of the loyal opposition.

Had interest groups and parties served solely as pure conduits of their members' diverse interests, this displacement would have barely registered a ripple. These two intermediaries, however, did far more than convey preferences to candidates. Partisan and interest-group leaders mixed and matched their members' preferences, adapting them to the politically possible. The key to their flexibility was the broad deference that voters granted party and interest-group leadership when it came to cutting deals with other elites. These insiders translated broad voter demand into narrowly drawn policy outcomes. These compromises added up to a broad social contract—at least for those Americans who were well represented at the ballot box and on K Street.

Public opinion polling, which by the 1980s was increasingly combined with big data, cut out the middle men. Increasingly secure in the likelihood of garnering a favorable response from a properly chosen fragment of the population, candidates were tempted to direct provocative messages at ever-narrowing slivers of the electorate, confident that a properly targeted appeal would be limited to that receptive audience. And as presidential elections became more competitive, turning out key fragments in battleground states could often mean the difference between winning and losing. It also meant the rise of polarized politics and the decline of pluralist bargaining.

Candidates no longer needed to work through the intermediaries of parties and interest groups to discern the preferences of voters. Instead, they could commission polls or combine polling data with a range of demographic data, voting histories, and consumption patterns in order to intuit directly what voters preferred. The political world we inhabit today is the product of this shift—a world in which candidates know more details about individual voters than they ever have yet lack the ability to build the kinds of coalitions that party and interest-group intermediaries were talented at crafting. Coalition building and compromise elude the grasp of public officials today as they seek to placate, or at least neutralize, the relatively unmediated, and often nonnegotiable, demands of their key constituents.

Scene 5: A Phone Conversation Between Frozen Food Mogul Clarence Birdseye and Rowe, Massachusetts, Realtor, Jack Williams, 1955

Shortly after hearing that a new commercial nuclear power plant would be built in Rowe, Massachusetts, Clarence Birdseye picked up the phone and called Jack Williams. Birdseye was certain that the future lay in irradiated food, and he was eager to build a huge processing plant that would capitalize on the surplus radiation from the new reactor.[28]

After all, the experts at the Atomic Energy Commission had assured Congress and the American public that commercial nuclear power was safe, that a technological solution to radioactive fuel disposal was around the corner, and that social benefits would one day flow from the same source that produced the massive destruction unleashed on Hiroshima and Naga-saki. Increasingly, decisions in the private and voluntary sectors, not to mention state and local government, hinged on knowledge, regulation, and administrative programs nurtured by the federal government. Nor was this source of power immediately subject to election returns. In this segment, electoral politics are eclipsed by bureaucratic politics—proministrative pol-itics to be exact.

Forged during the ongoing crisis of the Cold War, the proministrative state married *professional* expertise and ad*ministrative* capacity in agencies like the Atomic Energy Commission, the National Science Foundation, and the National Security Agency. Professionals were eager to capitalize on the resources of the national government, while federal administrators capital-ized on the prestige of postwar science, credited for winning the war by inventing the atomic bomb, mastering radar, and deploying penicillin. Fed-eral spending and administrative infrastructure grew dramatically following the war, from a reorganized national security sector that housed the newly minted Department of Defense and Central Intelligence Agency, to science-driven agencies, such as the Office of Naval Research and the National Institutes of Health. Even social science was represented through the Coun-cil of Economic Advisers.

The professions also expanded at a record pace, with the number of Ph.Ds awarded tripling between 1940 and 1960. Federal incentives, employ-ment in federal agencies, and direct funding for graduate education pro-duced a good deal of this expertise. And professional agendas pursued by the experts who were employed by the federal government drove new fed-eral agendas, from the quest for cures for cancer to identifying the causes of poverty. The symbiotic relationship forged between experts and adminis-trators in the post–World War II state altered the course of pluralist politics in mid-century America.

Proministrators preferred to work behind closed doors, in gray build-ings, far from the glare of publicity. Indeed, many of the newly created agencies and the policies that they worked on were shrouded by multiple levels of classification. While Cold War fears protected funding for projects that claimed a direct military application, civilian applications required publicity in order to demonstrate their value to tax-averse voters. Federal administrators and experts teamed up to promote public demand for the increasingly esoteric services that they had to offer. Rather than simply responding to social and economic demands, postwar administrators, armed with the ideas and ambitions of professionals, sought to *create* demand for the application of their knowledge—knowledge that grew out of their theories, experiments, and data sets. Precisely because the kinds of politics they engaged in excluded meaningful public participation in the details of complex policy decisions, general public support was crucial to the experts' success. That support could only be garnered through publicity, often facilitated through ambitious promises, such as electricity too cheap to meter.

The creation of expertise and the expanding organizational base that housed ambitious policy agendas pursued by these experts spawned specialization. Subdisciplines proliferated. Whether seeking or saddled with new responsibilities, the organizational infrastructure also subdivided at a breathtaking pace. As experts, professional disciplines, and organizational subdivisions proliferated, the insulated debate crucial to expert decision making spilled over into increasingly public forums. The elaboration of expertise into specialized units, the inevitable differences in perspective that arose when a number of disciplines examined the same problem, and the political agendas engaged by various host institutions brought disputes between experts to the public's attention. When combined with the high visibility that experts courted in order to promote demand for their services, these disputes ultimately helped undermine both the authority and subsequently the autonomy of experts.

The interplay of expertise and these structural factors created its own dynamic—a process that ultimately shattered public expert consensus and the nation's confidence in its experts. By the mid-1970s, expertise had been relegated to a necessary, but no longer decisive, condition for political success. With the federal government committed to the large-scale production of expertise, with research agendas incorporated wholesale into public policy, with each new subdiscipline looking at old problems from new perspectives, and, most significantly, with these once exclusively scholarly debates now reified in the halls of hundreds of agencies and subject to a thousand points of access, paradigmatic shifts have become a dime a dozen. They have undermined the once politically valuable authority of experts and left administrators and politicians alike in search, not for order, but for a new political resource with which to break the nation's painful policy stalemates.

This dynamic played out over the course of the 1960s and 1970s— decades that are still remembered for their sharp social divisions and countercultures. To attribute such tectonic shifts solely to the dynamics of the prominitrative state by ignoring the most important social revolution in the twentieth century—the civil rights movement; or one of America's most divisive wars, Vietnam; or the constitutional crisis of Watergate—would be delusional. All three events had profound effects on the course of partisan politics. To ignore the evolution of prominitrative politics, however, misses the underlying structural changes in the relationships among citizens, elected officials, administrators, and the way in which public policy was shaped over three pivotal post–World War II decades.

Scene 6: Town Hall Meeting in Simpsonville, South Carolina, on the Affordable Care Act, 2009

"How We Got Here" concludes with a town hall meeting on health care in South Carolina in the summer of 2009. That's where one outraged citizen warned conservative Congressman Robert Inglis to "keep your government hands off my Medicare."[29]

The phenomenon that Representative Inglis addressed was not new. Americans have been forgetting about the state since the founding. Because the nation was forged in opposition to British monarchical overreach, fear of intrusion into private and local affairs has always touched a particularly sensitive nerve in the United States. Thus, recognition of the role that the feds played is often the first casualty when historical narratives are constructed. The state has consistently been displaced by individual initiative and market mechanisms in personal and collective memory and, more often than not, scholarly interpretations as well.

Tea Party opponents of Obamacare are the latest in a long line of Americans who have erased the crucial role that the federal government has played in securing their well-being. The list ranges from settlers protected from the threat of Indian attack to farmers who financed their land with the aid of federally extended credit. Forgetting the national government's role and replacing it with heroic, rugged, or merely opportunistic individual initiative has punctuated the past two and a half centuries of American political development. As one of the leaders of the "New Western History," Richard White has noted, "In the imagination of modern America, the West has come to stand for independence, self-reliance, and individualism."[30] Yet, "more than any other section of the United States," White insists, the American West "is a creation not so much of individual or local efforts, but of federal efforts. More than any other region, the West has been historically a dependency of the federal government."[31]

Fast-forwarding a hundred years, a "Sunbelt synthesis" spotlights the crucial public decisions and resources ranging from redlining to highway construction that created racially segregated housing patterns in both the North and the South.[32] Yet, by the 1970s, white suburban beneficiaries of these policies loudly proclaimed "hands off our schools" when minorities challenged the racially bifurcated allocation of resources. Those same suburban homeowners, who had benefited disproportionately from the GI Bill and the redistributive engines of social security and Medicare, directed their wrath at a population that had been systematically excluded from these benefits, yet were characterized as beholden to big government. Matt Lassiter and his fellow contributors to the "New Suburban History" have shed light on important political and social phenomena, ranging from the emergence of Nixon's "silent majority" to the roots of suburban sprawl. In doing so, they have also documented a remarkable erasure—the collective amnesia about the powerful role that government programs played in forging the Sunbelt synthesis.[33]

*   *   *

A better understanding of the associational order that has structured the political economy for much of American history is ready for prime time. It is an opportune time to translate what is presently a series of scholarly insights into a user-friendly narrative because the long-running popular story starring liberalism versus conservatism explains less and less. Takeaways that illuminated politics during the New Deal, or its Great Society expansion, and analysis built around the conservative response to these liberal forays during the Age of Reagan miss the mark today. Because they echo the very rhetoric that politicians use to wage ideological warfare, the old narrative fails adequately to distinguish the actions of these very same politicians from their rhetorical excess. Bill Clinton's declaration that the age of big government is over or George W. Bush's nation building abroad (and heavy use of military contractors to do so) are just two of the many anomalies that a long-standing popular history pitting advocates of big government versus small government fails to explain. That failure intensifies frustration with politics today.

A popular historical narrative that replaces ideological difference as the driving force of political history might reorient the current political debate from big government versus small government to a discussion of ways to hold intermediary institutions in the voluntary and private sectors accountable for the outcomes of their actions. The public authority that has been delegated to universities, the professions, interest groups, trade associations, and private corporations constitutes a sacred trust. In many, perhaps most, instances, the delegated authority has been effectively deployed, not only satisfying the political objective of exercising power through outlets that are more widely trusted than the government, but also fulfilling substantive objectives as well—from the latest medical advance to projecting American foreign policy objectives through the light touch of a nongovernmental organization rather than a more overt State Department presence.

The financial meltdown of global proportions that froze credit markets at the end of the first decade in the twenty-first century and the revelations of Edward Snowden that the government regularly captures information about its citizens' phone calls and e-mails are stark reminders that an effective associational order requires constant vigilance and recalibration in order to correct the balance between citizen, private/voluntary sector intermediary, and the state. Whether the flurry of legislation to intensify public oversight of banks and insurance companies that proved "too big to fail" in the last financial panic will get that balance right, and whether the public outcry in response to the NSA's revelations of data mining will as well, remains to be seen. In either case, however, recognizing that Americans historically have preferred to parcel state power through a variety of intermediary institutions is a promising first step.

A popular reconceptualization of the nation's political history is timely because voters are tired of the partisan rancor that has prevailed for the past twenty years. No doubt, identifying ideologically committed voters at either end of the ideological spectrum is easier today due to public opinion polling and data mining. And reaching voters directly is less costly with the rise of digital media on the one hand and multiple television channels on the other hand. But stirring up the base is not the only way in which these new media can be deployed. Media can also be used to win back voters who have a less passionate interest in politics but who can provide a moderating influence and strong support for effective public policies delivered through familiar, trusted means. These same voters may well provide the margins to ensure that those private and voluntary intermediaries are held accountable for achieving the ends that their delegated authority was intended to secure.

When beneficiaries of employer-based health care ignore the billions of dollars of federal tax expenditures that support this system, when Medicare recipients consider their benefits to be the just fruits of payroll contributions and not a government program, and when these beneficiaries label visible reforms like the health care public option "big government," they are mobilizing one of the most potent framing devices in American history. That is the capacity to define *prospective* calls upon the nation's fiscal and plenary powers as selfish or reckless, while simultaneously insisting that the government keep its hands off *existing* subsidies of equal or greater value.

In order to break the current political logjam, public intellectuals and officials will have to get their history right. That history should be informed by an understanding of the ways in which elected officials and administrators take cues from citizens, the relationship between the federal government and intermediary institutions that both transmit those ideas and carry out programs in order to achieve collective ends, and the political culture that these intermediaries operate in, including the international context. While the relationship between ideology and partisan agendas explains some of this history, material interests, social mobilization, spatial analysis, professional agendas, organizational imperatives, new media that connect the electorate and their elected representatives, and the duration of crises explain a great deal more. With a historical explanation of how we got to where we are today at their disposal, the public will be better prepared to ensure the proper balance between citizens, intermediate institutions, and the state. This is a difficult balancing act, to be sure, but a good place to start is by rejecting history that obfuscates partisan behavior and that mirrors, rather than exposes, partisan rhetoric.

Notes

Introduction

I would like to thank the two anonymous readers for the University of Pennsylvania Press, Erica Ginsburg, Holly Knowles, Bob Lockhart, Tom Sugrue, and the following colleagues for their comments on this essay and others in this collection: Ed Ayers, Brent Cebul, Christy Chapin, Lis Clemens, Gareth Davies, Richard John, Mel Leffler, Chris Loss, Cathie Jo Martin, Evan McCormick, Andrew McGee, Andy Morris, Loren Moulds, Peter Onuf, Laura Phillips, Ed Russell, Herman Schwartz, and Jon Zimmerman. I would also like to thank the Miller Center.

1. On the history of business interests and liberal administrations' approaches to financing health care, see Christy Chapin, *Ensuring America's Health* (New York: Cambridge University Press, forthcoming).

2. Matt Lassiter recently cautioned those who sought to replace the Progressive synthesis with its mirror image—conservatism studies—by noting that "a future generation of scholars may well critique our reigning historiographical consensus for tendencies we identified in our predecessors—that the interpretations of political history have tracked too closely to the red-blue binaries of journalism and punditry; that the literature has taken the contradictions and fragmentation of liberalism as given but smoothed over the fissures within conservatism; the recent pendulum swing has overstated the case for a rightward shift in American politics by focusing too narrowly on partisan narratives and specific election cycles." Matthew D. Lassiter, "Political History Beyond the Red-Blue Divide," *Journal of American History* (December 2011): 760.

3. For a good example of a headline that was based on the "spatial turn" that I reference here, see Jennifer Schuessler, "Trove of Information from the 1930s, Animated by the Internet: Lab in Richmond Animates Comprehensive 1932 Atlas," *New York Times*, December 25, 2013.

4. On the historical origins and development of this rhetoric, see Brent Cebul, "Developmental State: The Politics of Business, Poverty, and Economic Empowerment from the New Deal to the New Democrats" (Ph.D. dissertation, University of Virginia, 2014). For the quote, see Lassiter, "Political History," 764.

5. Ellis W. Hawley, *The New Deal and the Problem of Monopoly: A Study in Economic Ambivalence* (New York: Fordham University Press, 1995), xxxii. For two recent explications of the associational approach as it frames regulatory policy, see Robert C. Lieberman, "Private Power and American Bureaucracy: The EEOC and Civil Rights Enforcement," paper presented at the Symposium on the State, Remarque Institute, New York University, New York, October 2010; and Quinn Mulroy, "The Regulatory Power of Private Litigation and the Equal Opportunity Commission," paper presented at the Spring Fellowship Conference, Miller Center of Public Affairs, University of Virginia, Charlottesville, May 2011.

6. On the origins of the organizational synthesis, see Louis Galambos, "The Emerging Organizational Synthesis in Modern American History," *Business History Review* 46, no. 1 (Autumn 1970): 279–90. In their haste to discover the sources of state autonomy, APD scholars, myself

included, used much of what the organizational synthesis had to offer when it came to understanding the resources that state agencies could muster to assert their autonomy. The inherently comparative perspective of APD, however, with its insistence that the American state was weak, defined many of the associations spawned by the state as private or voluntary, failing to appreciate the ways in which state power could be projected through such institutions and, more important, made more palatable to citizens wary of direct state administration of services. No doubt, the appeal of Hawley's approach was also limited because of the temporal "distinctiveness" of these associational arrangements and the truncated period of history that many of its scholarly advocates claimed for them. This approach was inaugurated with World War I and spectacularly terminated with the National Industrial Recovery Administration in the early New Deal, and even its advocates did not claim that associational relations dominated the broad sweep of American history. That little was done to explore whether such relations existed before and after the 1920s, however, also bears testimony to the staying power of Progressive historiography's cycles of reform interpretation and APD's initial foray into state capacity, which shared a common stake in defining state capacity as autonomous state power.

7. For a history of APD, see Karen Orren and Stephen Skowronek, *The Search for American Political Development* (New York: Cambridge University Press, 2004).

8. Suzanne Mettler and Andrew Milstein, "American Political Development from Citizens' Perspective: Tracking Federal Government's Presence in Individual Lives over Time," *Studies in American Political Development* 21, no. 1 (Spring 2007): 115; Theda Skocpol, *Protecting Soldiers and Mothers: The Political Origins of Social Policy in the United States* (Cambridge, MA: Belknap Press of Harvard University Press, 1992); Christopher Howard, *The Hidden Welfare State: Tax Expenditures and Social Policy in the United States* (Princeton, NJ: Princeton University Press, 1997); Marie Gottschalk, *The Shadow Welfare State: Labor, Business, and the Politics of Health Care in the United States* (Ithaca, NY: Cornell University Press, 2000). For a good summary of the transition from state autonomy to a state strengthened by its ties to intermediary institutions, see Desmond King and Robert C. Lieberman, "American State Building: The Theoretical Challenge," in *The Unsustainable American State*, ed. Lawrence Jacobs and Desmond King (New York: Oxford University Press, 2009), 299–322.

9. R. Jeffrey Lustig explicates this delicate balancing act by tracing the ideas of Herbert Croly. Croly was enamored of the modern corporation, because of its apparent efficiency and ability to control its environment. Yet Croly distinguished between the plenary power of the state and even the most efficient organizations within civil society. See R. Jeffrey Lustig, *Corporate Liberalism: The Origins of Modern American Political Theory, 1890–1920* (Berkeley: University of California Press, 1982), 196; and Herbert Croly, *The Promise of American Life* (New York: Macmillan, 1909).

10. For quotes, see Theda Skocpol, "Bringing the State Back In: Strategies of Analysis in Current Research," in *Bringing the State Back In*, ed. Peter B. Evans, Dietrich Rueschemeyer, and Theda Skocpol (New York: Cambridge University Press, 1985), 4, 9. See also Brian Balogh, "Reorganizing the Organizational Synthesis: Federal-Professional Relations in Modern America," *Studies in American Political Development* 5, no. 1 (Spring 1991): 119–72.

11. Stephen Skowronek, *Building a New American State: The Expansion of National Administrative Capacities, 1877–1920* (New York: Cambridge University Press, 1982).

12. Ibid., 286.

13. Brian Balogh, "The State of the State Among Historians," *Social Science History* 27, no. 3 (Fall 2003): 460.

14. Brian Balogh, "Securing Support: The Emergence of the Social Security Board as a Political Actor, 1935–1939," in *Federal Social Policy: The Historical Dimension*, ed. Ellis W. Hawley and Donald T. Critchlow (University Park: Pennsylvania State University Press, 1988), 71. See also Robert H. Wiebe, *The Search for Order, 1877–1920* (New York: Hill and Wang, 1967); Robert

D. Cuff, *The War Industries Board: Business-Government During World War I* (Baltimore, MD: Johns Hopkins University Press, 1973); Samuel P. Hays, *Conservation and the Gospel of Efficiency: The Progressive Conservation Movement, 1890–1920* (New York: Atheneum, 1969); "Political Choice in Regulatory Administration," in *Regulation in Perspective: Historical Essays*, ed. Morton Keller and Thomas K. McCraw (Boston: Division of Research, Graduate School of Business Administration, Harvard University, 1981), 24–154; Skowronek, *Building a New American State*; Ellis W. Hawley, "Secretary Hoover and the Changing Framework of New Era Historiography," introduction to *Herbert Hoover as Secretary of Commerce, 1921–1928: Studies in New Era Thought and Practice*, ed. Ellis W. Hawley (Iowa City: University of Iowa Press, 1981); Ellis W. Hawley, "Herbert Hoover, the Commerce Secretariat, and the Vision of an 'Associative State,' 1921–1928," *Journal of American History* 61, no. 1 (June 1974): 116–40; and Martha Derthick, *Policymaking for Social Security* (Washington, DC: Brookings Institution, 1979).

15. Daniel P. Carpenter, "The Political Foundations of Bureaucratic Autonomy," *Studies in American Political Development* 15, no. 1 (Spring 2001): 113. In a similar vein, Adam Sheingate documented the ways in which the entrepreneurial skills of a select group of public officials shifted the story of political development from exogenous shocks to one that turned on the innovations from within agencies. Sheingate, "Political Entrepreneurship, Institutional Change, and American Political Development," *Studies in American Political Development* 17, no. 2 (Fall 2003): 185–203.

16. Stephen Skowronek, "What's Wrong with American Political Development," *Studies in American Political Development* 17, no. 1 (Spring 2003): 110.

17. William J. Novak, "The American Law of Association: The Legal-Political Construction of Civil Society," *Studies in American Political Development* 15 (Fall 2001): 163–88; Theda Skocpol, *Diminished Democracy: From Membership to Management in American Civic Life* (Norman: University of Oklahoma Press, 2003); Brian Balogh, *A Government Out of Sight: The Mystery of National Authority in Nineteenth-Century America* (New York: Cambridge University Press, 2009).

18. Skocpol, "Bringing the State Back In," 20.

19. There was a difference in the way in which APD scholars, and those working in the progressive/conservative vein viewed "citizen" groups, especially social movements. APD scholars tended to categorize them as interests, for better or worse. Progressive historians tended to view them as representing a far broader swath of citizens than their membership or even public opinion polling supported, often placing them on the "people" side of the "people vs. the interests" equation.

20. Carpenter, "Political Foundations," 113.

21. Rogers Smith, *Civic Ideals: Conflicting Visions of Citizenship in U.S. History* (New Haven, CT: Yale University Press, 1997). See also Alexander Keyssar, *The Right to Vote: The Contested History of Democracy in the United States* (New York: Basic Books, 2000). While APD scholars like Suzanne Mettler and Vesla Weaver have documented the way race and gender operated informally to restrict the influence of women and African Americans, they are joined by some of the leading historians of the past twenty years in documenting this phenomenon. A truncated list includes Eugene D. Genovese, *Roll Jordan Roll: The World the Slaves Made* (New York: Random House, 1974); Glenda Elizabeth Gilmore, *Gender and Jim Crowe: Women and the Politics of White Supremacy in North Carolina, 1896–1920* (Chapel Hill: University of North Carolina Press, 1996); Linda K. Kerber, *Women of the Republic: Intellect and Ideology in Revolutionary America* (Chapel Hill: University of North Carolina Press, 1980); Mary P. Ryan, *Cradle of the Middle Class: The Family in Oneida County, New York, 1790–1865* (New York: Cambridge University Press, 1981).

22. David Plotke, *Building a Democratic Political Order: Reshaping American Liberalism in the 1930s and 1940s* (New York: Cambridge University Press, 1996); Stephen Skowronek, *The*

Politics Presidents Make: Leadership from John Adams to Bill Clinton (Cambridge, MA: Belknap Press of Harvard University Press, 1993); Paul Charles Milazzo, *Unlikely Environmentalists: Congress and Clean Water, 1945–1972* (Lawrence: University Press of Kansas, 2006); Julian E. Zelizer, *Taxing America: Wilbur D. Mills, Congress, and the State, 1945–1975* (New York: Cambridge University Press, 1998); Samuel Kernell, "Rural Free Delivery as a Critical Test of Alternative Models of American Political Development," *Studies in American Political Development* 15, no. 1 (Spring 2001).

23. Cathie Jo Martin, "Sectional Parties, Divided Business," *Studies in American Political Development* 20, no. 2 (Fall 2006): 160–61, 170.

24. Richard Franklin Bensel, *Yankee Leviathan: The Origins of Central State Authority in America, 1859–1877* (New York: Cambridge University Press, 1990) and *The Political Economy of American Industrialization, 1877–1900* (New York: Cambridge University Press, 2000); Richard R. John, *Spreading the News: The American Postal System from Franklin to Morse* (Cambridge, MA: Harvard University Press, 1995); Robin L. Einhorn, *Property Rules: Political Economy in Chicago, 1833–1872* (Chicago: University of Chicago Press, 1991) and *American Taxation, American Slavery* (Chicago: University of Chicago Press, 2006); William J. Novak, *The People's Welfare: Law and Regulation in Nineteenth-Century America* (Chapel Hill: University of North Carolina Press, 1996) and "The American Law of Association."

25. Brian Balogh, "Americans Love Government—As Long as They Can't See It," *History News Network*, June 15, 2009, http://hnn.us/articles/88154.html. See also Michael Mann, *The Sources of Social Power* (New York: Cambridge University Press, 1986).

26. Skocpol, *Diminished Democracy*, 70–71.

27. Andrew J. F. Morris, "I Gave at the Plant: How the State and Labor Saved Voluntary Funding," paper presented at the Social Science History Conference, Miami, FL, October 2008, 3. See also Morris, *The Limits of Voluntarism: Charity and Welfare from the New Deal Through the Great Society* (New York: Cambridge University Press, 2009).

28. See "Good Citizens of a Good Nation: Post-War Reconfigurations of the Obligation to Give," in *Boundaries of the State in U.S. History*, ed. William Novak, Stephen Sawyer, and James T. Sparrow (Chicago: University of Chicago Press, forthcoming), 8 for quote and 17 for "charitable citizenship."

29. Novak, "The American Law of Association," 166.

30. Eldon Eisenach, "Liberal Citizenship and American National Identity," *Studies in American Political Development* 13, no. 1 (Spring 1999): 206.

31. Marc Allen Eisner, "Markets in the Shadow of the State," in *Government and Markets: Toward a New Theory of Regulation*, ed. Edward J. Balleisen and David A. Moss (New York: Cambridge University Press, 2010), 513; Charles Lindbloom, "The Market as Prison," *Journal of Politics* 44, no. 2 (May 1982): 33, quoted in Eisner, "Markets in the Shadow," 519.

32. Eisner, "Markets in the Shadow," 519–21; Daniel Carpenter, "Confidence Games: How Does Regulation Constitute Markets?," in *Government and Markets*, ed. Balleisen and Moss, 167.

33. Gerald Berk, *Louis D. Brandeis and the Making of Regulated Competition, 1900–1932* (New York: Cambridge University Press, 2009), 1–2. On professional relations with the state generally, see Christopher D. McKenna, *The World's Newest Profession: Management Consulting in the Twentieth Century* (New York: Cambridge University Press, 2006).

34. Berk, *Brandeis*, 2–3.

35. David Harvey, *A Brief History of Neoliberalism* (New York: Oxford University Press, 2007); Novak, "The American Law of Association," 165.

36. Alfred P. Chandler Jr., *The Visible Hand: The Managerial Revolution in American Business* (Cambridge, MA: Harvard University Press, 1977). Large mass production corporations such as those in tobacco and steel thrived on technological breakthroughs, innovations in managerial techniques, and improved information flows. They integrated vertically with suppliers and horizontally with competitors to increase the efficiency of their "throughput." These were highly

concentrated industries that obtained their advantages by internalizing those factors that made the production process and the market unpredictable. They made visible the hands as they sought to manage transactions previously left to the market or chance. For challenges to this interpretation, see Louis Galambos and Joseph Pratt, *The Corporate Commonwealth: United States Business and Public Policy in the 20th Century* (New York: Basic Books, 1988) and Philip Scranton, *Endless Novelty: Specialty Production and American Industrialization, 1865–1925* (Princeton, NJ: Princeton University Press, 1997).

37. Scranton, *Endless Novelty*, 18. "Proprietors adopted and shared schemes for improving work flows through the shop, refining accounting to provide cost data for diverse outputs, or through collaborative efforts, creating hiring bureaus and common terms of sale," Scranton concluded. From specialty textiles to custom production of locomotives, creating systems and networks, rather than standardizing products, distinguished the specialty manufacturing segment of the economy from the mass production giants chronicled by Chandler.

38. Berk, *Brandeis*, 27–28 for cultivational approach, and 29 for reasons that institutionalists missed this development. For quotation, see 29.

39. Berk has long been interested in the systems these professionals devised. As early as 1980, he noted the importance of standard setting and the role that professionally generated information played in the loosely associated networks that relied upon these common data for cues about costs, pricing, and demand. Summing up the conclusions of scholars at a Harvard Business School conference on the history of public policy, Berk noted that there was strong consensus that standard setting for products and services was essential to regulatory regimes as it "increases reliability and certainty in market transactions." Gerald P. Berk, "Approaches to the History of Regulation," in *Regulation in Perspective*, ed. Keller and McCraw, 198.

40. Berk, "Approaches to the History of Regulation," 250, 252, and 254. See also Laura Phillips Sawyer, *American Fair Trade: Proprietary Capitalism, Networks, and the "New Competition," 1890–1940* (New York: Cambridge University Press, forthcoming).

Chapter 1

1. Brian Balogh, *A Government Out of Sight: The Mystery of National Authority in Nineteenth-Century America* (New York: Cambridge University Press, 2009).

2. Ellis W. Hawley, "Herbert Hoover, the Commerce Secretariat, and the Vision of an 'Associative State,'" *Journal of American History* 61, no. 1 (June 1974): 116–40.

3. Samuel H. Beer, "The Modernization of American Federalism," *Publius* 3, no. 2 (Autumn 1973): 49–95; Brian Balogh, "Introduction: Directing Democracy," in *A Legacy of Innovation: Governors and Public Policy*, ed. Ethan G. Sribnick (Philadelphia: University of Pennsylvania Press, 2008), 1–22.

4. Stephen Skowronek, *Building a New American State: The Expansion of National Administrative Capacities, 1877–1920* (New York: Cambridge University Press, 1982).

5. Eldon J. Eisenach, "Bookends: Seven Stories Excised from the Lost Promise of Progressivism," *Studies in American Political Development* 10, no. 1 (Spring 1996): 178.

6. Peter S. Onuf, "Introduction: State and Citizen in British America and the Early United States," in *State and Citizen: British America and the Early United States*, ed. Peter Thompson and Peter Onuf (Charlottesville: University of Virginia Press, 2013), 10.

7. Theda Skocpol, *Protecting Soldiers and Mothers: The Political Origins of Social Policy in the United States* (Cambridge, MA: Belknap Press of Harvard University Press, 1992).

8. Brian Balogh, "'Mirrors of Desires': Interest Groups, Elections and the Targeted Style in Twentieth-Century America," in *The Democratic Experiment*, ed. Meg Jacobs, William Novak, and Julian Zelizer (Princeton, NJ: Princeton University Press, 2003), 222–49.

9. Hawley, "Herbert Hoover," 117. See also Hawley, *The New Deal and the Problem of Monopoly: A Study in Economic Ambivalence* (New York: Fordham University Press, 1995) and

The Great War and the Search for a Modern Order: A History of the American People and Their Institutions, 1917–1933 (New York: St. Martin's, 1979).

10. Robert H. Wiebe, *The Search for Order, 1877–1920* (New York: Hill and Wang, 1967). See also Louis Galambos, "The Emerging Organizational Synthesis in Modern American History," *Business History Review* 44, no. 3 (Autumn 1970): 279–90.

11. Eisenach, "Bookends," 173; Julia Irwin, *Making the World Safe: The American Red Cross and a Nation's Humanitarian Awakening* (New York: Oxford University Press, 2013), 217 (for chartering).

12. For an overview of the ways in which pluralist politics changed over the course of the twentieth century, see Brian Balogh, "Making Pluralism 'Great': Beyond a Recycled History of the Great Society," in *The Great Society and the High Tide of Liberalism*, ed. Sidney M. Milkis and Jerry Mileur (Amherst: University of Massachusetts Press, 2005), 145–82; and Elisabeth S. Clemens, "Lineages of the Rube Goldberg State: Building and Blurring Public Programs, 1900–1949," in *Rethinking Political Institutions: The Art of the State*, ed. Ian Shapiro, Stephen Skowronek, and Daniel Galvin (New York: New York University Press, 2006), 187–215.

For a penetrating analysis of the strengths and weakness of the American Medical Association, see Christy Chapin, "The AMA and the Institutional Intersection of Political and Market Power, 1945–1957" (paper presented to the Institute for Applied Economics and the Study of Business Enterprise, Johns Hopkins University, Baltimore, MD, October 2008).

For a sophisticated discussion of the way in which the voluntary sector adapted to the rise of New Deal social service provision, see Andrew J. F. Morris, *The Limits of Voluntarism: Charity and Welfare from the New Deal Through the Great Society* (New York: Cambridge University Press, 2008).

In *The G.I. Bill* (New York: Cambridge University Press, 2009), Kathleen Jill Frydl effectively demonstrates how prodigious spending for veterans was obscured by the institutional mechanisms through which it was delivered (in this case, the states and private contractors) at the very time federal authority was expanded.

13. Daniel P. Carpenter argues that "the unprecedented multiplicity and diversity of civic and voluntary associations during the period 1880–1920 enabled bureaucratic officials to enter and occupy these unique positions." See *The Forging of Bureaucratic Autonomy: Reputations, Networks, and Policy Innovation in the Executive Agencies, 1862–1928* (Princeton, NJ: Princeton University Press, 2001), 365. See also Ellen M. Immergut, *Health Politics: Interests and Institutions in Western Europe* (New York: Cambridge University Press, 1992). Immergut argues that what matters is not the power of the groups involved in making a decision but the country's structure of representation (11).

14. Citations to the literature on the hidden welfare state, the carceral state, and the contractual states are in subsequent notes.

15. On the state-building impact of moral impulses, see James A. Morone, *Hellfire Nation: The Politics of Sin in American History* (New Haven, CT: Yale University Press, 2003).

16. As Stephen Skowronek has reminded us, a number of institutional logics are in operation at any given time, each of which usually owes its origins to a distinct period of political development. This is the normal state of affairs, a condition that political modelers and historians alike have been too eager to flatten into the regularities of one dominant regime or another. Thus, there are "the incorporation of ancient, common law rules of work relations into the liberal, market-oriented constitutions of the post-Revolutionary era; the incorporation in the Constitution of protection for the institutions of slavery within a regime of individual rights; the promulgation of a regime of individual rights in the context of the primordial norms of the patriarchal family; the development of a mass-based party system around a pre-democratic republican Constitution hostile to the very notion of political parties," and the development that Skowronek has studied in great detail, "the emergence of a national economy based on the

corporate organization of capitalism within the context of a decentralized system of economic regulation rooted in state judiciaries." Stephen Skowronek, "Order and Change," *Polity* 28, no. 1 (Fall 1995): 95–96.

17. Brian Balogh, "Scientific Forestry and the Roots of the Modern American State: Gifford Pinchot's Path to Progressive Reform," *Environmental History* 7, no. 2 (April 2002): 198–225.

18. Karen R. Merrill, *Public Lands and Political Meaning: Ranchers, the Government, and the Property Between Them* (Berkeley: University of California Press, 2002), 48, and ch. 2 generally.

19. For an excellent discussion of the U.S. Department of Agriculture as a "university," see Carpenter, *Forging*, ch. 7.

20. Ibid., 261–70. See also Gabriel Kolko, *The Triumph of Conservatism: A Re-interpretation of American History, 1900–1916* (New York: Free Press, 1963).

21. Eldon J. Eisenach, *The Lost Promise of Progressivism* (Lawrence: University Press of Kansas, 1994), 18.

22. Women were more prone than other members of the associative order to seek government assistance at the state and local levels. Elisabeth S. Clemens, *The People's Lobby: Organizational Innovation and the Rise of Interest Group Politics in the United States, 1890–1925* (Chicago: University of Chicago Press, 1997); Lorraine Gates Schuyler, *The Weight of Their Votes: Southern Women and Political Leverage in the 1920s* (Chapel Hill: University of North Carolina Press, 2006). See also Balogh, "'Mirrors of Desires.'" The story of federal and voluntary relationships in social services is picked up in Morris, *Limits of Voluntarism*.

23. The work of Christopher Loss has changed the way in which we think about universities in relationship to the state. Breaking out of the more traditional university research-military complex, Loss considers the ways in which universities reshaped American citizenship from the 1920s through the end of the Cold War. Christopher Loss, *Between Citizens and the State: The Politics of American Higher Education in the Twentieth Century* (Princeton, NJ: Princeton University Press, 2012).

24. For a fascinating account of what the Social Security Administration was able to do once it *did* acquire computers, see Andrew Meade McGee, "'Please, Mr. Machine, Give This to a Human to Read': Electronic Data Processing, Systems Management, and Great Society Idealism in the Social Security Administration, 1965–1974" (master's thesis, University of Virginia, 2007).

25. For analytical histories of the early social security program and its administrators, see Martha Derthick, *Policymaking for Social Security* (Washington, DC: Brookings Institution Press, 1979); Edward Berkowitz, *Robert Ball and the Politics of Social Security* (Madison: University of Wisconsin Press, 2003); and Berkowitz, *Mr. Social Security: The Life of Wilbur J. Cohen* (Lawrence: University Press of Kansas, 1995).

26. Brian Balogh, Joanna Grisinger, and Philip Zelikow, "Making Democracy Work: A Brief History of Twentieth Century Executive Reorganization" (Miller Center of Public Affairs Working Paper, July 2002); Brian Balogh, *Chain Reaction: Expert Debate and Public Participation in American Commercial Nuclear Power, 1945–1975* (New York: Cambridge University Press, 1991); Harold D. Lasswell, "The Garrison State," *American Journal of Sociology* 46, no. 4 (January 1941): 455–68. On the "contract state," see Aaron L. Friedberg, *In the Shadow of the Garrison State: America's Anti-Statism and Its Cold War Grand Strategy* (Princeton, NJ: Princeton University Press, 2000).

27. Peter F. Drucker, *The Unseen Revolution: How Pension Fund Socialism Came to America* (New York: Harper and Row, 1976), 46, quoted in Jacob S. Hacker, *The Divided Welfare State: The Battle over Public and Private Social Welfare Benefits in the United States* (New York: Cambridge University Press, 2002), 82. See also Hacker, *Divided Welfare State*, 11, 83. For other key interpretations of the hidden welfare state, see Chris Howard, *The Hidden Welfare State: Tax Expenditures and Social Policy in the United States* (Princeton, NJ: Princeton University Press, 1997); and Jennifer Klein, *For All These Rights: Business, Labor, and the Shaping of America's*

Public-Private Welfare State (Princeton, NJ: Princeton University Press, 2003). For an excellent example of the political culture that limited the kind of taxation and its extent, see Julian Zelizer, *Taxing America: Wilbur D. Mills, Congress, and the State, 1945–1975* (New York: Cambridge University Press, 1998).

28. Hacker, *Divided Welfare State*. On subsidies that have favored white middle-class constituents, see Ira Katznelson, *When Affirmative Action Was White: An Untold Story of Racial Inequality in Twentieth-Century America* (New York: W. W. Norton, 2005).

29. Philip Rucker, "Sen. DeMint of S.C. Is Voice of Opposition to Health-Care Reform," *Washington Post*, July 28, 2009, http://www.washingtonpost.com/wp-dyn/content/article/2009/07/27/AR2009072703066.html; Timothy Noah, "The Medicare-Isn't-Government Meme," *Slate .com*, August 5, 2009, http://www.slate.com/id/2224350/.

Chapter 2

I would like to thank Kendrick Clements, Thomas Dunlap, Louis Galambos, Steve Innes, Joe Kett, James Lewis, Karen Merrill, Char Miller, Peter Norton, Jenry Morsman, Adam Rome, Ed Russell, Bruce Schulman, Jessica Wang, and an anonymous reader for their comments and suggestions regarding Chapter 2. I would also like to thank the Forest History Society for the research grant that it provided, and the Grey Towers Foundation.

1. Char Miller, *Gifford Pinchot and the Making of Modern Environmentalism* (Washington, DC: Island, 2001). On the trend to place man within nature, see William Cronon, *Uncommon Ground: Rethinking the Human Place in Nature* (New York: W. W. Norton, 1995) generally; specifically, see Cronon, "The Trouble with Wilderness; or, Getting Back to the Wrong Nature," in *Uncommon Ground*, 69–90. See also Richard White, "The Current Weirdness in the West," *Western Historical Quarterly* 28 (Spring 1997): 13–14. I would like to thank the Lewis and Clark Faculty Colloquium at the University of Virginia for its valuable discussion of trends in Progressive Era Western history and environmental history. On the conservation versus preservation structure, see, for instance, Roderick Nash, *Wilderness and the American Mind* (1967; New Haven, CT: Yale University Press, 1982).

2. William Cronon, "Landscapes of Abundance and Scarcity," in *The Oxford History of the American West*, ed. Clyde A. Milner II, Carol A. O'Connor, and Martha Sandweiss (New York: Oxford University Press, 1994), 608–10; quotation on 610.

For the details of the "Pinchot story," see Pinchot's autobiography, *Breaking New Ground* (New York: Harcourt and Brace, 1947); M. Nelson McGeary, *Gifford Pinchot: Forester, Politician* (Princeton, NJ: Princeton University Press, 1960); Harold T. Pinkett, *Gifford Pinchot: Private and Public Forester* (Urbana: University of Illinois Press, 1970); and John Milton Cooper, "Gifford Pinchot Creates a Forest Service," in *Leadership and Innovation: A Biographical Perspective on Entrepreneurs in Government*, ed. Jameson W. Doig and Erwin C. Hargrove (Baltimore, MD: Johns Hopkins University Press, 1987), 63–95. Char Miller has begun to revise the Pinchot story in significant ways. For an overview of the ways in which forest history is being reconceptualized, see Miller, ed., *American Forests: Nature, Culture and Politics* (Lawrence: University Press of Kansas, 1997). Among Miller's many articles, see "The Greening of Gifford Pinchot," *Environment History Review* (Fall 1992): 1–20; and "Keeper of His Conscience? Pinchot, Roosevelt and the Politics of Conservation," in *Theodore Roosevelt: Many-Sided American*, ed. Natalie A. Naylor, Douglas Brinkley, and John Allen Gable (Interlaken, NY: Heart of Lakes, 1992), 231–44. I benefited from the first three chapters of Miller's *Gifford Pinchot: A Life in Progress* in manuscript form. For a useful account of Pinchot's early career (particularly as it touched on the creation of forestry as a profession), see James G. Lewis, "Trained by Americans in American Ways: The Establishment of Forestry Education in the United States, 1885–1911" (Ph.D. dissertation, Florida State University, 2001).

The Pinchot story, of course, is integrally connected to the story of forestry in the United States. For this story, see Harold K. Steen, *The U.S. Forest Service: A History* (Seattle: University of Washington Press, 1976); *Americans and Their Forests: A Historical Geography* (New York: Cambridge University Press, 1989); David A. Clary, *Timber and the Forest Service* (Lawrence: University Press of Kansas, 1986); William G. Robbins, *Lumberjacks and Legislators: Political Economy of the U.S. Lumber Industry, 1890–1941* (College Station: Texas A&M Press, 1982); William D. Rowley, *U.S. Forest Service Grazing and Rangelands: A History* (College Station: Texas A&M Press, 1985); and Nancy Langston, *Forest Dreams, Forest Nightmares: The Paradox of Old Growth in the Inland West* (Seattle: University of Washington Press, 1995). See also Miller, *American Forests*; and Harold K. Steen, ed., *The Origins of the National Forests: A Centennial Symposium* (Durham, NC: Forest History Society, 1992).

3. On the relationship between Progressive Era conservation and the national government, Samuel P. Hays led the way, with *Conservation and the Gospel of Efficiency: The Progressive Conservation Movement, 1890–1920* (Cambridge, MA: Harvard University Press, 1959), and took the story up to recent times in *Beauty, Health, and Permanence: Environmental Politics in the United States, 1955–1985* (New York: Cambridge University Press, 1987). Donald Worster and Donald J. Pisani have written masterful accounts of the relationships between water, land, and politics in Worster, *Rivers of Empire: Water, Aridity, and the Growth of the American West* (New York: Oxford University Press, 1985); and Pisani, *Water, Land and Law in the West: The Limits of Public Policy, 1850–1920* (Lawrence: University Press of Kansas, 1996). Pisani has also summed up the literature on late nineteenth-century conservation and early twentieth-century conservation in "Forests and Conservation, 1865–1890," *Journal of American History* 72, no. 2 (September 1985): 340–59; and "The Many Faces of Conservation: Natural Resources and the American State," 1900–1940," in *Taking Stock: American Government in the Twentieth Century*, ed. Morton Keller and R. Shep Melnick (New York: Cambridge University Press, 1999). Two important works that look at the conservation and preservation movements from the top down and bottom up are Stephen Fox, *The American Conservation Movement: John Muir and His Legacy* (Madison: University of Wisconsin Press, 1981); and Richard W. Judd, *Common Lands, Common People: The Origins of Conservation in Northern New England* (Cambridge, MA: Harvard University Press, 1997). Although this environmental history has yet to penetrate the American political development literature that focuses on state building in the late nineteenth and early twentieth centuries, Richard White, by examining the politics of conservation in the West, has made a powerful case for the significance of water, land, and forests in American state building. See White, *"It's Your Misfortune and None of My Own": A New History of the American West* (Norman: University of Oklahoma Press, 1991). See also Karen R. Merrill, "In Search of the 'Federal Presence' in the American West," *Western Historical Quarterly* 30, no. 4 (Winter 1999): 469. Merrill looks specifically at grazing issues in "Whose Home on the Range?" *Western Historical Quarterly* 27 (Winter 1996): 433–51. One last source to know about is Michael McCarthy, "The First Sagebrush Rebellion," in Steen, *Origins of the National Forests*, 187.

4. This essay is part of a larger manuscript entitled *Building a Modern State: Gifford Pinchot and the Tangled Roots of Modern Administration in the United States*. In addition to the themes dealt with here, the book argues that Pinchot's success in extending and actively managing the national forests depended on his ability to work closely with a number of special interests (a point made by Samuel P. Hays long ago), his cultivation of key congressional constituencies, and his sensitivity to and flexibility in dealing with local issues that often conflicted with the national mandates he sought to implement in the Forest Service.

5. Miller, *Gifford Pinchot*, chs. 1 and 2; Joseph A. Arnold, "James Wallace Pinchot," *1907 Yearbook of the United States Department of Agriculture* (Washington, DC: Government Printing Office, 1908), 495–96; M. Nelson McGeary, *Gifford Pinchot: Forester-Politician* (Princeton, NJ: Princeton University Press, 1960), 3–4; John Milton Cooper, "Gifford Pinchot Creates a Forest

Service," in *Leadership and Innovation: A Biographical Perspective on Entrepreneurs in Government*, ed. Jameson W. Doig and Erwin C. Hargrove (Baltimore, MD: Johns Hopkins University Press, 1987), 64.

6. Quoted in McGeary, *Gifford Pinchot*, 3.

7. On the Puritan attitude toward idleness, see Stephen Innes, *Creating the Commonwealth: The Economic Culture of Puritan New England* (New York: W. W. Norton, 1995), 13; James Pinchot to Gifford Pinchot, December 4, 1882, and June 3, 1883, Papers of Gifford Pinchot, "Family Members," Manuscript Division, Library of Congress, Washington, DC (hereafter, GPLCFAM); Max Weber, *The Protestant Ethic and the Spirit of Capitalism,* trans. Talcott Parsons (New York: Scribner's and Sons, 1958), 154, cited in Daniel T. Rodgers, *The Work Ethic in Industrial America, 1850–1920* (Chicago: University of Chicago Press, 1978), 9.

8. Gifford Pinchot to Mary Pinchot, November 2, 1883, GPLCFAM.

9. Stephen Fox, *John Muir and His Legacy: The American Conservation Movement* (Boston: Little, Brown, 1981), 122.

10. Innes, *Creating the Commonwealth*, 15, 58–59. For a good periodization of the social gospel movement, see Charles Howard Hopkins, *The Rise of the Social Gospel in American Protestantism, 1865–1915* (New Haven, CT: Yale University Press, 1940). See also Robert T. Handy, *A Christian America: Protestant Hopes and Historical Realities* (New York: Oxford University Press, 1984), 135–47; Ronald C. White Jr. and C. Howard Hopkins, *The Social Gospel: Religion and Reform in Changing America* (Philadelphia: Temple University Press, 1976). On Pinchot's attendance at Reverend Aitken's revivals, see Gifford Pinchot to "Nettie" Pinchot, November 23, 1880, GPLCFAM. See also Gifford Pinchot to Mary Pinchot, October 18, 1880; Mary Pinchot to Gifford Pinchot, October 17, 1880; and Mary Pinchot to Gifford Pinchot, November 28, 1880, GPLC-FAM, for Gifford's religious preferences. Also see Washington Gladden, *Where Does the Sky Begin?* (Boston: Houghton Mifflin, 1904), 14, quoted in William McGuire King, "An Enthusiasm for Humanity: The Social Emphasis in Religion and Its Accommodation in Protestant Theology," in *Religion and Twentieth Century American Intellectual Life*, ed. Michael J. Lacey (New York: Cambridge University Press, 1989), 53–54. On religious campaigns to improve man's environment, see Paul Boyer, *Urban Masses and Moral Order in America, 1820–1920* (Cambridge, MA: Harvard University Press, 1978). On America's collective mission, see John Higham, "Hanging Together: Divergent Unities in American History," *Journal of American History* 61 (June 1974): 13. For a discussion of how this fits into the larger Progressive agenda, see Brian Balogh, "Reorganizing the Organizational Synthesis: Federal-Professional Relations in Modern America," *Studies in American Political Development* 5, no. 1 (1991): 123. On the reform influence of the social gospel, see also Robert M. Crunden, *Ministers of Reform: The Progressives' Achievement in American Civilization, 1889–1920* (New York: Basic, 1982). For theological implications of social gospel, see King, "Enthusiasm for Humanity," 49–77.

11. Rodgers, *Work Ethic*, 9.

12. For movement to an intensive economy, see Louis Galambos, *America at Middle Age: A New History of the United States in the Twentieth Century* (New York: McGraw-Hill); Louis Galambos and Joseph Pratt, *The Rise of the Corporate Commonwealth: United States Business and Public Policy in the 20th Century* (New York: Basic, 1988); David Potter, *People of Plenty: Economic Abundance and the American Character* (Chicago: University of Chicago Press, 1954); and Samuel Haber, *Efficiency and Uplift: Scientific Management in the Progressive Era, 1890–1920* (Chicago: University of Chicago Press, 1964), 3 and chs. 3–6. See also Daniel Nelson, *Frederick W. Taylor and the Rise of Scientific Management* (Madison: University of Wisconsin Press, 1980).

Less publicized but more substantive was the movement toward efficient government. Here, the advance guard operated at the municipal level. They heralded the objectives of nonpartisanship, strong executives, and the separation of politics from administration and sought to achieve these ends through the scientific use of statistics, civil service reform, municipal research bureaus, and city structural changes in executive/legislative relations epitomized by the city manager form of government.

Americans not only had to work hard, but also had to work productively. On Earth, this was the key to ameliorating social problems; above, it demonstrated a collective movement toward the millennium. A disciple of Frederick W. Taylor, Morris L. Cooke, embodied the disparate strands of America's tortured relationship to work. Convinced that Taylor's ideas paved the way to social reconstruction, Cooke popularized the gospel of efficiency in what approximated a religious crusade. See Edwin T. Layton Jr., *The Revolt of the Engineers: Social Responsibility and the American Engineering Profession* (1971; Baltimore, MD: Johns Hopkins University Press, 1986), 144. Cooke juxtaposed Taylor's arcane prescriptions and popular appeal, and, as Philadelphia's director of public works in Mayor Randolph Blankenberg's reform administration, he also transposed Taylor's teachings from the private sector to a public policy forum. See Layton, *Revolt*, ch. 7.

13. For a good discussion of the relationship between the moral and technical roots of the efficiency movement and the appeal of the professions to men with Pinchot's background, see Haber, *Efficiency and Uplift*, 55. For Pinchot's career inclinations, see Pinchot, *Breaking New Ground*, 3.

14. For a subtle analysis of how a group of religious scholars transformed Yale into an institution that trained men for careers in the modern professions, see Louise L. Stevenson, *Scholarly Means to Evangelical Ends: The New Haven Scholars and the Transformation of Higher Learning in America, 1830–1890* (Baltimore, MD: Johns Hopkins University Press, 1986). On Pinchot's love of the forest, see Pinchot, *Breaking New Ground*, 2.

15. On the reconciliation of work and pleasure in the religious strain of American culture in the last part of the nineteenth century, see Rodgers, *Work Ethic*, 95–97 and ch. 4, "Play, Repose, and Plenty." See also Herbert Spencer, farewell banquet address, New York, November 9, 1882, quoted in Rodgers, *Work Ethic*, 94. On Wanamaker's church, see William Leach, *Land of Desire: Merchants, Power, and the Rise of a New American Culture* (New York: Pantheon, 1993), 199–200.

16. On Professor Brewer's comments, see Gifford Pinchot to James Pinchot, December 11, 1885, Papers of Gifford Pinchot, "General Correspondence," Manuscript Division, Library of Congress, Washington, DC (hereafter, GPLCGNCR). On being thrown out of first division, see Gifford Pinchot to Mary Pinchot, December 20, 1885, box 53, GPLCGNCR. In fact, Gifford was able to retain his place in the first division. See Gifford Pinchot to Mary Pinchot, September 26, 1886, box 53, GPLCGNCR. By December 1886, he was again worried about falling out. Gifford Pinchot to Mary Pinchot, December 8, 1886, box 53, GPLCGNCR. This time Pinchot's fears were confirmed. See James Pinchot to Gifford Pinchot, January 13, 1887, box 53, GPLCGNCR.

17. On the goal of universities to form character, see Peter Dobkin Hall, *The Organization of American Culture, 1700–1900: Private Institutions, Elites, and the Origins of American Nationality* (New York: New York University Press, 1982), 49, 252. On no U.S. forestry programs, see Harold T. Pinkett, *Gifford Pinchot: Private and Public Forester* (Urbana: University of Illinois Press, 1970), 16. On the Forestry Division dominated by Pinchot's Yale friends and graduates, see McGeary, *Gifford Pinchot*, 46, 49.

18. For the quote on Yale friends, see Pinchot, *Breaking New Ground*, 6. On Skull and Bones, see Pinchot to "Dear Pats of D'87," March 26, 1890, Papers of Gifford Pinchot, "Breaking New Ground," Manuscript Division, Library of Congress, Washington, DC (hereafter, GPLCBNG). Because of the club's secretive nature, it is not easy to find details about its practices. One useful starting point can be found in Bob Woodward and Walter Pincus, "Bush Opened Up to Secret Yale Society," *Washington Post*, August 7, 1988. George H.W. Bush and several of his family members were Bones men.

19. On Skull and Bones, see Woodward and Pincus, "Bush Opened Up," 1, 19. On Pinchot's experience in France, see Pinchot to "Dear Pats," March 26, 1890, GPLCBNG.

20. Pinchot offered financial help through loans to many of his less affluent Yale friends and other employees who did not attend Yale. See Pinkett, *Gifford Pinchot*, 51. Also see Dan A. Oren, *Joining the Club: A History of Jews and Yale* (New Haven, CT: Yale University Press, 1985), 23. For a good description of how the sophomore societies, junior fraternities, and senior societies winnowed the entering class, see George Wilson Pierson, *Yale College: An Educational History* (New Haven, CT: Yale University Press, 1952), 36. Most of Pinchot's brothers probably did not face pressing financial problems. But those with whom he formed lasting bonds often did. Among the poorer brothers was Walker, who planned to become a lawyer, providing that he could earn the money to get through law school (Gifford Pinchot to Mary Pinchot, March 13, 1889, GPCLGNCR). Henry Graves, who would become Pinchot's right-hand man at the Bureau of Forestry and the first dean of the School of Forestry at Yale, was another Bones man who faced financial difficulty after graduating (Graves to Pinchot, February 12, 1894, GPLCBNG). For a good summary of Pinchot's classmates' career plans, see Gifford Pinchot to Mary Pinchot, March 13, 1889, GPCLGNCR. For the story of affluent Yale men helping out classmates, see Holbrook cited in Helen Lefkowitz Horowitz, *Campus Life: Undergraduate Cultures from the End of the Eighteenth Century to the Present* (New York: Knopf, 1987), 51.

21. On Woodruff's correspondence with Pinchot, see Gifford Pinchot to Mary Pinchot, March 13, 1889, GPCLGNCR. Woodruff began to complain that he was not earning enough while practicing law in 1899, telling Pinchot that he was "the only person I can talk intelligently to about my affairs" (Woodruff to Pinchot, June 13, 1899, GPLCGNCR). In February 1900, Woodruff informed Pinchot that some friends were pushing him to run for assistant U.S. district attorney for the Eastern District of Pennsylvania. Would Pinchot mind exercising his influence? The letter closed with the Skull and Bones farewell "Yours in D 87" (Woodruff to Pinchot, February 1, 1900, GPLCGNCR). For further correspondence, see Woodruff to Pinchot, March 1, 1902, GPLCGNCR; Woodruff to Pinchot, May 26, 1902, GPLCGNCR; Pinchot to Woodruff telegram, May 28, 1902, GPLCGNCR; Pinchot to Taft, February 25, 1902, GPLCGNCR. On shelling peas, see Woodruff to Pinchot, May 25 and May 27, 1899, GPLCGNCR.

22. For Woodruff's inquiry to Pinchot, see Woodruff to Pinchot, November 28, 1902, GPLCGNCR. For Pinchot's hiring of Woodruff, see Maud Woodruff to Pinchot, December 23, 1902 [misdated as April 23, 1902], GPLCGNCR. For George Woodruff's apologies to Pinchot, see Woodruff to Pinchot, January 31, 1903, GPLCGNCR. For Pinchot's acceptance of Woodruff's proposal to work for him, see Pinchot to Woodruff, February 2, 1903, GPLCGNCR. For a summary of Woodruff's service, see Pinkett, *Gifford Pinchot*, 69. Woodruff began by reviewing the *Congressional Record*, looking for all matters that legally might affect the Forestry Division. As examples, Pinchot cited issues ranging from a resolution to investigate the lands of the Seneca to a bill granting land warrants to soldiers and sailors of the Spanish-American War. Pinchot offered Woodruff a salary of $1,500 and possibly as high as $1,800 (Pinchot to Woodruff, February 2, 1903, GPLCGNCR). For Woodruff as Pinchot's lifelong friend, see McGeary, *Gifford Pinchot*, 46. When Pinchot missed his fortieth class reunion, he blamed it on his buddy Woodruff. "Forty Years ago," Pinchot wrote the class, "George and I made a plan to go to the South Seas together in a schooner we were to own and sail." Pinchot fulfilled the plan in 1929; George backed out (*Fortieth Reunion of '89*, p. 48, Yale University Library). For Woodruff's declaration of loyalty, see Woodruff to Pinchot, January 31, 1903, GPLCGNCR.

23. For a brief biographical sketch of Graves, see Andrew Denny Rodgers III, *Bernhard Eduard Fernow: A Story of North American Forestry* (Durham, NC: Forest History Society, 1991), 218. On Pinchot's urging Graves to pursue forestry, see Graves, "Reflections of an Old Time Forester," undated [circa 1940], box 17, folder 208, Henry Solon Graves Papers, Yale University Archives, New Haven, CT (hereafter, Graves Papers).

Graves's financial concerns were well founded. As late as 1896, Graves was still struggling to pay off his graduate school debts while his father struggled to put his other son through school on a schoolteacher's salary. To make matters worse, Mrs. Graves was bedridden, making the task of caring for boarders especially onerous. See "Papa" to Graves, November 16, 1896, box 10, folder 122, Graves Papers. For Graves's concerns about the financial viability of a career in forestry, see Graves to Pinchot, June 28, 1895, GPLCBNG. For Walker's opposition to Graves working in forestry, see Walker to Pinchot, March 14, 1893, GPLCGNCR. For correspondence with Graves and his father, see "Papa" to Graves, November 8, 1896, box 10, folder 122, Graves Papers. For instance, in the spring of 1884 Pinchot convinced his father and two partners in Phelps Dodge to contribute money for Graves's salary. Graves used the funds to study the White Pine. See the Papers of Gifford Pinchot, the Diaries of Gifford Pinchot, April 8–9, 1894, Manuscript Division, Library of Congress, Washington, DC (hereafter, GPLCDIAR).

24. For Pinchot's correspondence with Vanderbilt, see Pinchot to Vanderbilt, September 8, 1893, reel 5, Papers of Gifford Pinchot, Letterbooks and Diaries, Manuscript Division, Library of Congress, Washington, DC (hereafter, GPLCLBDI). Graves raised money for the YMCA long after leaving Yale. See James Reynolds to Graves, June 11, 1896, and April 25, 1898, box 10, folder 122, and Henry Fowler to Graves, April 25, 1898, box 10, folder 123, Graves Papers. On Graves at Yale, see M. A. Huberman, "'G.P' and 'Harry'—Two Foresters," May 3, 1941, box 10, folder 126, Graves Papers.

25. On Graves going to do boundary work, see Graves to Pinchot, June 13, 1897, GPLC-BNG. On Graves as a Pinchot houseguest, see Graves to Pinchot, September 1 [1900—the year is not included but this is the most likely year], GPLCBNG. On Pinchot picking Graves to be the dean of the Yale School of Forestry, see McGeary, *Gifford Pinchot*, 49. On Yale's need of Graves, see Pinchot to Brandis, March 31, 1900, GPLCBNG. On Graves's gratitude to Pinchot, see Graves to Pinchot, September 1[, 1900], GPLCBNG.

26. On Graves's effectiveness, see Pinkett, *Gifford Pinchot*, 69.

27. McGeary, *Gifford Pinchot*, 19. For a description of Pinchot's cruise, see Pinchot to Mary Pinchot, October 14, 1889, GPLCBNG. For Pinchot's lack of plans, see Pinchot, *Breaking New Ground*, 6. The chief of the division, Bernhard Fernow, offered Pinchot a desk and use of the library but was unable to pay him anything. He did tell Pinchot that the prospect for a paying job in the future looked bright (Fernow to Pinchot, September 25, 1889, GPLCBNG). For a good review of the Forest Pavilion at the French Exposition, see *Garden and Forest*, January 15, 1890, pp. 26–27.

28. On Pinchot's road to meeting Brandis, see Gifford Pinchot to James Pinchot, October 18, 1889, GPLCBNG. On Brandis, see Pinchot, *Breaking New Ground*, 56.

29. On the length of Pinchot's training, see Gifford Pinchot to James and Mary Pinchot, January 5, 1890, GPLCBNG. On Brandis's opinion on the value of professional training, see Brandis to Pinchot, October 14, 1890, GPLCBNG.

30. Brandis to James Pinchot, March 20, 1890, GPLCBNG.

31. On Pinchot's stubbornness to return, see Gifford Pinchot to James and Mary Pinchot, January 5, 1890, GPLCBNG. On the lack of a need for extensive training, see Gifford Pinchot to Mary Pinchot, February 12, 1890, GPLCBNG. Pinchot wrote ecstatically in that letter that Forstmeister Meister approved of his return after a year. In his memoirs, Pinchot attributed Meister's wisdom to his citizenship in "the most democratic country in Europe" (Pinchot, *Breaking New Ground*, 20).

32. Drew Evan VandeCreek, "'Make It National!': Economic Expertise and the Development of the Progressive Economic Policymaking System, 1890–1933" (Ph.D. dissertation, University of Virginia, 1996). On Pinchot being recognized as a forestry authority, see Pinchot, *Breaking New Ground*, 33, 36, and also January 11, 1891, GPLCDIAR.

33. *Garden and Forest*, August 6, 1890, p. 386. For Brandis's view that forests must not just be preserved but also made economically productive, see Gifford Pinchot to James and Mary Pinchot, January 5, 1890, GPLCBNG.

34. Gifford Pinchot, "The Forest: Forest Policy Abroad," *Garden and Forest* 4, nos. 150 (January 7, 1891), 151 (January 14, 1981), and 152 (January 21, 1981). The quotations about the most profitable forests, "forest policy abroad," facts learned from India, and the value of state control are from, respectively, 152, p. 34; 152, p. 35; 152, p. 34; and 150, p. 8.

35. For Brandis's ideas on private funding of forest management, see Brandis to James Pinchot, March 20, 1890, GPLCBNG. For efforts to convince Amos Eno to purchase forests for Pinchot to manage, see Gifford Pinchot to James Pinchot, July 31, 1890, GPLCBNG; and Gifford Pinchot to Mary Pinchot, September 21, 1890, GPLCBNG.

36. On discussing forest management with Biltmore, see October 12, 1891, GPLCDIAR. On the goal of managing Biltmore Forest, see December 6, 1891, GPLCDIAR.

37. Fernow to Pinchot, February 2, 1892, GPLCBNG; Fernow to Pinchot, September 19, 1892, GPLCBNG.

38. October 15, 1891, GPLCDIAR; February 4, 1892, GPLCDIAR.

39. Brandis to Pinchot, January 7, 1895, GPLCBNG. On the failed planting experiment, see Pinkett, *Gifford Pinchot*, 27.

40. On difficulty finding interest in Biltmore Forest, see Gifford Pinchot to James Pinchot, September 12, 1892, GPLCLBDI.

41. For Pinchot's exhibit, see Char Miller, "The Prussians Are Coming!" *Journal of Forestry* 91 (March 1991): 42; Miller quotes B. C. Truman, *History of the World's Fair* (New York: Arno, 1983), 610. On forestry building in Chicago, see Ben W. Twight, "Bernhard Fernow and Prussian Forestry in America," *Journal of Forestry* 88, no. 2 (February 1990): 23. On Pinchot's display, see Pinchot, *Breaking New Ground*, 56–57; and Pinkett, *Gifford Pinchot*, 26. Regarding Pinchot's delight with the display, see Gifford Pinchot to Mary Pinchot, January 2, 1892, GPLCBNG. Pinchot also agreed to prepare an exhibit of forestry for the state of North Carolina (Harold T. Pinkett, "Gifford Pinchot at Biltmore," *North Carolina Historical Review* 34, no. 3 [July 1957]: 352).

42. On the decision to use photographs in the exhibit, see Gifford Pinchot to James Pinchot, August 15, 1892, GPLCLBDI. Also see Julie K. Brown, *Contesting Images: Photography and the World's Columbian Exposition* (Tucson: University of Arizona Press, 1994), ch. 3; Robert W. Rydell, *All the World's a Fair: Visions of Empire at American International Expositions, 1876–1916* (Chicago: University of Chicago Press, 1984), 45.

43. *Garden and Forest*, February 21, 1894, p. 71.

44. For a description of Pinchot's exhibit as the principal exhibit on forestry, see Truman, *History of the World's Fair*, 285. Pinchot's juxtaposition of utilitarian rationale and the romantic medium was particularly effective, given its intended constituency. It reinforced for its primarily eastern audience a sense of immediacy about a problem that was located thousands of miles to the West. Nancy K. Anderson, "The Kiss of Enterprise: The Western Landscape as Symbol and Resource," in *The West as America: Reinterpreting Images of the Frontier, 1820–1920*, ed. William H. Truettner (Washington, DC: Smithsonian Institution Press), 241. Anderson concludes from her survey of Western imagery that Americans were deeply ambivalent about the tension between preservation and use. The tension was often resolved by the assumption that resources, like the nation's redwoods, were inexhaustible (275–76, 281). For a good discussion of the way in which socially realist photographs were used in campaigns of social reform during the Progressive Era, see Eileen Boris's discussion of Lewis Hine in *Home to Work: Motherhood and the Politics of Industrial Homework in the United States* (New York: Cambridge University Press, 1994), 95.

45. For Fox's invitation, see Fox to Pinchot, February 26, 1894, GPLCBNG. See also *Buffalo Express*, February 23, 1894, Papers of Gifford Pinchot, "Scrap Books," Manuscript Division, Library of Congress, Washington, DC (hereafter, GPLC Scrap Books), 7.

46. Southorth to Pinchot, October 10, 1895, GPLCBNG.

47. *Garden and Forest*, February 21, 1894, p. 71. For financial results in the pamphlet, see Schenck, "Biltmore Forest," in Papers of Carl Alwin Schenck, State University of North Carolina, Raleigh, NC (hereafter, Schenck Papers), 37, 40; *Garden and Forest*, February 21, 1894, p. 71.

48. "Trip to Whittier w/Whitney," March 2, 1892, box 959, Biltmore Forest file, GPLCBNG; and Schenck, "Biltmore Forest," 38.

49. One exception to the acceptance of Pinchot's accounting is Ben W. Twight, who, in an exchange with Char Miller, cited Schenck's memoirs as evidence that Pinchot might have fudged the numbers. Ben W. Twight, " 'Fernow' Author Responds," *Journal of Forestry* 91 (March 1991): 25–27 , in response to Miller, "The Prussians Are Coming!" 23–27, 42. It appears that by fiscal year 1905, more than a decade after Pinchot arrived, Biltmore Forest had begun to produce an operating surplus. See Schenck to Vanderbilt, budget submission, November 1, 1905, Schenck Papers.

50. Robert E. Wolf, "National Forest Timber Sales and the Legacy of Gifford Pinchot: Managing a Forest and Making It Pay," in Miller, *American Forests*, 87–105. For information about the Pinchot profitability promise that led to control over national forest reserves, see p. 88. For Pinchot's House testimony, see p. 88. For Forest Service losses, see p. 89.

51. Daniel Rodgers identified three "clusters of ideas," three distinct "social languages" that tied disparate parts of the Progressive program together. They were the "rhetoric of antimonopolism," an "emphasis on social bonds," and the "language of social efficiency." See Rodgers, "In Search of Progressivism," *Reviews in American History* 10, no. 4 (December 1982): 123. These social languages are usually portrayed, understandably, as arrayed against the social language of the market. Yet if we are to understand the popular political appeal of Progressives, it is essential that we consider the ways in which they adapted their programs and appeals to the powerful language of market choice in the United States in the early twentieth century. Doing so "naturalizes" our conception of Progressivism, adapting it to the specific historical constraints faced by those who would extend the reach of the national government into the lives of millions of Americans.

Four relatively recent interpretations have resurrected Progressive historiography. Intellectual historians, led by James Kloppenberg, have charted the formal ideational foundations of the Progressive social agenda. See Kloppenberg, *Uncertain Victory: Social Democracy and Progressivism in European and American Thought, 1870–1920* (New York: Oxford University Press, 1986). Political scientists and sociologists, often referred to as the "new institutionalists," have concentrated on the relationship between political structure and the ability of national administrative agencies to carve out autonomy required to pursue public policies. See, for instance, Theda Skocpol, *Protecting Soldiers and Mothers: The Political Origins of Social Policy in the United States* (Cambridge, MA: Harvard University Press, 1992); and Stephen Skowronek, *Building a New American State: The Expansion of National Administrative Capacities, 1877–1920* (New York: Cambridge University Press, 1982). Eldon Eisenach melds an intellectual history of Progressivism to an institutional base in *The Lost Promise of Progressivism* (Lawrence: University of Kansas Press, 1994). Eisenach's conception of "parastate institutions" is particularly useful in understanding the Progressive conception of political power. Gendered interpretations have reconceptualized a number of Progressive mainstays, from the meaning of citizenship to the foundations of the modern welfare state. See, for instance, Linda Gordon, *Pitied but Not Entitled: Single Mothers and the History of Welfare, 1890–1935* (Cambridge, MA: Harvard University Press, 1995); Robyn Muncy, *Creating a Female Dominion in American Reform, 1890–1935* (New York: Oxford University Press, 1991); and Skocpol, *Protecting Soldiers and Mothers*. Most recently, Daniel Rodgers's *Atlantic Crossings* has offered an exhaustive and elegant account of Progressive cross-fertilization. Rodgers, *Atlantic Crossings: Social Politics in a Progressive Age* (Cambridge, MA: Harvard University Press, 1998). As Rodgers puts it, the "transatlantic moment was occupied by a range of amateurs" (26). The amateurs served as "salad makers," to use Henry Demarest

Lloyd's term, "of all good ideas in Europe and Australia" (Lloyd quoted in Rodgers, *Atlantic Crossings*, 67).

Chapter 3

I would like to thank Ed Ayers, Lou Galambos, Mark Hansen, Shelly Kaplan, Meg Jacobs, Ira Katznelson, Mike Lacey, Chuck McCurdy, Sid Milkis, Jim Morone, Bill Novak, Peter Onuf, Elizabeth Sanders, Lori Gates Schuyler, Gil Troy, Hal Wells, and Julian Zelizer for their comments and suggestions. I would also like to thank the staff at the Hoover Presidential Library for their archival assistance. Participants both in seminars at the Johns Hopkins University and the University of Virginia and in Organization of American Historians and Policy History Conference panels made valuable comments. I am also grateful for the support of the Woodrow Wilson Center for International Affairs, the Hoover Presidential Library Foundation, and the University of Virginia School of Arts and Sciences.

1. Alex Keyssar, *The Right to Vote: The Contested History of Democracy in the United States* (New York: Basic, 2000); Michael McGerr, *The Decline of Popular Politics: The American North, 1865–1928* (New York: Oxford University Press, 1986); Mark Lawrence Kornbluh, *Why America Stopped Voting: The Decline of Participatory Democracy and the Emergence of Modern American Politics* (New York: New York University Press, 2000).

2. Gil Troy, *See How They Ran: The Changing Role of the Presidential Candidate* (New York: Free Press, 1991); Richard Jensen, *The Winning of the Midwest: Social and Political Conflict, 1888–1896* (Chicago: University of Chicago Press, 1971), 165; McGerr, *Decline of Popular Politics*, ch. 6; Robert Westbrook, "Politics as Consumption: Managing the Modern American Election," in *Culture of Consumption*, ed. Richard Wightman Fox and T. J. Jackson Lears (New York: Pantheon, 1983), 143–74. On "going public," see Samuel Kernell, *Going Public: New Strategies of Presidential Leadership*, 2nd ed. (Washington, DC: Congressional Quarterly Press, 1993).

On the decline of the party system and the rise of alternatives, see Richard L. McCormick, "The Party Period and Public Policy: An Exploratory Hypothesis," *Journal of American History* 66 (1979): 279–98; Sidney M. Milkis, *Political Parties and Constitutional Government: Remaking American Democracy* (Baltimore: Johns Hopkins University Press, 1999), 4–8; Gerald Gamm and Renee M. Smith, "Presidents Parties and the Public: Evolving Patterns of Interaction, 1877–1929," in *Speaking to the People: The Rhetorical Presidency in Historical Perspective*, ed. Richard J. Ellis (Amherst: University of Massachusetts Press, 1998), 90–93; Jeffrey K. Tulis, *The Rhetorical Presidency* (Princeton, NJ: Princeton University Press, 1987); and Sidney M. Milkis and Daniel J. Tichenor, "'Direct Democracy' and Social Justice: The Progressive Campaign of 1912," *Studies in American Political Development* 8, no. 2 (Fall 1994): 282–340.

3. Gamm and Smith, "Presidents, Parties and the Public," 104–8.

4. On "consumption communities," compare Daniel J. Boorstin, *The Americans: The Democratic Experience* (1973; New York: Vintage, 1974), 89–164; and Olivier Zunz, *Why the American Century?* (Chicago: University of Chicago Press, 1998), ch. 4. See also the examples of consumption transcending geographical boundaries in Edward L. Ayers, *The Promise of the New South: Life After Reconstruction* (New York: Oxford University Press, 1992), 81–103; and Lizbeth Cohen, *Making a New Deal: Industrial Workers in Chicago, 1919–1939* (New York: Cambridge University Press, 1990), ch. 3. On the prevalence of business and professional groups, see Jack L. Walker Jr., *Mobilizing Interest Groups in America: Patrons, Professions, and Social Movements* (Ann Arbor: University of Michigan Press, 1991), 12.

5. Brian Balogh, "The State of the State Among Historians," *Social Science History* (Fall 2003): 455–63; Louis Galambos, *America at Middle Age* (New York: McGraw-Hill, 1983); Louis Galambos, *Competition and Cooperation: The Emergence of a National Trade Association* (Baltimore, MD: Johns Hopkins University Press, 1966); Robert Wiebe, *Business Men and Reform: A Study of the Progressive Movement* (Cambridge, MA: Harvard University Press, 1962); Robert

Wiebe, *The Search for Order, 1877–1920* (New York: Hill and Wang, 1967); and Samuel P. Hays, *The Response of Industrialism, 1885–1914* (Chicago: University of Chicago Press, 1957).

For an explanation and critique of the "organizational synthesis," see Brian Balogh, "Reorganizing the Organizational Synthesis: Federal-Professional Relations in Modern America," *Studies in American Political Development* 5, no. 1 (1991): 119–72. Stephen Skowronek relies heavily on the "organizational" approach in *Building a New American State: The Expansion of National Administrative Capacities, 1877–1920* (New York: Cambridge University Press, 1982). In *The Politics That Presidents Make: Leadership from John Adams to Bill Clinton* (Cambridge, MA: Belknap Press of Harvard University Press, 1997), Skowronek carves out a far greater role for ideas, replacing some of the organizational baggage of his earlier work with the concept of policy regimes. Like my own work, and that of most scholars who focus on policy, the electoral basis for these policy regimes is not as well grounded.

Although Theda Skocpol conceptualizes an electorate integrally connected to the policy-making system in *Protecting Soldiers and Mothers: The Political Origins of Social Policy in the United States* (Cambridge, MA: Harvard University Press, 1992) and notes the politically convenient way in which veterans' benefits were funneled to Republican constituents after the Civil War, this is not the case for Part III of *Protecting*, where women are effective politically before gaining the right to vote. Thus, Progressive women could set agendas in terms of their own ideals as long as they did *not* have the vote. "Ironically," Skocpol writes, "this situation prevailed only as long as women were collectively mobilized for styles of politics that did not depend primarily on voting. . . . [A]fter the franchise was fully won, politically active American women faced the same choices and obstacles 'within the system' as other U.S. citizens" (319). What Skocpol neglects to say is that they also now had the same clout when it came to voting.

Anna L. Harvey, in *Votes Without Leverage: Women in American Electoral Politics, 1920–1970* (New York: Cambridge University Press, 1998), also sees a marked decline in the influence of women by the mid-1920s. In a recent synthesis of the role played by women in politics during the 1920s, Kristi Anderson (as do Skocpol and Harvey) documents the ways in which the political system adapted to women, redefining the boundary that distinguished men and women in public life in *After Suffrage: Women in Partisan and Electoral Politics Before the New Deal* (Chicago: University of Chicago Press, 1996). But Anderson too concludes that suffrage resulted in declining clout for women by the late 1920s (102–9). For a good discussion of the long-standing presumption among scholars that women's influence declined after gaining the vote, see Anderson, *After Suffrage*, 5–9. For its origins, see William Henry Chafe, *The American Woman: Her Changing Social, Economic, and Political Roles, 1920–1970* (New York: Oxford University Press, 1972), 299–300.

Nancy Cott, in *The Grounding of Modern Feminism* (New Haven, CT: Yale University Press, 1987), sees more continuity with "voluntarist" politics continuing from the Progressive Era through the 1920s. Because Cott frames the question as whether a "woman bloc" would emerge and whether it would elect women to office—something that clearly did not happen—rather than whether the power of the vote would make those lobbying for issues disproportionately supported by women more effective, she concludes that acquiring the vote mattered little. Voluntarist politics "continued as women's principal political mode" (Cott, *Grounding*, 114 and ch. 3). The most striking of these continuities was "women's favoring the pursuit of politics through voluntary associations over the electoral arena" (Cott, *Grounding*, 85). This bifurcation of associations and the electoral arena is characteristic of the more general tendency within political history to separate policy from the electoral sphere.

Cott and Robin Muncy also distinguish women's voluntary groups—even after women obtained the vote—from traditional interest groups because the women's groups did not have the capacity to make huge monetary contributions to political campaigns. See Cott, *Grounding*, 99; and Robin Muncy, *Creating a Female Dominion in American Reform, 1890–1935* (New York:

Oxford University Press, 1991), 128. Paula Baker, in "The Domestication of Politics: Women and American Political Society, 1780–1920," *American Historical Review* 89 (June 1984): 639, argues that because women created a separate sphere in politics, they were the first to craft "interest-group tactics," providing a model that men would follow as partisan politics declined in the twentieth century. I take issue with this argument on two grounds. First, it ignores the rich history of male interest groups that proliferated in the late nineteenth century, alongside the dominant party system. Second, and more relevant to this chapter, it neglects the crucial connection between votes and interest-group effectiveness.

Even the more recent revisionist literature, which seeks to restore some agency to women after they gained suffrage, implicitly suggests that women settled for the politics of symbolism. Anderson sums this up succinctly, writing that, by the late 1920s, "male leaders responded to women's concerns on a primarily symbolic basis" (*After Suffrage*, 105). This fits squarely within the traditional politics of consumption, which views candidates in Lippmann-esque terms as manipulators of symbols, adept at appealing to homogeneous audiences.

For impressive evidence that the votes of women *did* matter during the 1920s, see Lori Gates Schuyler, "The Weight of Their Votes: Southern Women and Politics in the 1920s" (Ph.D. dissertation, University of Virginia, 2001).

David B. Truman refers to "widely held attitudes that are not expressed in interaction" as "potential interest groups." The Hoover campaign provided the organizational catalyst to forge behavior and action, ideally resulting in a vote for Hoover. See Truman, *The Governmental Process: Political Interests and Public Opinion* (1951; Berkeley, CA: Institute of Governmental Studies, 1993), 35.

6. Truman, *Governmental Process*, 33; Walker, *Mobilizing Interest Groups*, 12–13.

7. John Mark Hansen, *Gaining Access: Congress and the Farm Lobby, 1919–1981* (Chicago: University of Chicago Press, 1991), 228–29; Wiebe, *Search for Order*; Gabriel Kolko, *The Triumph of Conservatism: A Reinterpretation of American History* (New York: Free Press, 1977); Elisabeth S. Clemens, *The People's Lobby: Organizational Innovation and the Rise of Interest Group Politics in the United States, 1890–1925* (Chicago: University of Chicago Press, 1997), 6–7, 207.

8. On policy feedback, see Skocpol, *Protecting Soldiers and Mothers*, 57–60.

9. Jean M. Converse, *Survey Research in the United States: Roots and Emergence, 1890–1960* (Berkeley: University of California Press, 1987); Susan Herbst, *Numbered Voices: How Opinion Polling Has Shaped American Politics* (Chicago: University of Chicago Press, 1993).

10. Susan Strasser, *Satisfaction Guaranteed: The Making of the American Mass Market* (New York: Pantheon, 1989), 161, and ch. 5. See also a review of Strasser by Lizbeth Cohen, "The Mass in Mass Consumption," *Reviews in American History* (December 1990): 549–55; Hal Wells, "Remapping America: Market Research and American Society, 1900–1940" (Ph.D. dissertation, University of Virginia, 1999); Richard Tedlow, *New and Improved: The Story of Mass Marketing in America* (New York: Basic, 1990), 6; Roland Marchand, *Advertising the American Dream: Making Way for Modernity, 1920–1940* (Berkeley: University of California Press, 1985); The President's Research Committee on Social Trends, *Recent Social Trends in the United States*, vol. 2 (New York: McGraw-Hill, 1933), 866; and Cohen, *Making a New Deal*, ch. 3.

11. Herbert Croly, *The Promise of American Life* (1909; Cambridge, MA: Harvard University Press, 1965), 270; Eldon Eisenach, *The Lost Promise of Progressivism* (Lawrence: University Press of Kansas, 1994), ch. 1.

12. Eisenach, *Lost Promise*, chs. 1, 4; Harwood Lawrence Childs, *Labor and Capital in National Politics* (1930; New York: Arno Press, 1974), 243; E. Pendleton Herring, *Group Representation Before Congress* (Baltimore, MD: Johns Hopkins University Press, 1929), 2; "Electioneering on the Air," *New Republic* (September 3, 1924): 9, quoted in Clayton R. Koppes, "The Social Destiny of the Radio: Hope and Disillusionment in the 1920s," *South Atlantic Quarterly* 68, no. 3 (Summer 1969): 366.

13. Walter Lippmann, *Public Opinion* (1922; New York: Free Press, 1965), Part III, ch. 15; Robert Westbrook, *John Dewey and American Democracy* (Ithaca, NY: Cornell University Press, 1991), 294–96; Richard Jensen, *The Winning of the Midwest: Social and Political Conflict, 1888–1896* (Chicago: University of Chicago Press, 1971), 165; McGerr, *Decline of Popular Politics*, ch. 6; Troy, *See How They Ran*; Westbrook, "Politics as Consumption," 143–74.

14. Childs, *Labor and Capital*, 247.

15. Arthur F. Bentley, *The Process of Government* (1908; Cambridge, MA: Harvard University Press, 1967), 204, 209–10, 223.

16. Michael J. Lacey and Mary O. Furner, eds., *The State and Social Investigation in Britain and the United States* (New York: Woodrow Wilson Center Press and Cambridge University Press, 1993), 40–49; Herring, *Group Representation*, 60; Edward Bernays, *Crystallizing Public Opinion* (New York: Boni and Liveright, 1923), 146, cited in Wells, "Remapping America," 338; President's Research Committee, *Recent Social Trends*, 1515; Barry D. Karl, *Charles E. Merriam and the Study of Politics* (Chicago: University of Chicago Press, 1974), 201. Estimates cited in Mark P. Petracca, "The Rediscovery of Interest Group Politics," in *The Politics of Interests: Interest Groups Transformed*, ed. Mark P. Petracca (Boulder, CO: Westview, 1992), 13.

17. Peri Ethan Arnold, "Herbert Hoover and the Continuity of American Public Policy," *Public Policy* 20 (Fall 1972): 525–44.

18. Joan Hoff Wilson, *Herbert Hoover: Forgotten Progressive* (1975; Prospect Heights, IL: Waveland Press 1992), 46; Craig Lloyd, *Aggressive Introvert: A Study of Herbert Hoover and Public Relations Management, 1912–1932* (Columbus: Ohio State University, 1972), 37, 45–52; Frederick M. Feiker, "Washington as a Date Line Is News" and "What Business May Expect," Speeches and Articles 1928, box 16, Feiker Papers, Herbert Hoover Presidential Papers, West Branch, IA (hereafter, HHPL).

19. Wells, "Remapping America," chs. 3 and 5; William Leach, *Land of Desire: Merchants, Power, and the Rise of a New American Culture* (New York: Pantheon, 1993), 364–65; Ellis Hawley, "Herbert Hoover, the Commerce Secretariat, and the Vision of an 'Associative State,' 1921–1928," *Journal of American History* 61, no. 1 (1974): 116–40; David E. Hamilton, "Building the Associative State: The Department of Agriculture and American State-Building," *Agricultural History* 64, no. 2 (Spring 1990): 207–18; Colin Gordon, *New Deals: Business, Labor, and Politics in America, 1920–1935* (New York: Cambridge University Press, 1994).

20. Correspondence between Arthur Rule and Lewis Strauss, general manager of the Federated Fruit and Vegetable Growers, box 67; and Aaron Sapiro and Lewis Strauss, box 68 and Subject File I—Accretions, Herbert Hoover, 1927, box 68, Papers of Lewis L. Strauss, HHPL; Monahan to Matthews, April 30, 1925, Department of Commerce Files, box 2, Advertising 1925 folder; Assistant to Feiker to Tay, reporting on "Camp Cooperation," September 11, 1925, Advisory Committee on Statistics (2), 1924–25, box 1; Frederick M. Feiker, "What Business May Expect from the Next President," November 25, 1928, Speeches and Articles, 1928 folder, box 16, Frederick M. Feiker Papers, HHPL; "Associations" correspondence, Department of Commerce files, HHPL; April 12, 1921, Associations Information, 1921, box 38, Commerce Collection, HHPL; May 5, 1921, Associations Information, 1921, box 38, Commerce Collection, HHPL; MacChesney to Dear Sir, October 25, 1928, Republican Party—1928, Final Report of National Committee, box 38, MacChesney Papers, HHPL; Hoover to Bradfute, February 14, 1923, American Farm Bureau Federation, 1922–1927 folder, Department of Commerce Collection, box 24, HHPL.

21. Gary Dean Best, "The Hoover-for-President Boom of 1920," *MidAmerica* 53, no. 4 (October 1971): 227.

22. Roy V. Peel and Thomas C. Donnelly, *The 1928 Campaign: An Analysis* (New York: Richard R. Smith, 1931), 87; David Burner, *Politics of Provincialism: The Democratic Party in Transition, 1918–1932* (1968; Cambridge, MA: Harvard University Press, 1986), 179–80. For an

opposing view on the possibility of a Smith victory, see Allan J. Lichtman, *Prejudice and Old Politics: The Election of 1928* (Chapel Hill: University of North Carolina Press, 1979), 245; and Paul A. Carter, "Deja Vu; or Back to the Drawing Board with Alfred E. Smith," *Reviews in American History* 8, no. 2 (1980): 272–76.

See also *St. Louis Globe-Democrat*, September 25, 1928; Edward Flesh to George Barr Baker, October 1, 1928, Baker folder, box 7, Campaign and Transition Files, HHPL; unattributed note, September 27, 1928, Work, Hubert file, box 72, Campaign and Transition (hereafter, C&T) Files, HHPL; Colored People 1928 files, box 7, Akerson Papers, HHPL (particularly A. L. Holsey, secretary to the principal, Tuskegee Normal and Industrial Institute, to Akerson, March 29, 1928; Akerson to Richey telegram, January 26, 1929, Akerson folder, box 2, C&T Files, HHPL; Akerson to Richey, February 7, 1929, Strauss folder, box 66, C&T Files, HHPL; Akerson to Mr. Graves, March 27 [1928], Fox folder, box 8, Akerson Papers, HHPL; Fox to Akerson, March 26, 1928, Fox folder, box 8, Akerson Papers, HHPL; and Akerson to Fox, March 28, 1928, Fox folder, box 8, Akerson Papers, HHPL); "Fort Memo," undated, Fort file, box 27, C&T Files, HHPL; Rickard diaries, memo, August 1, 1928, HHPL.

"My general impression," Edgar Rickard, Hoover's close personal friend, confided to his diary, is "that HH is so completely absorbed in winning nomination that absolutely nothing else at the moment counts and I am sorry to see how completely this dominates his every action." As if to confirm Rickard's worst fears, Hoover wrote the Republican National Committee chair Hubert Work in July 1928 that he "must get some more political people here." Having come this far with his friend, Rickard could hardly object when Hoover handed him $5,000 in cash that had been given to the chief for "campaign purposes." On Rickard's concern regarding Hoover's political operatives, see Rickard Diaries, February 12, 1928; and on Hoover's funds for "campaign purposes," see Rickard Diaries, June 7, 1928; Hoover to Work, July 14, 1928, Work folder, box 73, C&T Files, HHPL.

23. Rickard diaries, August 24, 1928; Irwin to Hoover, September 13, 1928, Irwin folder, box 38, C&T Files, HHPL; "Me and the Movies," 3, *Baloney Knife* folder, box 1, Akerson Papers, HHPL; Bruce Barton to Hoover, February 23, 1929, Barton folder, box 8, HHPL.

24. Edward Anthony, *Oral History*, 25–27, 74, HHPL; "Back Stage in Washington," January 2, 1929, no citation, Akerson folder, box 1, Akerson Papers, HHPL; Henry C. Morris to Hunt, September 28, 1928, and Henry C. Morris to Hunt, September 28, 1928, Hunt folder, box 9, Strother Papers, HHPL.

25. Keyssar, *Right to Vote*, 218; Baker, "Domestication," 643–47; Muncy, *Creating a Female Dominion*, 128; "Women's Page Service," in Anthony to Akerson, March 10, 1928, Anthony folder, box 5, Akerson Papers, HHPL; Victoria French Allen, "Some Pages from Hoover History," Edward Anthony Papers, Women's Page Service folder, box 1, HHPL; Maloney to Rosenwald, July 31, 1928, misc. M folder, box 14, Strauss papers, Campaign of 1928 Collection, HHPL.

26. Capper statement, August 20, 1928, Capper folder, box 8, C&T Files, HHPL; Hill to Alan Fox, November 24, 1928 Rickard folder, box 58, C&T Files, HHPL; *New York Times*, November 25, 1928; Akerson to Anthony, April 9, 1928, Anthony folder, box 5, Akerson Papers, HHPL; Harvey, *Votes Without Leverage*, ch. 4.

27. Lawrence Richey to unstated [most likely J. Bennett Gordon], undated [November 1928], box 157, C&T Papers, HHPL; J. Bennett Gordon to Lawrence Richey, January 3, 1929, box 157, C&T Papers, HHPL, p. 5; Harvey, *Votes Without Leverage*, ch. 4.

28. Gordon to Richey, January 3, 1929, 7; Harvey *Votes Without Leverage*, 130.

29. MacChesney to Work, November 12, 1928, Work folder, box 73, C&T Files, HHPL; MacChesney to Hoover, October 19, 1928, MacChesney folder, box 45, C&T Files, HHPL; Goodrich to Hoover and attached, February 9, 1929, Goodrich folder, box 29, C&T Files, HHPL; Nagel to Hoover, November 12, 1928, Nagel folder, box, C&T Files, HHPL.

30. Anthony, *Oral History*, 41–47, HHPL; Goodrich to Hoover, August 24, 1928, Goodrich folder, box 29, C&T Files, HHPL; Hoover to Work, February 7 [1929], Work folder, box 73, C&

T Files, HHPL; Kruesi to J. R. R. Nutt, RNC, October 8, 1928, Negroes folder, box 14, Straus Campaign 1928 Collection, HHPL; Wellford to Kruesi, October 5, 1928, Negroes folder, box 14, Strauss Campaign 1928 Collection, HHPL; Kirchoffer to Hoover, August 24, 1928, Kirchoffer folder, box 41, C&T Files, HHPL.

31. Hawley, "Herbert Hoover."

32. Herbert Hoover, "The Engineer's Place in the World," January 10, 1924, p. 3, HHPL; Herbert Hoover, May 24, 1923, p. 1, HHPL.

33. MacChesney to James W. Good, November 7, 1928, "Final Report," Hoover-Curtis Organization Bureau, MacChesney Papers, HHPL; MacChesney to Hoover, July 5, 1921, and Jackson to Hoover, October 29, 1925, MacChesney 1921–1925 folder, Commerce Collection, HHPL; MacChesney to Good, November 7, 1928, "Final Report," MacChesney Papers, HHPL; MacChesney to Work, November 12, 1928, Work folder, box 72, C&T Files, HHPL.

34. MacChesney to Good, November 7, 1928, 8.

35. MacChesney, "Special Bulletin," MacChesney Papers, HHPL.

36. Harry H. Culver to Hoover, August 29, 1928; Hoover to Work, August 31, 1928, Work folder, box 72, C&T Files, HHPL; undated form letter from Hollingsworth, "Special Bulletin."

37. S. G. Rubinow to Akerson, September 14, 1928, and Attachment B, Hoover Waterways Club folder, box 35, C&T Files, HHPL; Rand to Grocers, October 16, 1928, "Special Bulletin," MacChesney Papers, HHPL.

38. Brockman to Dear Sir, "Special Bulletin"; E. Percy Miller to Dear Friends, undated, "Special Bulletin."

39. Ibid. See also Voiland to Mr. L.C. Biglowe, September 15, 1928, "Special Bulletin."

40. Harvey, *Votes Without Leverage*, 107, 115, 119, 122; Rebecca Edwards, *Angels in the Machinery: Gender in American Party Politics from the Civil War to the Progressive Era* (New York: Oxford University Press, 1997); MacChesney to Good, November 7, 1928, "Final Report."

41. "Women's Activities," Hoover-Curtis Organization Bureau, Final Report, HHPL.

42. Ibid.

43. "Hoover-Curtis Organization Bureau Hoover Hostesses," Final Report.

44. Ibid. (emphasis added).

45. Mrs. Silas H. Strawn, "Final Report"; "The Master of Emergencies Film," Herbert Hoover 1921–1920, box 15, MacChesney Papers, HHPL.

46. *New York Times*, November 8, 1928, 2; Peel and Donnelly, *1928 Campaign*, 170; Lichtman, *Prejudice*, 160–62.

47. Hollingsworth, "Special Bulletin."

48. Skocpol, *Protecting Soldiers and Mothers*, 519–22; Harvey, *Votes Without Leverage*, 7–12, quotation from 7; Lichtman, *Prejudice*, 165.

Chapter 4

Portions of this essay were presented to a panel at the 1989 meeting of the Organization of American Historians and Harvard University's Twentieth Century American History Workshop. I thank the participants of those forums, the editors of *Studies in American Political Development*, and Louis Galambos for their criticism and insights.

1. Louis Galambos, "The Emerging Organizational Synthesis in Modern American History," *Business History Review* 44 (Autumn 1970): 279–90.

2. Louis Galambos, "Technology, Political Economy, and Professionalization: Central Themes of the Organizational Synthesis," *Business History Review* 57 (Winter 1983): 471–93. Although this article refined the organizational scholars' original emphasis on broad social forces attributed to modernization, modernization remained the engine that drove the organizational interpretation.

3. Alan Brinkley, "Writing the History of Contemporary America: Dilemmas and Challenges," *Daedalus* 113, no. 3 (Summer 1984): 134.

4. Michael McGerr, "Organization, Individualism, and Class Conflict: Redefining Early Twentieth-Century America," paper presented to the Seminar, Department of History, Johns Hopkins University, October 20, 1986, p. 5.

5. There are some notable exceptions. In 1988, Samuel P. Hays once again broke new ground by pushing his study of administrative decision-making forums into the Reagan administration in *Beauty, Health, and Permanence: Environmental Politics in the United States, 1955–1985* (New York: Cambridge University Press, 1987). Robert Wiebe, in *The Segmented Society: An Introduction to the Meaning of America* (New York: Oxford University Press, 1975), and Louis Galambos, in *America at Middle Age: A New History of the U.S. in the Twentieth Century* (New York: McGraw-Hill, 1983), have sketched the contours of post–World War II American state-society relations.

6. Brinkley, "Writing the History," 134.

7. Galambos, "Emerging Organizational Synthesis."

8. For a good summary of that field, see Daniel T. Rodgers, "In Search of Progressivism," *Reviews in American History* (December 1982): 113–32; David P. Thelen, "Social Tensions and the Origins of Progressivism," *Journal of American History* 56 (1969): 323–41. The seminal revision before the organizational scholarship was Richard Hofstadter, *The Age of Reform: From Bryan to F.D.R.* (New York: Knopf, 1955).

9. On the Progressive synthesis, see John Higham, *History* (Englewood Cliffs, NJ: Prentice-Hall, 1965), 171–232; and Richard Hofstadter, *The Progressive Historians: Turner, Beard, Parrington* (New York: Knopf, 1968).

10. Herbert Croly, *The Promise of American Life* (New York: Macmillan, 1909; reprint, Indianapolis: Bobbs-Merrill, 1965), 6. The transition from natural abundance to constructed abundance is emphasized by David Potter in *People of Plenty: Economic Abundance and the American Character* (Chicago: University of Chicago Press, 1954), 86–90, and it is applied directly to the growth of the twentieth-century state in Galambos, *America at Middle Age,* ch. 2.

11. John Higham, "Hanging Together: Divergent Unities in American History," *Journal of American History* 61 (June 1974): 13.

12. Ibid., 23.

13. Ibid., 24. See also Henry May, "The Religion of the Republic," in *Ideas, Faiths, and Feelings: Essays on American Intellectual and Religious History, 1952–1982,* ed. Henry May (New York: Oxford University Press, 1983).

14. Charles A. Beard and Mary R. Beard describe the "progressive wave" that brought about reforms toward "direct government" in *The Rise of American Civilization* (New York: Macmillan, 1939), 556–62.

15. Higham, "Hanging Together," 25.

16. Walter Lippmann, review of William English Walling's *Larger Aspect of Socialism, Call,* May 11, 1913, quoted in Ronald Steel, *Walter Lippmann and the American Century* (Boston: Little, Brown, 1980), 79. See also Lippmann, *Drift and Mastery: An Attempt to Diagnose the Current Unrest* (New York: Mitchell Kennerley, 1914; reprint, Madison: University of Wisconsin Press, 1985), 87.

17. Rodgers, "In Search of Progressivism," 123–24.

18. Samuel P. Hays, *The Response to Industrialism, 1885–1914* (Pittsburgh: Pittsburgh University Press, 1957); Robert Wiebe, *The Search for Order, 1877–1920* (New York: Hill and Wang, 1967); Glenn Porter, *The Rise of Big Business, 1860–1910* (Arlington Heights, IL: AHM, 1973).

19. In a detailed elaboration of precisely how this alliance worked, Richard L. McCormick has described how professional regulation of big business proceeded hand in hand with the less scientific but more deeply held public conviction that big business corrupted. See "The Discovery

That Business Corrupts Politics: A Reappraisal of the Origins of Progressivism," *American Historical Review* 86 (1981): 247–74.

20. Ibid., 265.

21. Ibid., 265–70.

22. Samuel P. Hays, *Conservation and the Gospel of Efficiency: The Progressive Conservation Movement, 1890–1920* (Cambridge, MA: Harvard University Press, 1959); Samuel P. Hays, "The Politics of Reform in Municipal Government in the Progressive Era," *Pacific Northwest Quarterly* (October 1964): 157–69; Gabriel Kolko, *Railroads and Regulation, 1877–1916* (Princeton, NJ: Princeton University Press, 1965); Gabriel Kolko, *The Triumph of Conservatism: A Reinterpretation of American History, 1900–1916* (New York: Macmillan, 1963). See also Robert Wiebe, *Businessmen and Reform* (Cambridge, MA: Harvard University Press, 1962); and Louis Galambos, *Competition and Cooperation: The Emergence of a National Trade Association* (Baltimore, MD: Johns Hopkins University Press, 1966).

23. Other central works include Alfred D. Chandler, *The Visible Hand: The Managerial Revolution in American Business* (Cambridge, MA: Harvard University Press, 1977); and Samuel P. Hays, *The Response to Industrialism, 1885–1914* (Pittsburgh: Pittsburgh University Press, 1957).

24. Hays documents how the business community used the techniques of direct democracy to break the hold of ward politicians in "The Politics of Reform."

25. Wiebe, *Search for Order*, 223.

26. Theda Skocpol, "Bringing the State Back In: Strategies of Analysis in Current Research," in *Bringing the State Back In*, ed. Peter B. Evans, Dietrich Rueschemeyer, and Theda Skocpol (New York: Cambridge University Press, 1985), 4. On Weberian roots, see Brinkley, "Writing the History," 132. See also Louis Galambos, "Parsonian Sociology and Post-Progressive History," *Social Science Quarterly* 50, no. 1 (June 1969): 25–45.

27. David B. Truman was probably the most influential political scientist in this regard. See Truman, *The Government Process*, 2nd ed. (1951; New York: Knopf, 1971).

28. For a good summary of this literature and the most recent scholarship on issue networks, see Thomas L. Gais, Mark A. Peterson, and Jack L. Walker, "Interest Groups, Iron Triangles and Representative Institutions in American National Government," *British Journal of Political Science* 14 (April 1984): 161–85. Grant McConnell's *Private Power and American Democracy* (New York: Knopf, 1966), which comes down squarely on the "capture" end of the spectrum, is still one of the best examples of this bipolar framework. The classic formulation of "capture" theory is Marver H. Bernstein, *Regulating Business by Independent Commission* (Princeton, NJ: Princeton University Press, 1955).

29. Skocpol, "Bringing the State Back In," 4.

30. The best statement of the Weberian ideal can be found in Max Weber, *The Theory of Social and Economic Organization* (Glencoe, IL: Free Press, 1947).

31. Peter Blau has emphasized informal practices that operate under the surface in bureaucracies that often violate the official rules and alter officially stated objectives. See Peter M. Blau, *Bureaucracy in Modern Society* (New York: Random House, 1956), 53–57. He has also stressed the link between competent officials' work satisfaction and the expansion of their responsibilities and their agencies' jurisdictions in *The Dynamics of Bureaucracy: A Study of Interpersonal Relations in Two Government Agencies* (Chicago: University of Chicago Press, 1955), 198–202. James G. March and Herbert A. Simon, in *Organizations* (New York: Wiley, 1958), 172–210, have used the concept of "bounded rationality" to introduce the limitations of human rationality into the study of organizations.

32. Skocpol, "Bringing the State Back In," 4. Samuel Beer noted in 1973 that the old pressure-group model did not apply to what he called "technocratic" politics. The merger of science and public policy, according to Beer, "shifts the initiative in government from the economic and social environment of government to government itself." Samuel H. Beer, "The Modernization of American Federalism," *Publius* 3 (Fall 1973): 75.

33. Samuel P. Hays, "Political Choice in Regulatory Administration," in *Regulation in Perspective: Historical Essays*, ed. Thomas K. McCraw (Cambridge, MA: Harvard University Press, 1981).

34. Skocpol, "Bringing the State Back In." Among historians, Hays himself has led the way with his pathbreaking study of politics and the environment, *Beauty, Health, and Permanence*. Other examples include Stephen Skowronek's *Building a New American State* (New York: Cambridge University Press, 1982), Christopher L. Tomlin's *The State and the Unions* (New York: Cambridge University Press, 1985), and my "Securing Support: The Emergence of the Social Security Board as a Political Actor, 1935–1939," in *Federal Social Policy: The Historical Dimension*, ed. Donald T. Critchlow and Ellis W. Hawley (University Park: Pennsylvania State University Press, 1988).

History informed by "supply-side" organizational theory has pushed the discovery of bureaucratic political agendas to its extreme. Carolyn Weaver's *The Crisis in Social Security: Economic and Political Origins* (Durham, NC: Duke University Press, 1982) is a good example.

35. Skowronek, *Building a New American State*, 287.

36. The Budgeting and Accounting Act of 1921, for instance, did create a beachhead for expert advice on fiscal matters and an administrative apparatus for managing the budget within the executive branch. But for each executive structure established, there seemed to be a congressional counterweight as well. In the case of fiscal advice, it was the General Accounting Office. In the case of the President's Civil Service Commission, it was the Congressional Bureau of Efficiency. Ibid., chs. 3 and 6.

37. Ellis Hawley, "Social Policy and the Liberal State in Twentieth Century America," in Critchlow and Hawley, *Federal Social Policy,* 127.

38. This relationship to the state bears certain similarities to the relationship of the professions to capitalism during this period, as suggested in the writings of Charles Peirce and as interpreted by Thomas L. Haskell in "Professionalism versus Capitalism: R. H. Tawney, Emil Durkheim, and C. S. Peirce on the Disinterestedness of Professional Communities," in *The Authority of Experts: Studies in History and Theory*, ed. Thomas L. Haskell (Bloomington: Indiana University Press, 1984), 214–19.

39. Skocpol, "Bringing the State Back In," 4.

40. The exception was Samuel Hays's account of the rise of scientific conservation (in *Conservation*). While the profession of forestry that Gifford Pinchot pioneered ultimately achieved a degree of expertise, credentials, and autonomy, it was hardly born professional, as Hays describes in impressive detail. Its influence was the product of a series of political, organizational, and intellectual struggles during which the very nature of the profession was altered.

In treating professionalization and the application of professional values and knowledge as a struggle with the outcome far from determined, Hays anticipated the thrust of much recent scholarship. Along these lines, see John Milton Cooper Jr., "Gifford Pinchot Creates a Forest Service," in *Leadership and Innovation*, ed. Jameson W. Doig and Erwin C. Hargrove (Baltimore, MD: Johns Hopkins University Press, 1990).

41. The best summary of this literature is Eliot Friedson, "Are Professions Necessary?" in Haskell, *Authority of Experts.*

42. Burton J. Bledstein, "Discussing Terms: Professions, Professionals and Professionalism," paper presented to the Organization of American Historians, April 1984.

43. The best example of this is Thomas Haskell's *The Emergence of Professional Social Science: The American Social Science Association and the Nineteenth-Century Crisis of Authority* (Urbana: University of Illinois Press, 1977).

44. Samuel P. Hays, "Introduction—The New Organizational Society," in *Building the Organizational Society: Essays on Associational Activities in Modern America*, ed. Jerry Israel (New York: Free Press, 1972), 1.

45. Magali Sarfatti Larson, *Rise of Professionalism: A Sociological Analysis* (Berkeley: University of California Press, 1977), 25.

46. Ibid., introduction.

47. See, for example, Talcott Parsons, "The Professions and Social Structure," *Social Forces* 17, no. 4 (May 1939): 457–67.

48. Wiebe, *Search for Order*, ch. 6.

49. Higham, "Hanging Together"; McCormick, "Discovery That Business Corrupts." In both the Higham and McCormick models, the technical and professional interests outlasted the wave of broader public concern and involvement. But as both Thomas McCraw, in *Prophets of Regulation: Charles Francis Adams, Louis Brandeis, James M. Landes, Alfred E. Kahn* (Cambridge, MA: Harvard University Press, 1984), and Chris Tomlins, in *The State and the Unions*, have shown in their studies of regulators, the professionals were hardly insensitive to popular beliefs. Perhaps the best example, however, of how cultural values influenced professional perspectives is Allan M. Brandt's *No Magic Bullet: A Social History of Venereal Disease in the United States Since 1880* (New York: Oxford University Press, 1987). Prevailing attitudes about sexual practices and class bias, Brandt argues, helped shape how doctors and scientists defined and treated venereal diseases. This proved to be a major factor in explaining why venereal disease failed to join the list of infectious diseases eradicated by medicine in the early twentieth century.

50. This tension is explored by Wayne K. Hobson in "Professionals, Progressives and Bureaucratization: A Reassessment," *The Historian* 39 (1977): 639–58.

51. Hays, *Response*, ch. 9; Wiebe, *Search for Order*, chs. 2–3; Haskell, *Emergence*; and Galambos, *America at Middle Age*, ch. 2.

52. Hays, "Introduction."

53. Underpinning the organizational revolution was an intellectual phenomenon that Wiebe labeled bureaucratic thought, in which process and adaptation replaced an earlier emphasis on fixed rules. See Wiebe, *Search for Order*, ch. 6, and *The Segmented Society*.

54. Wiebe, *Search for Order*, 115; Paul Starr, *The Social Transformation of American Medicine* (New York: Basic, 1982), 108–12.

55. Wiebe, *Search for Order*, 117.

56. Andrew Walsh, "Hartford Seminary and the Training of a Modern Ministry" (unpublished paper, Harvard University, 1988), 8.

57. Ibid., 12; see also Haskell, *Emergence*, 83.

58. Rather than crediting the specialization of knowledge exclusively for the profession's reconstituted authority, Thomas Haskell suggests that scholars "might construe both specialization and professionalization as strategies that people who claim to possess esoteric knowledge are likely to adopt when confronted with rising levels of competition" (Haskell, "Are Professors Professional?" [review essay], *Journal of Social History* 14, no. 3 [Spring 1981]: 489).

59. Jerold S. Auerbach, *Unequal Justice: Lawyers and Social Change in Modern America* (New York: Oxford University Press, 1976), 85.

60. Haskell, *Emergence*, 24.

61. Ibid., 40.

62. Ibid., 246–56.

63. Ibid., 236, 239–40.

64. Dorothy Ross, "American Social Science and the Idea of Progress," in Haskell, *Authority of Experts*, 160–61.

65. Ibid., 157.

66. Ibid., 161.

67. Magali Sarfatti Larsen, *Rise of Professionalism: A Sociological Analysis* (Berkeley: University of California Press, 1977), 34.

68. Ibid., xiii.

69. E. Richard Brown, *Rockefeller Medicine Men: Medicine and Capitalism in America* (Berkeley: University of California Press, 1979), 77.

70. Ibid., 75.

71. Starr, *Social Transformation*, 135–37.

72. Ibid., 141.

73. David F. Noble, *America by Design: Science, Technology, and the Rise of Corporate Capitalism* (New York: Oxford University Press, 1979), 26–38.

74. As the president of the Society for the Promotion of Engineering Education put it, "First, the principles of science were regarded as principles of truth whose study was ennobling because it attempted to solve the mystery of the universe; second, the laws of the forces of nature were recognized as important to be understood in order to advance the prosperity and happiness of man. The former point of view led to the introduction of experimental work, it being recognized that the truth of nature's laws could be verified by experience alone; the latter point of view led to the application of these laws in industrial and technical experimentation" (quoted in ibid., 24).

75. Edwin T. Layton, *The Revolt of the Engineers: Social Responsibility and the American Engineering Profession* (Baltimore, MD: Johns Hopkins University Press, 1971), ch. 1.

76. Noble, *America by Design*, 41; Larsen, *Rise of Professionalism*, 28. Engineers may have been the first science-based profession to face this dilemma, but they were not the last. This was precisely the choice ultimately confronted by basic scientists after World War II when colossal costs and federal funding served to consolidate the clients for the kinds of large-scale projects dictated by professional agendas.

77. Noble, *America by Design*, 130.

78. Ibid., 139.

79. Robert Kohler, *From Medical Chemistry to Biochemistry: The Making of a Biomedical Discipline* (Cambridge: Cambridge University Press, 1982).

80. Ibid., 158–65.

81. Ibid., 217.

82. Ibid., 288–89, 334.

83. Naomi R. Lamoreaux, "The Regulatory Agencies," in *Encyclopedia of American Political History*, ed. Jack Greene (New York: Scribner's, 1984).

84. "Predominant" agency is Hunter A. Dupree's characterization. See "Central Scientific Organization in the United States Government," *Minerva* (Summer 1963): 453–69.

85. Skowronek, *Building a New American State*, 142, 149–50. By including both an antipooling clause (intended to promote competition) and a prohibition on long-haul and short-haul discrimination (the primary means available to railroads for realizing such competition), Congress merely shifted the conflict to a slightly more insulated forum.

86. Ibid., 151–52.

87. Ibid., 160–61. Hadley and his colleagues gained a strong and effective supporter in Theodore Roosevelt. Roosevelt had little faith in the capacities of the courts or the Congress to rationalize railroad regulation. It was the president's duty to ensure that this difficult task was left to experts serving in an independent administrative agency (ibid., 254). Insulated independent professionals were the only group capable of embodying the broader public interest at stake in regulatory questions.

88. Ibid., 256, 264, 269.

89. Martin J. Sklar, *The Corporate Reconstruction of American Capitalism, 1890–1916: The Market, the Law, Politics* (New York: Cambridge University Press, 1988).

90. Ibid., 315.

91. Ibid., 422.

92. Ibid., 428.

93. Ibid., 426.

94. Ibid., 420–21.

95. Ibid., chs. 3 and 6.

96. Hawley, "Social Policy," 129.

97. Barry D. Karl, *The Uneasy State: The United States from 1915 to 1945* (Chicago: University of Chicago Press, 1983).

98. Michael B. Katz, *In the Shadow of the Poorhouse: A Social History of Welfare in America* (New York: Basic, 1986), 121, 128, 135.

99. David J. Rothman, *Conscience and Convenience: The Asylum and Its Alternatives in Progressive America* (Boston: Little, Brown, 1980), ch. 2.

100. Katz, *Shadow*, 139.

101. Andrew J. Polsky, "The Odyssey of the Juvenile Court: Policy Failure and Institutional Persistence in the Therapeutic State," *Studies in American Political Development* 3 (February 1989): 157–98.

102. Ibid., 173.

103. Ibid., 174.

104. Ibid.

105. Ibid., 177.

106. Ibid., 178.

107. Ibid., 122.

108. David B. Walker, *Toward a Functioning Federalism* (Boston: Little, Brown, 1981), 62.

109. Edward D. Berkowitz and Kim McQuaid, "Bureaucrats as 'Social Engineers': Federal Welfare Programs in Herbert Hoover's America," *American Journal of Economics and Sociology* 39, no. 4 (October 1980): 325.

110. Walker, *Toward a Functioning Federalism*, 62.

111. Berkowitz and McQuaid, "Bureaucrats as 'Social Engineers,'" 325.

112. Hays, "The Politics of Reform."

113. For a brief history of the rise in grants-in-aid, see Walker, *Toward a Functioning Federalism*, ch. 3.

114. There is a vast political science literature on these enduring relationships. One of the earliest commentators, Arthur Maass, in *Muddy Waters: The Army Engineers and the Nation's Rivers* (New York: Da Capo, 1974), documents the power of the Army Corps of Engineers. Other early commentators include J. Leiper Freeman, *The Political Process* (New York: Random House, 1965); and David Truman, *The Governmental Process* (New York: Knopf, 1963). There is an equally vast political science literature criticizing these pluralist models. See, for instance, E. E. Schattschneider, *The Semi-Sovereign People: A Realist's View of Democracy in America* (New York: Holt Rinehart and Winston, 1960); and Theodore J. Lowi, *The End of Liberalism: Ideology, Policy, and the Crisis of Public Authority* (New York: W. W. Norton, 1969). John Mark Hansen's work on policy networks in agriculture is unique in that it applies the theoretical framework of a political scientist to primary sources in tracing the historical development of a crucial policy network. See, for instance, Hansen, "Choosing Sides: The Creation of an Agricultural Policy Network in Congress, 1919–1932," *Studies in American Political Development* 2 (1987): 183–229; and Hansen, "Creating a New Politics: Development and Change of an Agricultural Policy Network in Congress, 1919–1980" (Ph.D. dissertation, Yale University, 1987). Louis Galambos has also used these three-sided relationships between agency, congressional committee, and interest group to describe the development of the twentieth-century American state, labeling them "triocracies" in *America at Middle Age*.

115. On the professionalization of the federal government, see Frederick C. Moser, *Democracy and the Public Service* (New York: Oxford University Press, 1968), 99–133. See also Beer, "Modernization," 74–80, for a discussion of "technocratic politics." Two classic studies of

administrative trends before World War II are Leonard D. White, *Trends in Public Administration* (New York: McGraw-Hill, 1933); and Dwight Waldo, *The Administrative State: A Study of Political Theory of American Public Administration* (New York: Ronald, 1948).

116. Frederick C. Mosher, *Democracy and Public Service* (New York: Oxford University Press, 1982), 104–5.

117. For a good example of how "state capacity" can be measured, see Theda Skocpol and Kenneth Finegold, "State Capacity and Economic Intervention in the Early New Deal," *Political Science Quarterly* 97 (Summer 1982): 255–74. I agree with Skocpol and Finegold that state capacity encompasses expertise. For the purposes of this essay, however, I distinguish between the two in order to understand better the relationship between experts and the administrative infrastructure in which they work.

118. Friedson, "Are Professions Necessary?" 10. For a general discussion of sources of professional autonomy, see Friedson, *Professional Powers: A Study of the Institutionalization of Formal Knowledge* (Chicago: University of Chicago Press, 1986).

119. Barry D. Karl and Stanley N. Katz argue that foundations filled a need for national organization that, for political reasons, the federal government was unable to fill in "The American Private Philanthropic Foundation and the Public Sphere, 1890–1930," *Minerva* 19, no. 2 (Summer 1981): 254. See also Robert E. Kohler, "Philanthropy and Science," and Barry D. Karl, "Philanthropy and the Social Sciences," both in *Proceedings of the American Philosophical Society* 129, no. 1 (1985): 9–13 and 14–19, respectively. Ellis Hawley has summed up the need for "quasiprivatist" machinery in "Social Policy and the Liberal State." Guy Alchon's *The Invisible Hand of Planning: Capitalism, Social Science and the State in the 1920s* (Princeton, NJ: Princeton University Press, 1985) is the most detailed account of how such mechanisms operated during the 1920s and of their limits in the 1930s.

120. Beer, "Modernization," 75.

121. Skocpol, "Bringing the State Back In," 18.

122. Ira Katznelson and Kenneth Prewitt, "Constitutionalism, Class, and the Limits of Choice in U.S. Foreign Policy," in *Capitalism and the State in U.S.-Latin American Relations*, ed. Richard Fagen (Stanford, CA: Stanford University Press, 1979), 38.

123. Margaret W. Rossiter, "The Organization of Agricultural Sciences," in *The Organization of Knowledge in Modern America*, ed. John Voss and Alexandra Oleson (Baltimore, MD: Johns Hopkins University Press, 1979), 215.

124. Skocpol and Finegold, "State Capacity," 271.

125. Ibid., 270–73. The USDA's department status dated back to the Civil War. It became a cabinet-level department in 1889.

126. Ibid., 274 (emphasis in original).

127. Quotation from ibid. On agricultural science initiating policy, see Don F. Hadwiger, *The Politics of Agricultural Research* (Lincoln: University of Nebraska Press, 1982), 15–22; and Richard S. Kirkendall, *Social Scientists and Farm Politics in the Age of Roosevelt* (Columbia: University of Missouri Press, 1966).

128. Dupree, "Central Scientific Organization," 457–58. The definitive account of those scientific fields in which the federal government was active before World War II and an analysis of the nature of federal support is Dupree's *Science in the Federal Government: A History of Policies and Activities to 1940* (Cambridge, MA: Harvard University Press, 1957).

129. Skocpol and Finegold, "State Capacity," 273; Walker, *Toward a Functioning Federalism*, 60.

130. Rossiter, "Organization of Agricultural Sciences," 215.

131. Skocpol and Finegold, "State Capacity," 272.

132. Ibid.

133. Victoria A. Harden, *Inventing the NIH: Federal Biomedical Research Policy, 1887–1937* (Baltimore, MD: Johns Hopkins University Press, 1986), 3, 42.

134. Roger L. Geiger, *To Advance Knowledge: The Growth of American Research Universities, 1900–1940* (New York: Oxford University Press, 1986), 29, 59.

135. Harden, *Inventing the NIH*, 42.

136. Ibid., 3.

137. Geiger, *To Advance Knowledge*, 29, 59.

138. Dupree, "Central Scientific Organization," 462.

139. Robert Kargon and Elizabeth Hodes, "Karl Compton, Isaiah Bowman, and the Politics of Science in the Great Depression," *Isis* 76 (1985): 316. For an account of some of the funding pressures facing the sciences and the failed effort to organize industrial support, see Lance E. Davis and Daniel J. Kevles, "The National Research Fund: A Case Study in the Industrial Support of Academic Science," *Minerva* 12, no. 2 (April 1974): 207–20.

140. Kargon and Hodes, "Karl Compton," 316.

141. Kargon, "Karl Compton." See also Lewis E. Auerbach, "Scientists in the New Deal: A Pre-war Episode in Relations Between Science and Government in the United States," *Minerva* 3, no. 4 (Summer 1965); and Daniel J. Kevles, *The Physicists: The History of a Scientific Community in Modern America* (New York: Knopf, 1978), ch. 17.

142. See, for instance, Alchon, *Invisible Hand of Planning*; and Donald T. Critchlow, *The Brookings Institution, 1916–1952* (DeKalb: Northern Illinois University Press, 1985).

143. Katz, *Shadow*, 167.

144. Galambos, *America at Middle Age*, 42–47.

145. Martin Bulmer and Joan Bulmer, "Philanthropy and Social Science in the 1920s: Beardsley Ruml and the Laura Spelman Rockefeller Memorial, 1922–29," *Minerva* 19, no. 3 (Autumn 1981): 362.

146. Ibid., 363, 386. See also Martin Bulmer, "Governments and Social Science: Patterns of Mutual Influence," and Theda Skocpol, "Government Structures, Social Science and the Development of Economic and Social Policies," in *Social Science Research and Government*, ed. Martin Bulmer (Cambridge: Cambridge University Press, 1987).

147. Barry D. Karl and Stanley N. Katz, "The American Private Philanthropic Foundation and the Public Sphere, 1890–1930," *Minerva* 19, no. 2 (Summer 1981): 238. See also Karl, "Philanthropy and the Social Sciences"; and Kohler, "Philanthropy and Science," 14–19.

148. Karl and Katz, "American Private Philanthropic Foundation," 243.

149. David M. Kennedy, *Over Here: The First World War and American Society* (Oxford: Oxford University Press, 1982), 50. For a good discussion of Progressive ambivalence toward the impact of war on American domestic politics, see Vincent Tompkins, "The Pragmatic Dilemma: Jane Addams, John Dewey, Randolph Bourne and World War I," paper presented to the Twentieth Century American History Workshop, Harvard University, July 26, 1989.

150. Karl, *Uneasy State*, 46.

151. Kevles, *Physicists*, 137.

152. Ibid., 95.

153. Ibid., ch. 9.

154. Skowroneck, *Building a New American State*, 274–76.

155. Robert Cuff, *The War Industries Board: Business-Government Relations During World War I* (Baltimore, MD: Johns Hopkins University Press, 1973), chs. 5–6; Cuff, "Bernard Baruch: Symbol and Myth in Industrial Mobilization," *Business History Review* 18, no. 2 (Summer 1969).

156. Karl, *Uneasy State*, 46.

157. Alchon, *Invisible Hand of Planning*, 68–75. Two institutions set up in response to the crisis did survive the war intact. The National Research Council turned from government sponsorship to corporate and foundation support in order to fund its research projects. The National Advisory Committee for Aeronautics survived the war and established an important precedent following the war, funneling federal dollars to university laboratories. It proved to be an important model in meeting the scientific and technical demands of World War II, foreshadowing the

National Defense Research Committee and the Office of Scientific Research and Development (John L. Heilbron and Daniel J. Kevles, "Science and Technology in U.S. History Textbooks: What's There—and What Ought to Be There," unpublished paper presented to the American Historical Association Annual Meeting, December 1987, p. 13).

158. Skowronek, *Building a New American State*, 279–83.

159. Ibid.

160. See, for instance, Ellis W. Hawley, "Herbert Hoover, the Commerce Secretariat and the Vision of an 'Associative State,' 1921–1928," *Journal of American History* 61, no. 1 (1974): 116–40; and Hawley, "The Discovery and Study of a Corporate Liberalism," *Business History Review* 52, no. 3 (Autumn 1978): 308–20.

161. Peri E. Arnold, "Herbert Hoover and the Continuity of American Public Policy," *Public Policy* 20 (Fall 1972): 525–44; Galambos, *Competition and Cooperation*.

162. Alchon, *Invisible Hand of Planning*, chs. 5–8.

163. Though I view Hoover's thinking as growing directly out of one strand of Progressive thought, not as a sharp break with Progressive thought, I was led to reexamine Progressive attitudes about interest groups by reading McConnell, *Private Power*; on the distinction between the "Progressive" view and the "orthodox" view, see McConnell, *Private Power*, 3–4.

164. Kevles, *Physicists*, ch. 16.

165. Ibid., 250–58.

166. Ibid., 260, 265.

167. Philip Selznick, *TVA and the Grass Roots: A Study of Politics and Organization* (Berkeley: University of California Press, 1984).

168. Sidney Baldwin, *Poverty and Politics: The Rise and Decline of the Farm Security Administration* (Chapel Hill: University of North Carolina Press, 1968).

169. Kevles, *Physicists*, 285.

170. Robert E. Kohler, "Management of Science: The Experience of Warren Weaver and the Rockefeller Foundation Programme in Molecular Biology," *Minerva* 14 (August 1976): 279–306; Bulmer and Bulmer, "Philanthropy and Social Science," 406, 403.

171. Bulmer and Bulmer, "Philanthropy and Social Science," 406.

172. Kirkendall, *Social Scientists*.

173. Bulmer and Bulmer, "Philanthropy and Social Science," 347; Samuel Z. Klausner and Victor M. Lidz, eds., *The Nationalization of the Social Sciences* (Philadelphia: University of Pennsylvania Press, 1986), 5.

174. Klausner and Lidz, *Nationalization of the Social Sciences*, 5.

175. Karl, *Uneasy State*, 113.

176. Ibid.

177. William E. Leuchtenburg, *Franklin D. Roosevelt and the New Deal, 1932–1940* (New York: Harper and Row, 1963), 48, chs. 7–8.

178. Ibid., 244, 250.

179. Ibid., 249.

180. Ibid., 256–57.

181. On the influence of World War II on the acceptance of Keynesian economics, see Herbert Stein, *The Fiscal Revolution in America* (Chicago: University of Chicago Press, 1969), 169–70. Robert M. Collins, in *The Business Response to Keynes, 1929–1964* (New York: Columbia University Press, 1981), 115–72, finds a more divided response, in the immediate wake of the war. But by the mid-1950s, Keynesians had carried the day.

182. Karl, *Uneasy State*, 163.

183. Critchlow, *Brookings Institution*, 108–9, 131–36.

184. Balogh, "Securing Support."

185. Walker, *Toward a Functioning Federalism*, 78.

186. Ibid., 79.

187. Arnold, "Herbert Hoover," 541.

188. Karl, *Uneasy State*, 160–68.

189. For the challenge to institutionalization of many of the New Deal programs that had relied on social science expertise, see James T. Patterson, *Congressional Conservatism and the New Deal* (Lexington: University of Kentucky Press, 1967), 288–324; and Baldwin, *Poverty and Politics*, 365–94.

190. Dupree, "Central Scientific Organization," 457–58; Dupree, *Science in the Federal Government*.

191. The best work on the "crisis" attributed to the shortage of highly trained experts, the major role played by the federal government in both publicizing and responding to this shortage, and the ultimate inflation of categories of expertise considered crucial to the state is an outstanding Ph.D. dissertation by Frank J. Newman, entitled "The Era of Expertise: The Growth, the Spread and Ultimately the Decline of the National Commitment to the Concept of the Highly Trained Expert: 1945 to 1970" (Stanford University, July 1981).

On the professionalization of the postwar state, see Mosher, *Democracy and the Public Service*, 99–133. Don K. Price comments on the trend of scientists moving into administrative positions in *The Scientific Estate* (Cambridge, MA: Harvard University Press, 1965), 66–71.

On the wartime mobilization model, see Kevles, *Physicists*, ch. 20. Joseph Stefan Dupré and Sanford Lakoff, *Science and the Nation: Policy and Politics* (Englewood Cliffs, NJ: Prentice Hall, 1962), 9–11; and Price, *Scientific Estate*, 32–38, document wartime scientific breakthroughs. On the Manhattan Project's impact on funding for science, see David Dickson, *The New Politics of Science* (Chicago: University of Chicago Press, 1984), 5–6. As Robert Gilpin put it in *American Scientists and Nuclear Weapons Policy* (Princeton, NJ: Princeton University Press, 1962), 25, "those wartime projects initiated a military revolution which changed irrevocably the relationship of science and war." For a good comparison to the impact of science on World War I, see ibid., 10–11.

192. Edward Everett Hazlett to Eisenhower, September 24, 1952, Dwight D. Eisenhower Personal Papers (1916–1953), Presidential Library, Abilene, KS.

193. On military spending, see John Lewis Gaddis, *Strategies of Containment: A Critical Appraisal of Postwar American National Security Policy* (Oxford: Oxford University Press, 1982), 23. On Eisenhower's battle, see Charles C. Alexander, *Holding the Line: The Eisenhower Era, 1952–1961* (Bloomington: Indiana University Press, 1975).

194. U.S. National Science Foundation, *Federal Funds for Science: III; The Federal Research and Development Budget, Fiscal Years 1953, 1954, and 1955* (Washington, DC: Government Printing Office), 15. For Eisenhower's farewell address, see *New York Times*, January 18, 1961. The quotation from Eisenhower to the directors and chiefs of the War Department, April 30, 1946, is from *The Papers of Dwight David Eisenhower*, vol. 7, *Chief of Staff*, ed. Louis Galambos (Baltimore, MD: Johns Hopkins University Press, 1970–79), 1046–47.

195. James B. Conant, "The Problems of Evaluation of Scientific Research and Development for Military Planning," speech to the National War College, February 1, 1952, quoted in James G. Hershberg, "'Over My Dead Body': James B. Conant and the Hydrogen Bomb" (unpublished paper presented to the Conference on Science, Military and Technology, Harvard and MIT, revised draft, June 1987), 50.

196. For case studies on how the Cold War stimulated demand for centralized expertise in space and weaponry, see Walter McDougall, *The Heavens and the Earth: A Political History of the Space Age* (New York: Basic, 1985); Gregg Herken, *Counsels of War* (Oxford: Oxford University Press, 1987); Herken, *The Winning Weapon: The Atomic Bomb in the Cold War, 1945–1950* (Princeton, NJ: Princeton University Press, 1988); and Herbert F. York, *The Advisors: Oppenheimer, Teller and the Superbomb* (San Francisco: W. H. Freeman, 1976). Hershberg's "'Over My

Dead Body'" is an excellent study of one of the nation's leading scientist administrators and his response to Cold War weaponry. See also Dickson, *New Politics of Science*, 26, 119–23. Price's *The Scientific Estate* is a testimonial to the increased authority and political clout of scientists in postwar America. Price correctly attributes to the new role of science in the federal government several major changes, including the narrowing gap between the public and private sectors, greater autonomy for and more initiative by executive agencies as a result of this expertise, and the adaptation of the research contract, leading to federal support for open-ended research (15–21, 36–40, 46–51). Gilpin contrasts the revolution in scientific participation in weapons development during World War II and after, to the case of World War I in *American Scientists and Nuclear Weapons Policy*, 9–12.

The best survey of the wide range of responses across disciplines is Paul Boyer, *By the Bomb's Early Light: American Thought and Culture at the Dawn of the Atomic Age* (New York: Pantheon, 1985). See also Newman, "Era of Expertise." On the impact of Sputnik, see Walter A. McDougall, *The Heavens and the Earth: A Political History of the Space Age* (New York: Basic, 1985), chs. 6 and 7; McDougall, "NASA, Prestige, and Total Cold War: The Expanded Purview of National Defense" (paper delivered to the History of Science Society, Chicago, December 1984), and McDougall, "Technocracy and Statecraft in the Space Age—Toward the History of a Salvation," *American Historical Review* 87, no. 4 (October 1982). For Bert the Turtle, see Federal Civil Defense Administration, "Bert the Turtle Says 'Duck and Cover'" (Washington, DC, 1950), quoted in JoAnne Brown, "'A Is for Atom, B Is for Bomb': Civil Defense in American Public Education, 1948–1963," *Journal of American History* 75, no. 1 (June 1988): 84. The quotation on experts is from Joseph Veroff, Richard A. Kulka, and Elizabeth Douvan, *The Inner American: A Self-Portrait from 1957 to 1976* (New York: Basic, 1981), 194. For statistics on counseling, see Elaine Tyler May, *Homeward Bound: American Families in the Cold War Era* (New York: Basic, 1988), 27

197. Statistics on federal growth are from Matthew A. Crenson and Francis E. Rourke, "By Way of Conclusion: American Bureaucracy Since World War II," in *The New American State: Bureaucracies and Policies Since World War II*, ed. Louis Galambos (Baltimore, MD: Johns Hopkins University Press, 1987), 147. On the military and foreign policy bureaucracy, see Charels E. Neu, "The Rise of the National Security Bureaucracy," in Galambos, *New American State*, 85–108; Anna Kasten Nelson, "President Truman and the Evolution of the National Security Council," *Journal of American History* 72, no. 2 (September 1985): 360–78; Bert A. Rockman, "America's Departments of State: Irregular and Regular Syndromes of Policy Making," *American Political Science Review* 75 (1981); and Crenson and Rourke, "By Way of Conclusion," 142. On new and expanded institutions that housed science, see Dickson, *New Politics of Science*, introduction and ch. 1; Price, *Scientific Estate*; Daniel S. Greenberg, *The Politics of Pure Science* (New York: New American Library, 1967); Detlev W. Bronk, "Science Advice in the White House: The Genesis of the President's Advisers and the National Science Foundation," *Technology in Society* 2, nos. 1 and 2 (1980): 245–56; Margaret W. Rossiter, "Science and Public Policy Since World War II," *Osiris* 1 (1985): 273–94; and Kevin Michael Saltzman, "Countdown to Sputnik: The Institutionalization of Scientific Expertise in the White House, 1945–1957" (undergraduate honors thesis in history, Harvard University, March 1988), ch. 3. On the social sciences, see Klausner and Lidz, *Nationalization of the Social Sciences*.

198. See Newman, "Era of Expertise," 55, for statistics; 59, for quotation; and ch. 3, for transformation of academic community vis-à-vis federal support.

199. Politics in the prominitrative state is the topic of my book *Chain Reaction: Expert Debate and Public Participation in American Commercial Nuclear Power, 1945–1975* (New York: Cambridge University Press, 1991). That monograph continues to trace the evolution of professional-federal political development after World War II.

200. Don K. Price, "Endless Frontier or Bureaucratic Morass?" *Daedalus* 107, no. 2 (Spring 1978): 75–92.

201. For a provocative account that argues that civil rights groups gained influence in insulated forums even as broad political support for their agenda subsided, see Abigail M. Thernstrom, *Whose Votes Count? Affirmative Action and Minority Voting Rights* (Cambridge, MA: Harvard University Press, 1987). Gary Orfield also demonstrates the significance of organizational resources applied for similar ends in a far different set of insulated forums in *The Reconstruction of Southern Education: The Schools and the 1964 Civil Rights Act* (New York: Wiley-Interscience, 1969). Even when civil rights leaders self-consciously played to the public, their campaigns worked better when they were closely coordinated with an interest-group approach directed toward narrow legislative ends. On the coordination between these two political techniques, see David Garrow, *Protest at Selma: Martin Luther King and the Voting Rights Act of 1965* (New Haven, CT: Yale University Press, 1978).

202. Compare, for instance, to the emphasis in William Chafe, *The Unfinished Journey: America Since World War II* (New York: Oxford University Press, 1986).

Chapter 5

1. Brian Balogh, "'Keep Your Government Hands Off My Medicare': A Prescription That Progressives Should Fill," *Forum* 7, no. 4, article 3 (2009): 1–21.

2. Ellis W. Hawley, "The New Deal and Business," in *The New Deal: The National Level*, ed. John Braeman, Robert Bremner, and David Brody (Columbus: Ohio State University Press, 1975), 51.

3. Colin Gordon, *New Deals: Business, Labor, and Politics in America, 1920–1935* (New York: Cambridge University Press, 1994), 1–2.

4. Brian Balogh, *A Government Out of Sight: The Mystery of National Authority in Nineteenth-Century America* (New York: Cambridge University Press, 2009), 12.

5. Balogh, *Government Out of Sight*, 13; Balogh, "The Origins and Legacy of the Associative State in Modern America," paper presented at the History and Sociology of Science Seminar, University of Pennsylvania, Philadelphia, February 15, 2010, 14–15.

6. Gordon, *New Deals*, 167; Elliot A. Rosen, *Roosevelt, the Great Depression and the Economics of Recovery* (Charlottesville: University of Virginia Press, 2005), 3, 116; Mary O. Furner, *Advocacy and Objectivity: A Crisis in the Professionalization of American Social Science, 1865–1905* (Lexington: University Press of Kentucky, 1975), 111; Hawley, "New Deal and Business," 60.

7. Hawley, "New Deal and Business," 69; Gordon, *New Deals*, 167, 194–200; Ellis W. Hawley, "Three Facets of Hooverian Associationalism: Lumber, Aviation, and Movies, 1921–1930," in *Regulation in Perspective: Historical Essays*, ed. Thomas K. McCraw (Cambridge, MA: Harvard University Press, 1981), 121.

8. Adam D. Sheingate, "Institutions and the Interest Group Power: Agricultural Policy in the United States, France, and Japan," *Studies in American Political Development* 14, no. 2 (Fall 2000): 194.

9. Christopher P. Loss, *Between Citizens and the State: The Politics of American Higher Education in the Twentieth Century* (Princeton, NJ: Princeton University Press, 2012), 60–62; Henry Wallace, "A Message to All County Agents," *Extension Service Review* 6 (July 1935): 97, as quoted in Loss, *Between Citizens*, 62. See also Wayne D. Rasmussen, *Taking the University to the People: Seventy-Five Years of Cooperative Extension* (Ames: Iowa State University Press, 1989); and Daniel P. Carpenter, *The Forging of Bureaucratic Autonomy: Reputations, Networks, and Policy Innovation in Executive Agencies, 1862–1928* (Princeton, NJ: Princeton University Press, 2001).

10. American Farm Bureau Federation, "Administrative Report," *Minutes of the Board of Directors*, June 5–6, 1935, quoted in Sheingate, "Institutions and the Interest Group Power," 195.

11. Wallace as quoted in Loss, *Between Citizens*, 68; Richard S. Kirkendall, *Uncle Henry: A Documentary Profile of the First Henry Wallace* (Ames: Iowa State University Press, 1993), 90.

12. Ellis W. Hawley, *The New Deal and the Problem of Monopoly: A Study in Economic Ambivalence* (Princeton, NJ: Princeton University Press, 1966), 28, 195.

13. Anthony J. Badger, *The New Deal: The Depression Years, 1933–40* (New York: Macmillan, 1989), 118, 120.

14. Theda Skocpol, *Diminished Democracy: From Membership to Management in American Civic Life* (Norman: University of Oklahoma Press, 2004), 71.

15. Hawley, *New Deal*, 195.

16. Gordon, *New Deals*, 86, 237, 238.

17. Ibid., 239; Hawley, "New Deal and Business," 70.

18. Louis Galambos, *The Creative Society—and the Price Americans Paid for It* (New York: Cambridge University Press, 2011), 102–3. See also Edwin T. Layton, *Revolt of the Engineers: Social Responsibility and the American Engineering Profession* (Baltimore, MD: Johns Hopkins University Press, 1986); and David F. Noble, *America by Design: Science, Technology, and the Rise of Corporate Capitalism* (New York: Knopf, 1977).

19. Christopher D. McKenna, *The World's Newest Profession: Management Consulting in the Twentieth Century* (New York: Cambridge University Press, 2006), 17–18.

20. Ibid., 28.

21. Herbert Croly, *The Promise of American Life* (1909; New York: Macmillan, 1911), 132, quoted in Daniel Ernst, "Lawyers, Bureaucratic Autonomy, and Securities Regulation During the New Deal," paper presented at The State in U.S. History Symposium, Remarque Institute, New York University, New York, October 22, 2010, 3–4; Ernst, "Lawyers," 17; Galambos, *Creative Society*, 102–3; Christopher L. Tomlins, *The State and the Unions: Labor Relations, Law, and the Organized Labor Movement in America, 1880–1960* (New York: Cambridge University Press, 1985), 154, as quoted in Galambos, *Creative Society*, 103.

22. Ernst, "Lawyers," 5, 18; John C. Coffee Jr., *Gatekeepers: The Professions and Corporate Governance* (New York: Oxford University Press, 2006), 204, quoted in Ernst, "Lawyers," 5.

23. Ernst, "Lawyers," 16.

24. Brian Balogh, *Chain Reaction: Expert Debate and Public Participation in American Commercial Nuclear Power, 1945–1975* (New York: Cambridge University Press, 1991), 5.

25. Balogh, *Government Out of Sight*, 390.

26. Ibid., 391–92.

27. Rebecca S. Lowen, *Creating the Cold War University: The Transformation of Stanford* (Berkeley: University of California Press, 1997), 32, 31 for Wilbur quotation. See also Loss, *Between Citizens*, 73.

28. Loss, *Between Citizens*, 75, 76–79.

29. Ibid., 86. For an excellent example of the type of network that relied on universities as intermediaries slightly after the period covered by this essay, see Dominique A. Tobell, *Pills, Power, and Policy: The Struggle for Drug Reform in Cold War America and Its Consequences* (Berkeley: University of California Press, 2012).

30. Ibid., 91–93.

31. Ibid., 73.

32. Jason Scott Smith, *Building New Deal Liberalism: The Political Economy of Public Works, 1933–1956* (New York: Cambridge University Press, 2006), 1–5, 121.

33. Ibid., 3. In this regard, Smith's work fits well with James Sparrow. 34. Smith, *Building New Deal Liberalism*, 4–5.

35. Lewis Schwellenbach speech, July 15, 1938, "Speeches and Writings file. 1938" folder, box 3, Schwellenbach Papers, Library of Congress, as quoted in Smith, *Building New Deal Liberalism*, 121.

36. "Fifth Night-Radio Series" transcript, no date (probably after February 11, 1937), "Addresses" folder, box 2, entry 34, "Records of the Projects Control Division. File of Lloyd N.

Beeker, Assistant Director of the Projects Control Division, 1936–1941," Record Group 135, National Archives, Washington, DC, as quoted in Smith, *Building New Deal Liberalism*, 111. See Smith, *Building New Deal Liberalism*, 110–11, generally.

37. Smith, *Building New Deal Liberalism*, 78, 103.

38. Jerome Frank, address before the Harvard Business Club, December 8, 1938, "Special Files. New Deal Era. Speeches and Writings Files. Speech File. Frank, Jerome N. 1938–1940" folder, box 218, Thomas G. Corcoran Papers, Manuscript Division, Library of Congress, as quoted in Smith, *Building New Deal Liberalism*, 118–19.

39. Smith, *Building New Deal Liberalism*, 98.

40. Frank, address before the Harvard Business Club, as quoted in Smith, *Building New Deal Liberalism*, 119.

41. Franklin D. Roosevelt, "A Suggestion for Legislation to Create the Tennessee Valley Authority," April 10, 1933, New Deal Network, Franklin and Eleanor Roosevelt Institute, http://newdeal.feri.org/speeches/1933j.htm, as quoted in Steven M. Neuse, *David E. Lilienthal: The Journey of an American Liberal* (Knoxville: University of Tennessee Press, 1996), 67; Neuse, *Lilienthal*, 68–69.

42. Neuse, *Lilienthal*, 69.

43. Ibid., 80; Erwin C. Hargrove, "David Lilienthal and the Tennessee Valley Authority," in *Leadership and Innovation: A Biographical Perspective on Entrepreneurs in Government*, ed. Jameson W. Doig and Erwin C. Hargrove (Baltimore, MD: Johns Hopkins University Press), 39; David E. Lilienthal, *TVA: Democracy on the March* (New York: Pocket, 1944), 5.

44. Neuse, *Lilienthal*, 84, 109–11.

45. Hargrove, "David Lilienthal," 53.

46. Philip Selznick, *TVA and the Grass Roots: A Study in the Sociology of Formal Organization* (Berkeley: University of California Press, 1949), 37.

47. David Lilienthal, *The Journals of David E. Lilienthal*, vol. 1, *The TVA Years, 1940* (New York: Harper & Row, 1964), 213.

48. Selznick, *TVA and the Grass Roots*, 49.

49. Franklin D. Roosevelt, letter to Conference on Economic Conditions of the South, July 5, 1938, in U.S. National Emergency Council, *Report on Economic Conditions of the South* (Washington, DC, 1938), 1–2, as quoted in Bruce J. Schulman, *From Cotton Belt to Sun Belt: Federal Policy, Economic Development, and the Transformation of the South, 1938–1980* (Durham, NC: Duke University Press, 1994), 3. See also Schulman, *From Cotton Belt to Sun Belt*, 135.

50. Quotation from Ira Katznelson, *Fear Itself: The New Deal and the Origin of Our Times* (New York: Liveright Publishing Corporation, 2013), 16; Jill S. Quadagno, "From Old Age Assistance to Supplemental Security Income: The Political Economy of Relief in the South, 1935–1972," in *The Politics of Social Policy in the United States*, ed. Margaret Weir, Ann Shola Orloff, and Theda Skocpol (Princeton, NJ: Princeton University Press, 1988), 235–64; Linda Gordon, *Pitied but Not Entitled: Single Mothers and the History of Welfare* (Cambridge, MA: Harvard University Press, 1994), 274–77. On the impact of federalism on social provision, see Edwin Amenta, *Bold Relief: Institutional Politics and the Origins of Modern American Social Policy* (Princeton, NJ: Princeton University Press, 1998), 162–90. For an outstanding comparison of southern and northern approaches to economic development and the varied uses of federalism in that quest, see Brent Cebul, "Developmental State: The Politics of Business, Poverty, and Economic Empowerment from the New Deal to the New Democrats" (Ph.D. dissertation, University of Virginia, 2014).

51. Schulman, *From Cotton Belt to Sun Belt*, 3.

52. Ibid., 72.

53. Ibid., 92–95.

54. Ibid., 95, 97–98; Roosevelt memorandum to Nelson, October 22, 1942, Records of the Works Progress Board, RG 179, no. 314.4342, as quoted in Schulman, *From Cotton Belt to Sun Belt*, 97.

55. Schulman, *From Cotton Belt to Sun Belt*, 99.

56. Ibid., 100, 101, 116–17, 135–36.

57. Stephen B. Adams, *Mr. Kaiser Goes to Washington: The Rise of a Government Entrepreneur* (Chapel Hill: University of North Carolina Press, 1997), 1; see 2 for quote.

58. Ibid., 2; see Balogh, *Government Out of Sight*.

59. Adams, *Mr. Kaiser*, 15, 21.

60. Ibid., 23, 24.

61. Ibid., 26–27.

62. *Engineering News-Record* as quoted in Adams, *Mr. Kaiser*, 25; see also 3, 11.

63. Paul A. C. Koistinen, *Arsenal of World War II: The Political Economy of American Warfare (1940–45)* (Lawrence: University Press of Kansas, 2004), 444–88, 501–3.

64. Ibid., 467, 486; Bartholomew H. Sparrow, *From the Outside In: World War II and the American State* (Princeton, NJ: Princeton University Press, 1996), 175–91. See also Gregory Hooks, *Forging the Military-Industrial Complex: World War II's Battle of the Potomac* (Urbana: University of Illinois Press, 1991).

65. Aaron L. Friedberg, *In the Shadow of the Garrison State: America's Anti-Statism and Its Cold War Grand Strategy* (Princeton, NJ: Princeton University Press, 2000), 57; quotation on 29 (emphasis added). On fear of the garrison state, see also Michael J. Hogan, *A Cross of Iron: Harry S. Truman and the Origins of the National Security State, 1945–1954* (New York: Cambridge University Press, 1998). On procurement contracts as market exchange, see Friedberg, *In the Shadow of the Garrison State*, 201.

66. On Stanford and MIT, see Lowen, *Creating the Cold War University*; and Stuart W. Leslie, *The Cold War and American Science: The Military-Industrial-Academic Complex at MIT and Stanford* (New York: Columbia University Press, 1994). See also Hogan, *Cross of Iron*, 470–71. On the general relationship between science and universities, see Balogh, *Chain Reaction*; Daniel J. Kevles, *The Physicists: The History of a Scientific Community in Modern America* (New York: Knopf, 1978); and Loss, *Between Citizens*, 160–61.

Chapter 6

I would like to thank Ed Ayers, Catherine Gavin Loss, Chris Loss, Chi Lam, Mike Lynch, Paul Milazzo, Sid Milkis, and Ed Sermier for their assistance with this essay.

1. Hugh Heclo, "Sixties Civics," in *The Great Society and the High Tide of Liberalism*, ed. Sydney M. Milkis and Jerome M. Mileur (Amherst: University of Massachusetts Press, 2005), 71.

2. Ibid., 60.

3. Lyndon B. Johnson, "Remarks at the University of Michigan, May 22, 1964," *Public Papers of the Presidents of the United States: Lyndon Johnson, 1963–1964* (Washington, DC: U.S. Government Printing Office, 1965), 704.

4. Ibid., 704, 706.

5. The quotation is from Lewis Strauss. For background on Strauss and the context for his statement, see Brian Balogh, *Chain Reaction: Expert Debate and Public Participation in American Commercial Nuclear Power, 1945–1975* (New York: Cambridge University Press, 1991), 113.

6. For quotes, see Johnson, "Remarks at the University of Michigan," 706. On the assumption that the Great Society would not require a redistribution of income and power, see Allen J. Matusow, *The Unraveling of America: A History of Liberalism in the 1960s* (New York: Harper and Row, 1984).

7. James T. Patterson, *Grand Expectations: The United States, 1945–1974* (New York: Oxford University Press, 1996), 562.

8. Ibid., 536, 563, 569; Peter Marris and Martin Rein, *Dilemmas of Social Reform: Poverty and Community Action in the United States* (Chicago: University of Chicago Press, 1982), 24–25.

9. Patterson, *Grand Expectations*, 569.

10. Edward Berkowitz, "Medicare: The Great Society's Enduring National Health Insurance Program," in Milkis and Mileur, *Great Society*, 329.

11. Ibid.

12. Gareth Davies, *From Opportunity to Entitlement: The Transformation and Decline of Great Society Liberalism* (Lawrence: University of Kansas Press, 1996), as cited in Eileen Boris, "Contested Rights: The Great Society Between Home and Work," in Milkis and Mileur, *Great Society*, 118.

13. Patrick McGuinn and Frederick Hess, "Freedom from Ignorance? The Great Society and the Evolution of the Elementary and Secondary Education Act of 1965," in Milkis and Mileur, *Great Society*, 289–90.

14. See Gary Orfield, *The Reconstruction of Southern Education: The Schools and the 1964 Civil Rights Act* (New York: Wiley, 1969). See also Gary Orfield, *Must We Bus? Segregated Schools and National Policy* (Washington, DC: Brookings Institution, 1978) for statistics on southern desegregation. That the shift from opportunity to achievement endured long beyond the Great Society is illustrated by the willingness of both liberals and conservatives to support federal expansion. The No Child Left Behind Act, passed in 2002 and supported by both George Bush and Ted Kennedy, significantly increased the federal government's presence in secondary and elementary education.

15. "Special Message to Congress on Natural Beauty," February 8, 1965, *Public Papers of the Presidents: Lyndon Baines Johnson, 1965*, vol. 1 (Washington, DC: Government Printing Office, 1966), 155–65, cited in Paul Milazzo, "Legislating the Solution to Pollution: Congress and the Development of Water Pollution Control Policy" (Ph.D. dissertation, University of Virginia, 2001), ch. 3.

16. Milazzo, "Legislating the Solution," ch. 3.

17. Paul Milazzo, "Congress and the Environment," in *The American Congress: The Building of Democracy*, ed. Julian Zelizer (Boston: Houghton Mifflin, 2004).

18. Thomas Byrne Edsall with Mary D. Edsall, *Chain Reaction: The Impact of Race, Rights, and Taxes on U.S. Politics* (New York: W. W. Norton, 1991).

19. Wilson Carey McWilliams, "Great Empires and Great Societies: Lyndon Johnson and Vietnam," in Milkis and Mileur, *The Great Society*, 215.

20. H. W. Brands, *The Strange Death of American Liberalism* (New Haven, CT: Yale University Press, 2001); Robert Higgs, *Crisis and Leviathan: Critical Episodes in the Growth of American Government* (New York: Oxford University Press, 1987); Mary L. Dudziak, *Cold War Civil Rights: Race and the Image of American Democracy* (Princeton, NJ: Princeton University Press, 2000).

21. Robert Dallek, *Lone Star Rising: Lyndon Johnson and His Times, 1908–1960* (New York: Oxford University Press, 1991), cited in McWilliams, "Great Empires," 215. On some of the unfortunate consequences of this mindset, see Patricia N. Limerick, *Legacies of Conquest: The Unbroken Past of the American West* (New York: W. W. Norton, 1987).

22. McWilliams, "Great Empires," 216–17 (though he certainly does not use the word *chutzpah*).

23. Rogers M. Smith, *Civic Ideals: Conflicting Visions of Citizenship in U.S. History* (New Haven, CT: Yale University Press, 1997).

24. John Dittmer, *Local People: The Struggle for Civil Rights in Mississippi* (Urbana: University of Illinois Press, 1994). African Americans improved their relative economic condition during the New Deal era due to general relief programs, but not because of programs specifically aimed at improving race relations.

25. Hugh Davis Graham, "The Great Society's Civil Rights Legacy: Continuity 1, Discontinuity 3," in Milkis and Mileur, *Great Society*, 371.

26. This is not to suggest that they had to start from scratch. Roosevelt had laid the foundation for rights-based liberalism in his Commonwealth Club address of September 1932. Sidney M. Milkis, *The President and the Parties: The Transformation of the American Party System Since the New Deal* (New York: Oxford University Press, 1993), 38–51.

27. Boris, "Contested Rights," 129–37; the quote is from 129.

28. Johnnie Tillmon, "Welfare Is a Women's Issue," *Liberation News Service* no. 415, February 26, 1972, reprinted in *America's Working Women: A Documentary History, 1600 to the Present*, ed. Rosalyn Baxandall and Linda Gordon (New York: W. W. Norton, 1995), 31.

29. Sydney M. Milkis, "Lyndon Johnson, the Great Society, and the 'Twilight' of the Modern Presidency," in Milkis and Mileur, *Great Society*, 3–5.

30. Ibid., 5, and Frances Fox Piven and Richard A. Cloward, "The Great Society in Action: The Politics of the Great Society," in Milkis and Mileur, *Great Society*.

31. David M. Shribman, "Means and Ends: Lyndon Johnson and What His Presidency Means in the End," in Milkis and Mileur, *Great Society*, 17.

32. Milkis, "Lyndon Johnson," 6.

33. Balogh, *Chain Reaction*.

34. J. Edgar Hoover, "The Twin Enemies of Freedom: Crime and Communism," address before the 28th Annual Convention of the National Council of Catholic Women, Chicago, IL, November 9, 1956, cited in Elaine Tyler May, *Homeward Bound: American Families in the Cold War Era* (New York: Basic, 1988), 137.

35. Dudziak, *Cold War Civil Rights*, 13–14. Robert M. Collins, *The Business Response to Keynes, 1929–1964* (New York: Columbia University Press, 1981). On the impact of National Security Council Report 68 on growthmanship, see Robert M. Collins, *More: The Politics of Economic Growth in Postwar America* (New York: Oxford University Press, 2000), 24–25.

36. Godfrey Hodgson, *America in Our Time* (Garden City, NY: Doubleday, 1976); and Richard H. Pells, *The Liberal Mind in a Conservative Age: American Intellectuals in the 1940s and 1950s* (New York: Harper and Row, 1985).

37. Walter Lippmann, *A Preface to Morals* (New York: Macmillan, 1929), as cited in Heclo, "Sixties Civics," 66.

38. Ibid., 67.

39. On *Goldberg v. Kelley*, see R. Shep Melnick, *Between the Lines: Interpreting Welfare Rights* (Washington, DC: Brookings Institution, 1994), 42–43.

40. Milkis, "Lyndon Johnson," 16–19.

41. Baxandall, "The New Politics of Participatory Democracy Viewed Through a Feminist Lens," in Milkis and Mileur, *Great Society*, 277.

42. On the succession of activist movements, a classic work is Sara Evans, *Personal Politics* (New York: Knopf, 1979). See also Terry Anderson, *The Movement and the Sixties: Protest in America from Greensboro to Wounded Knee* (New York: Oxford University Press, 1995). On the electronic media, see David Garrow, *Protest at Selma: Martin Luther King, Jr., and the Voting Rights Act of 1965* (New Haven, CT: Yale University Press, 1978); and Todd Gitlin, *The Whole World Is Watching: Mass Media in the Making and Unmaking of the New Left* (Berkeley: University of California Press, 1980).

43. Graham, "Great Society's Civil Rights Legacy," 367.

44. Hugh Davis Graham, *The Civil Rights Era: Origins and Development of National Policy* (New York: Oxford University Press, 1990); Abigail Thernstrom, *Whose Votes Count? Affirmative Action and Minority Voting Rights* (Cambridge, MA: Harvard University Press, 1987).

45. Thernstrom, *Whose Votes Count?*

46. Baxandall, "New Politics," 275–76.

47. Linda Gordon, as quoted in Baxandall, "New Politics," 284.

48. Heclo, "Sixties Civics," 71.

49. Ibid., 77; and R. Shep Melnick, "From Tax and Spend to Mandate and Sue: Liberalism after the Great Society," in Milkis and Mileur, *Great Society*, 403–4.

50. Nader as cited in Melnick, "Tax and Spend," 404–5; quoted from Hugh Heclo, "The Sixties False Dawn," in *Integrating the Sixties*, ed. Brian Balogh (University Park: Pennsylvania State University Press, 1996), 50–52.

51. Milkis, "Lyndon Johnson," 9.

52. Ibid., 8.

53. Melnick, "Tax and Spend," 405.

54. Ibid. On rights talk, see Mary Ann Glendon, *Rights Talk: The Impoverishment of Political Discourse* (New York: Free Press, 1991).

55. Robert Kagan, *Adversarial Legalism: The American Way of Law* (Cambridge, MA: Harvard University Press, 2001), cited in Melnick, "Tax and Spend," 405.

56. Milkis, "Lyndon Johnson," 1–2.

57. McGuinn and Hess, "Freedom from Ignorance?" 306. The No Child Left Behind Act, passed in January 2002, confirmed the national government's central role in elementary and secondary education. Richard Elmore has called it "the single largest expansion of federal power over the nation's education system in history." See Elmore, "Unwarranted Intrusion," *Education Next* 2, no. 1 (Spring 2002): 31–35, as cited in McGuinn and Hess, "Freedom from Ignorance?" 312. See also 311–13 generally, and Boris, "Contested Rights," 137–38.

58. Boris, "Contested Rights."

59. Graham, "Great Society's Civil Rights Legacy," 368; and John David Skrentny, *The Ironies of Affirmative Action* (Chicago: University of Chicago Press, 1996), to which Graham also refers.

60. James Q. Wilson, as cited in Melnick, "Tax and Spend," 391. There is strong consensus among many of the authors cited here that the Great Society systematically expanded the range of public policies in which the national government engaged. In doing so, the Great Society resembled the New Deal, which was decidedly "illegitimate" in the eyes of its opponents. At the same time, the barriers to legitimacy lowered by the Great Society were precisely those established by the New Deal and its offspring.

61. Falk quoted in Milkis, *President and the Parties*, 245n79.

62. Melnick, "Tax and Spend," 391–92.

63. Ibid., 391.

64. Dan Morgan, "Senators Tried to Balance Deluge of Needs, Ceiling on Spending," *Washington Post*, January 26, 2003, A4.

65. On social services, see Martha Derthick, *Uncontrollable Spending for Social Service Grants* (Washington, DC: Brookings Institution, 1975); on services and mental health, see Andy Morris, "Therapy and Poverty: Private Social Service in the Area of Public Welfare" (Ph.D. dissertation, University of Virginia, 2003). On mental health, see Peter Sheehy, "The Triumph of Group Therapeutics: Therapy, the Social Self, and Liberalism in America, 1910–1960" (Ph.D. dissertation, University of Virginia, 2002). On the therapeutic in education, see Catherine Gavin Loss, "Public Schools, Private Lives: American Education and Psychological Authority, 1945–1975" (Ph.D. dissertation, University of Virginia, 2005).

66. Heclo, "Sixties Civics," 74.

67. Sheehy, "Triumph of Group Therapeutics."

68. Baxandall, "New Politics," 14.

69. Ibid., 280–81.

70. Graham, "Great Society's Civil Rights Legacy," 367.

71. Melnick, "Tax and Spend," 402.

72. Orfield, *Reconstruction of Southern Education.*

73. See Martha Derthick, "Crossing Thresholds: Federalism in the 1960s," in Balogh, *Integrating the Sixties*; Martha Derthick, *Keeping the Compound Republic* (Washington, DC: Brookings Institution, 2001).

74. McGuinn and Hess, "Freedom from Ignorance?" 300–301.

75. Ibid., 304.

76. Brian Balogh, Joanna Grisinger, and Philip Zelikow, *Making Democracy Work: A Brief History of Twentieth-Century Federal Executive Reorganization* (Charlottesville: University of Virginia, 2002), 67.

77. Melnick, "Tax and Spend," 398–99.

78. Ibid., 393–94.

79. Ibid., 392.

80. Quoted in ibid., 406.

81. Ibid.

82. Milazzo, "Legislating the Solution"; Paul Milazzo, "U.S. Water Pollution," in *Water and the Environment Since 1945: Global Perspectives*, ed. Char Miller, Mark Cioc, and Kate Showers (Detroit: St. James, 2001), 257–63.

83. Graham, "Great Society's Civil Rights Legacy," 367.

84. McGuinn and Hess, "Freedom from Ignorance?" 294–95.

85. Brian Balogh, "'Mirrors of Desires': Interest Groups, Elections and the Targeted Style in Twentieth Century America," in *The Democratic Experiment*, ed. Meg Jacobs, William Novak, and Julian Zelizer (Princeton, NJ: Princeton University Press, 2003). Pluralism has undergone significant change during the twentieth century. From the late nineteenth century onward, it has adapted to the quantity and styles of its participants. Four distinct phases of pluralism dominated twentieth-century American political culture: business/professional pluralism, labor pluralism, Cold War pluralism, and democratic pluralism. Each phase added a new layer of complexity to the existing structure but hardly displaced those interests that had previously staked a claim.

See also John Mark Hansen, *Gaining Access: Congress and the Farm Lobby, 1919–1981* (Chicago: University of Chicago Press, 1991); and Lorraine Gates Schulyer, "The Weight of Their Votes: Southern Women and Politics in the 1920s" (Ph.D. dissertation, University of Virginia, 2001). In a brilliant history of pluralist adaptation, Elisabeth Clemens underscores the ways in which the political history of each nascent interest group shaped its strategy, modifying the nature of pluralism as new groups joined the "club." Women and farmers ultimately moved away from failed populist and social democratic efforts. But they behaved differently than long-standing pluralist stalwarts like business interests. Women and farmers were far more likely to call for state intervention in public policy. Nevertheless, both groups narrowed the scope of their agendas and created permanent homes in Washington, DC, for the American Farm Bureau Federation and the League of Women Voters. In the 1920s organizations like these groups walked, talked, and lobbied more like interest groups than populist movements. See Elisabeth S. Clemens, *The People's Lobby: Organizational Innovation and the Rise of Interest Group Politics in the United States, 1890–1925* (Chicago: University of Chicago Press, 1997).

86. On labor commitment to interest-group bargaining, see Jacob Hacker, *The Divided Welfare State: The Battle over Public and Private Social Benefits in the United States* (New York: Cambridge University Press, 2002).

87. These are the adjectives used by Nelson Lichtenstein in "Pluralism, Postwar Intellectuals, and the Demise of the Union Idea," in Milkis and Mileur, *Great Society*.

88. For fighting faith, see Arthur M. Schlesinger Jr., *The Vital Center: The Politics of Freedom* (Cambridge, MA: Riverside, 1949).

89. Louis Galambos, *America at Middle Age: A New History of the United States in the Twentieth Century* (New York: New Press, 1983), 67.

90. Heclo, "Sixties Civics," 67.

91. McWilliams, "Great Empires," 225.

92. Byron C. Hulsey, *Everett Dirksen and His Presidents: How a Senate Giant Shaped American Politics* (Lawrence: University Press of Kansas, 2000). See also Jerome M. Mileur, "The Great Society and the Demise of New Deal Liberalism," in Milkis and Mileur, *Great Society*, 438. Lichtenstein provides a good description of this system in his section on labor during the Cold War in "Union Idea," 93–101. Pluralism provides a mechanism for formulation of limited issues, where the parties still disagree on principles.

93. E. E. Schattschneider, *The Semisovereign People: A Realist's View of Democracy in America* (1960; Hinsdale, IL: Dreyden, 1975), 34–35.

94. For an extended discussion of Cold War liberalism and the attack on it, see Brian Balogh, "Introduction," in Balogh, *Integrating the Sixties*, 13–17.

95. Dittmer, *Local People*.

96. Samuel Hays, *Beauty, Health, and Permanence: Environmental Politics in the United States, 1955–1985* (New York: Cambridge University Press, 1987).

97. On the concept of scope of debate, see Schattschneider, *Semisovereign People*.

98. The Port Huron Statement is a good example of this. See http://coursesa.matrix .msu.edu/~hst306/documents/huron.html.

99. Graham, "Great Society's Civil Rights Legacy," 370–71. See also John David Skrentny, *The Minority Rights Revolution* (Chicago: University of Chicago Press, 2002), as cited by Graham.

100. Graham, "Great Society's Civil Rights Legacy," 372–75. David Mann, however, retained a great deal of discretion. Even though Native American groups were reluctant at the time to be officially designated as protected groups, Mann added them anyway.

101. Graham, "Great Society's Civil Rights Legacy," 375.

102. "Society" is in quotation marks because there never had been consensus and society had been quite diverse. But that portion of society engaged in active policy making had indeed been more consensual and far less diverse.

103. Peter Skerry, "We're All Moralists Now: Racial Politics in the American Administrative State," paper presented at The Great Society: Then and Now conference, November 17–18, 2000, University of Virginia, Charlottesville, 7.

104. Clemens, *People's Lobby*.

105. Lichtenstein, "Union Idea"; Heclo, "Sixties Civics." It is ironic that the rise of "identity" politics would mean the demise of pluralism because in the United States ethnic politics long served as one of the foundations of pluralism.

106. Lichtenstein, "Union Idea," 108.

Conclusion

1. Renee Montagne, "In Michigan, Businessmen and Politicians Agree on Medicaid," National Public Radio, January 20, 2014, http://www.npr.org/templates/transcript/transcript .php?storyId=263467886.

2. Ellen Nakashima and Greg Miller, "Obama Calls for Significant Changes in Collection of Phone Records of U.S. Citizens," *Washington Post*, January 17, 2014.

3. "Transcript of President Obama's January 17 Speech on NSA Reforms," January 17, 2014, http://www.washingtonpost.com/politics/full-text-of-president-obamas-jan-17-speech-on -nsa-reforms/2014/01/17/fa33590a-7f8c-11e3-9556-4a4bf7bcbd84_story.html.

4. Ibid.

5. William J. Novak, *The People's Welfare: Law and Regulation in Nineteenth-Century America* (Chapel Hill: University of North Carolina Press, 1996); Richard R. John, *Spreading the News: The American Postal System from Franklin to Morse* (Cambridge, MA: Harvard University Press, 1995); James Sparrow, *Warfare State: World War II Americans and the Age of Big Government* (New York: Oxford University Press, 2011); Suzanne Mettler, *Submerged State: How Invisible Government Policies Undermine American Democracy* (Chicago: University of Chicago Press, 2011); Michael Mann, *The Sources of Social Power* (New York: Cambridge University Press, 1986).

6. William G. Robbins, *Lumberjacks and Legislators: Political Economy of the U.S. Lumber Industry, 1890–1941* (College Station: Texas A&M University Press, 1982), 43.

7. See Julia F. Irwin, *Making the World Safe: The American Red Cross and a Nation's Humanitarian Awakening* (New York: Oxford University Press, 2013), 119–21 for uniform and ranking decisions. The "American character" quote is from Chester Aldrich as quoted in Irwin, *Making the World Safe*, 119.

8. Ibid., 27.

9. Ibid., 27.

10. Ibid., 30–32.

11. Ibid., 30.

12. Ibid., 31–32.

13. Ibid., 32–34.

14. Ibid., 96–102, 111–12.

15. Quoted in ibid., 156.

16. Ibid., 185–87.

17. Ibid., 208.

18. Emily S. Rosenberg, *Spreading the American Dream: American Economic and Cultural Expansion 1890–1945* (New York: Hill and Wang, 1982); Melvyn P. Leffler, *The Elusive Quest: America's Pursuit of European Stability and French Security, 1919–1933* (Chapel Hill: University of North Carolina Press, 1979).

19. Clara Altman, "Courtroom Colonialism: Philippine Law and U.S. Rule" (Ph.D. dissertation, Brandeis University, 2014), 3.

20. Ibid., 5.

21. Ibid. (emphasis added).

22. Harwood L. Childs, *Labor and Capital in National Politics* (Columbus: The Ohio State University Press, 1930), 247.

23. The remainder of this section is excerpted from Brian Balogh, "From Corn to Caviar: The Evolution of Presidential Electoral Communications, 1960 to 2000," in *America at the Ballot Box: Elections and American Political History*, ed. Gareth Davies and Julian E. Zelizer (Philadelphia: University of Pennsylvania Press, forthcoming).

24. On the role of television, see James L. Baughman, *Same Time, Same Station: Creating American Television, 1948–1961* (Baltimore, MD: Johns Hopkins University Press, 2007), 202–3; see also Nicholas Lemann, "Tune In Yesterday," *New Yorker* 83, no. 10 (April 30, 2007): 80. On media oligopoly, see Kernell, *Going Public*, 138. For debate figures, see George C. Edwards III, *On Deaf Ears: The Limits of the Bully Pulpit* (New Haven, CT: Yale University Press, 2006), 188.

25. Robert J. Pitchell, "The Influence of Professional Campaign Management Firms in Partisan Elections in California," *Western Political Quarterly* 11, no. 2 (June 1958): 289.

26. D. Sunshine Hillygus, "The Evolution of Election Polling in the United States," *Public Opinion Quarterly* 75, no. 5 (2011): 963.

27. Robert M. Groves, "Three Eras of Survey Research," *Public Opinion Quarterly* 75, no. 5 (2011): 861; Hillygus, "Evolution of Election Polling," 976 for quote, along with Lawrence Jacobs and Robert Shapiro, "Polling Politics, Media, and Election Campaigns," *Public Opinion Quarterly* 69 (Special Issue No. 5): 635–41. In *Post-Broadcast Democracy: How Media Choice Increases Inequality in Political Involvement and Increases Polarization* (New York: Cambridge University Press, 2007), Markus Prior argues that media choice has allowed more citizens to avoid political discourse entirely, thus placing a premium on likely voters. This makes microtargeting efforts worth the effort. See also D. Sunshine Hillygus and Todd Shields, *The Persuadable Voter* (Princeton, NJ: Princeton University Press, 2008). For an excellent and highly engaging overview of the social science foundation on which microtargeting was built, see Sasha Issenberg, *The Victory Lab: The Secret Science of Winning Elections* (New York: Crown, 2012).

28. Brian Balogh, *Chain Reaction: Expert Debate and Public Participation in American Commercial Nuclear Power, 1945–1975* (New York: Cambridge University Press, 1991), 268.

29. Philip Rucker, "SC Senator Is a Voice of Reform Opposition," *Washington Post*, July 28, 2009. The remainder of this essay is excerpted from Brian Balogh, "'Keep Your Government Hands Off My Medicare': A Prescription That Progressives Should Fill," *Forum* 7, no. 4, article 3 (2009) 1–21.

30. Richard White, *"It's Your Misfortune and None of My Own": A New History of the American West* (Norman: University of Oklahoma Press, 1991), 57.

31. Ibid., 57.

32. Matthew D. Lassiter, *The Silent Majority: Suburban Politics in the Sunbelt South* (Princeton, NJ: Princeton University Press, 2006), 10–14.

33. For an excellent range of this work, see Kevin M. Kruse and Thomas J. Sugrue, *The New Suburban History* (Chicago: University of Chicago Press, 2006). For an overview of the northern corollary to the "Sunbelt synthesis," see Sugrue, *Sweet Land of Liberty: The Forgotten Struggle of Civil Rights in the North* (New York: Random House, 2008).

Index

accounting profession, 152–53

Adams, Stephen B., 167, 168

Affordable Care Act (ACA) ("Obamacare"), 1, 2, 200–201, 218

African Americans: and the Great Society, 178–79, 195–96; Hoover and Republican coalition in the South, 78; and the New Deal state, 259n24. *See also* civil rights legislation; civil rights movement

Agricultural Adjustment Act (AAA) (1933), 147–49, 208

Agricultural Marketing Act (1929), 147

Alchon, Guy, 250n119

Altman, Clara, 206–7

American Association for Labor Legislation, 26

American Bar Association, 102

American Economics Association, 31

American Engineering Council, 79

American Farm Bureau Federation (AFBF), 126, 148–49, 155, 208, 262n85

American Federation of Labor, 73, 83, 149

American Forestry Association, 55, 56, 60

"The American Law of Association: The Legal-Political Construction of Civil Society" (Novak), 15–16

American Medical Association (AMA), 24, 26, 34, 35, 102

American National Live Stock Association, 33

American Political Development (APD) scholarship, 6–22, 223–24n6; analyses of business-government relations, 13; and the associational synthesis, 3–6; and the associational turn, 18–22; background (and organizational synthesis), 223–24n6; and bureaucratic autonomy, 10; citizenship studies, 12; effect of historical developments on, 7; Eisenach's concept of

"parastates," 16, 25, 28, 34–35, 237n51; and the organizational synthesis, 6–11; perspectives on the state and the market, 16–17; on the professions, 7, 17–18, 19–21, 153, 227n39; and Progressive historiography/Progressive synthesis, 7–8, 9, 11, 225n19; regime studies, 13; relationship between citizen and civil society (and state-civil society boundaries), 7, 10–18, 225n19; and state capacity (state authority, state autonomy), 8–12, 147; and the USDA, 147

American Red Cross (ARC), 31, 204–6; carrying out American humanitarian diplomacy during World War I, 204–6; congressional charter, 205; and the social work profession, 205

American Social Science Association (ASSA), 104

American Society of Civil Engineers, 106

American Telephone and Telegraph (AT&T), 106, 107, 120

American War of Independence, 29, 30

American Wholesale Grocers' Convention, 79

Anderson, Kristi, 240–41n5

Anderson, Nancy K., 61, 236n44

ARC. *See* American Red Cross (ARC)

Arizona Wool Growers Association, 33

Armstrong, George, 153

Army Corps of Engineers, 114, 160, 168, 193

Arthur Andersen (firm), 153

Associated Business Papers, 75

associational order, 23–40; emergence of, 23–40; and federalism, 31–32; five enduring patterns/legacies of nineteenth-century governance, 28–30; Hawley on the associative state, 24, 27–28; and the "hidden welfare state," 32–38; Hoover's vision of the